'SOULED!'

BOOKS I & II

'SOULED!'

BOOKS I & II

Stories of
Striving and Yearning

by
HANOCH TELLER

in collaboration with
Marsi Tabak

New York City Publishing Company

ISBN 0-9614772-1-0

12   11   10   9   8   7   6   5   4   3   2

Available through:

NYC Publishing Co.
37 W. 37th St. 4th floor
NY, NY 10018

CIS Distributors
P.O.B. 26
Lakewood N.J. 08701

J. Lehmann
Hebrew Booksellers
20 Cambridge Terrace
Gateshead
Tyne & Wear

Kollel Bookshop
22 Muller St.
Yeoville Johannesburg 2198

*To our brethren whose stories
can only be whispered.*

ALSO BY HANOCH TELLER
Once Upon a Soul
Soul Survivors

APPROBATION FROM HAGAON HARAV MOSHE FEINSTEIN SHLITA

RABBI MOSES FEINSTEIN	מ ש ה פ י י נ ש ט י י ן
455 F. D. R. DRIVE	ר״מ תפארת ירושלים
New York, N. Y. 10002	בנוא יארק
—	
ORegon 7-1222	בע״ה

ב' ניסן תמש״ה

לכבוד מוהר״ר העניך מעללער שליט״א, בברכת שלום וברכה וכט״ס.

אחדשה״ט Due to the delicate state of my health, it is difficult for
me to delve into books sent to me for endorsement.
הנה מחמח However, I heard wonderful tidings regarding your most
לפני recent as well as your earlier book, from my grandson
להסכמה, HaRav Mordechai Tendler, Shlita. He praised the books
י הו י ג as ones which can provide a great service in drawing the
מוהר״ר פ hearts of many of our brethren to their Father in Heaven.
להמשיך לבות Therefore, I offer my blessings that the Almighty will
של הרבה award you with much success with this book, and that
שיצליחן you may merit to increase and glorify the Torah I have
השי״ח בט instructed that my seal be impressed upon this letter.

Moshe Feinstein

וצותי שישימו הרחמתי על מכתב זה.

APPROBATION FROM HAGAON HARAV SHLOMO ZALMAN AUERBACH SHLITA

הרב שלמה זלמן אויערבאך
פעיה"ק ירושלים תובב"א

ב"ה, יום ...

I hereby express my most heartfelt blessing to my dear friend, Rabbi Hanoch Yonason Teller, who studies in the *Kollel* of the Mirrer Yeshiva. I know him very well and can veritably testify that he is a fearer of sin and a Torah scholar.

Since he is in the category of a *talmid chacham* who does not allow anything improper to emanate from his hands, not to mention knows how to word things pleasantly and correctly, his intention to publish a book of his stories about Torah leaders and loving ones fellow Jew, etc.; in order to strengthen faith in God and enhance mitzva observance for an English reading audience receives my thorough endorsement. I extol his actions and extend my blessings that his words will penetrate the hearts of his readers and influence them to uplift and improve their deeds and purify their outlook for their own everlasting benefit.

May the author be blessed for his efforts from the source of blessing as he so desires, and I so fervently wish.

Shlomo Zalman Auerbach

BOOK I

Contents

ב"ה

Preface

LTHOUGH I HAVE published close to one hundred stories over the past three years, one aspect of the writing has not become easier with experience: the ending. English Composition teachers of our youth seem to still hold us captive to the lesson that every story we pen must include three basic elements, without which we could not hope for a passing grade: a Beginning, a Middle and an End. The Roman numerals I, II and III, inscribed on the blackboards of our mind, were to guide us aspiring writers down the path we were to faithfully trudge. No matter what the route, however, we had to arrive at III and there, summarize the journey.

The lesson is an important one, for it forces one to bear in mind that *every* piece of writing should have a logical design which introduces and fully develops a theme. But this lesson, fundamental to "How To Write A Story," misses the *point* of a story, or at least the point of the ending.

The function of the "ending," it was understood quite literally, was to conclude the story. *We* contend that the end of a story must bring its reader to a new beginning — to the realization that there *is* no ending, only a continuation. If the story has no lasting impact, if its message fails to stimulate thoughts and ideas which the reader will carry with him, then either the author or his reader were remiss.

Stories are related for the purpose of inspiring, motivating and teaching with a clarity and effect that cannot be achieved through other pedagogic techniques. This is accomplished by evoking in the reader a sense of identification with the characters whose actions he will want to either emulate or avoid. And when the author has achieved this goal, he may end... so that his reader may begin.

THE PUBLICATION of 'SOULED!', the concluding volume of the Soul Series, is approached with an overwhelming sense of gratitude to the Almighty. With the help of God I have written four books in the last two years. I pray that I may be deserving of His benevolence. Through the many letters and calls I've received from readers expressing their appreciation of *Once Upon a Soul* and *Soul Survivors* — the preceding two volumes of this series — I understand that my stories have made a modest impact on our People, and for this I feel especially blessed. It is the vindication I had hoped for. I only regret that I could not touch more of the subjects about which people need to hear.

A deliberate attempt was made in this volume to collate stories pertinent to contemporary Jewry. I sincerely hope their message will live on and continue to inspire generations to come. An author once commented that he would gladly exchange one hundred readers today for one reader one hundred years hence. I heartily concur.

In this volume, each chapter is comprised of three stories bound by a common theme. Perhaps King Solomon's advice that "the three-ply strand will not quickly be severed," will apply here as well, thus endowing my message with greater potency and durability. Book II of 'SOULED!' was designed for youngsters — and their parents! — making this a family book suitable for every home.*

There is no doubt that the characters portrayed in, and the messages transmitted by these stories embody everlasting truths. Be they dedicated men who rush to the aid of those in need at any time of day or night, courageous women who defied the savage Nazi monsters, or children whose faith was strong enough to challenge death itself: these lofty-SOULED individuals set a shining example for all to follow.

❀

Those who gave of their time over the years to help and guide me, specifically my Rebbeim, and the Mirrer Rosh Yeshiva in whose kollel I learn, are the first to receive my accolades. My dear parents have been no less instrumental in my education and development, and have allowed me to pester them incessantly throughout the preparation of this work. Plaudits go once again to the dedicated team at NYC Publishing Company, and my appreciation for them is exceeded only by my gratitude for the assistance I received from the people mentioned below.

Zelda Goldfield, Jack Bieler, Douglas Davis, David Grossman, and especially Reuven Abedon were kind enough to scrutinize portions of the manuscript, and return them in far better condition than when they received them. Likewise Daniel Taub's insightful comments bountifully

---

* Please note that certain parts of Book I might be considered inappropriate for youngsters. Parental discretion is advised.

grace this book. The skill and style of the two giants of the graphic world, Ben Gasner and Alex Berlyne, have again found expression in this volume. Lisa Stein, an incorrigible "workaholic," gave her every waking hour in the fight against the deadline clock.

I offer my profound appreciation to Rabbi Nisson Wolpin, who has gone to great lengths to prove that distance cannot diminish a friendship. Likewise I must thank the kind people at the "Bookstop," Jerusalem, for their invaluable research. Similar recognition is extended to Hillel Goldberg for his article about Novardok which appeared in *Mussar Anthology*.

I am also indebted to Dr. Yaakov Tendler for his patience and assistance. Preparation of the stories in "Three on Nobility" would have been impossible without his help.

And above all my deepest thanks are extended to MARSI TABAK, whose input to this book was equalled only by her unremitting dedication and immeasurable talents.

As long as the above list is, I regret that two of the most deserving of recognition prefer anonymity. Similarly, the vast "computer complex" of Bayit Vegan, whose "memory banks" unfailingly produced vital data and background material. I hope these three realize how heartfelt my gratitude is.

Acknowledgement must also be made of my seminary students, an insatiable audience when it comes to stories ("*Rabbi Teller, tell us a story!*") who proved to be the finest testing ground and sounding board a writer could ever hope to have.

Achron, achron I bow in gratefulness and deference to the noblest soul I know, who also happens to be the surpassingly patient wife of the author. May the Almighty grant us the privilege of seeing our children and children's children fulfill the concepts and ideals reflected in these stories.

As I go to press I pray with fervor for a *refuah sheleimah* for *Rabeinu* Reb Nisson Alpert *shlit'a,* a *Gaon* whose imprint can be discerned in every line of this book.

※

When people ask me what I am working on, I am wont to reply, "*Gemara Pesachim.*" Now that this series is complete, I hope, with the help of God, to resume my work...

עם חיתום סידרה משולשת זו, ספר וספר וסיפור, הריני כולל הודאה עם בקשה: כאשר זיכני קב״ה שנתקבלו דברי כותיבתי עד הנה, חדרו ללבות אשר חדרו ונשאו פרי באשר נשאו; כה יתן ה׳ וכה יוסיף כהנה וכהנה, ולוואי יישירו ליבותינו לאבינו שבשמים.

Hanoch Teller
Jerusalem ת״ו
Rosh Chodesh Adar Sheini/March 1986

Introduction

THE AILING REBBE knew he was dying, but it was not that knowledge which caused his immense sorrow. As he looked around him at the bedraggled, beleaguered handful of chassidim at his bedside, he wondered how he could raise their flagging spirits. Life for Jews in Russia had never been easy but now they – particularly the chassidim – were besieged from every side: by the Ukrainians who hoped to annihilate them; by the "Haskala," which threatened to decimate them; and by the misnagdim who ridiculed the very foundations of their faith.

The Rebbe sighed deeply. "איך האב שוין אלץ פראבירט - I have tried everything to unite my People and strengthen their beliefs. I have taught them Torah and mussar, I have shown them how to serve the Almighty in song and dance. Yet I have failed. I have not provided them with the fortitude to withstand the onslaughts and attacks that have always been a part of our destiny, assaults from within and without. I have tried everything else, איצטער וויל איך אנפאנגען דערצעלען מעשהס - now I will begin telling stories."

XX

Thus began Rabbi Nachman of Breslov — one of the most famous storytellers who ever lived — to spin the profound, enchanting tales which have captivated and inspired his followers for nearly two centuries.

The Holy Torah is like a beacon of Heavenly light, illuminating a dark existence and arousing mankind from its spiritual and intellectual slumber. However, when one who sleeps is suddenly awakened by a bright beacon of light, he might instinctively shield his eyes — and never see the source of the light. When the beam's intensity is diffused and allowed to seep in gently, the sleeper may take longer to arise, but he will not need to hide his eyes. Awake at last, mankind can gaze in joy and wonder at the Heavenly Light.

Some say a story is the best way to induce sleep. I say a story is the best way to rouse a sleeping soul.

Now I will begin telling stories...

three on altruism

ת״ר בשלשה דברים גדולה גמילות חסדים יותר מן הצדקה. צדקה
בממונו גמילות חסדים בין בגופו בין בממונו, צדקה לעניים גמילות
חסדים בין לעניים בין לעשירים, צדקה לחיים גמילות חסדים בין לחיים
בין למתים.

סוכה מט

✽ Our Sages taught, in three respects is Gemilus
Chassadim superior to charity: charity can be only
with one's money, but Gemilus Chassadim can be
performed with one's person and one's money.
Charity can be given only to the poor, Gemilus
Chassadim, is for both the rich and the poor. Charity
can be given only to the living, Gemilus Chassadim
can be extended to both the living and the dead.

Sukkah 49

Heart Beat

HE CALL WAS clocked in at 11:26:00 and the dispatcher depressed the TRANSMIT key on his mike: "FLATBUSH units vicinity Avenue O and East Ten; respond." He held the caller on the line and five seconds later repeated his transmission: "Any F units vicinity O, East Ten: respond."

11:26:08 "F-98 here." It was Zev Stein, one of the Flatbush drivers. "I'm at Ocean Parkway and X."

"Ten-four, F-98. Proceed to 913 Avenue O. Code Blue."

The term "Code Blue" evoked a flurry of responses. When it crackled out of the walky-talky in Moish Weinberg's inside jacket pocket during a business meeting on Fourteenth Avenue, he leaped from his seat. His chair went skating across the polished office floor and smashed into the wall six feet away. Without so much as a "Pardon

---

Copy — receive message **ten-four** — end of transmission **D.O.A.** — dead on arrival **EMT** — emergency medical technician **Smokeys** — highway patrolmen **CPR** — cardio-pulmonary resuscitation **thumper**— automatic CPR device **EKG**— electro-cardiogram **ETA**— estimated time of arrival **IV**— intravenous

me," Moish was out the door. "B-83 here," he reported, "I'm at Fourteenth Avenue and Fifty-first. Do you copy?"

"Ten-four, B-83."

Joe Rosen was in the shower when his walky-talky gasped the message from the edge of the bathroom sink. He raced out of the stall and into his clothes, zipping up his coveralls in the elevator down. As the floor indicator marked his descent, Joe checked his watch: 11:27:14. Not too bad, he thought. From dripping wet to fully dressed and on his way in one minute, six seconds. Still, he'd have to hustle if he hoped to make it in time. He plotted the route in his head as he ran through the lobby. "This is F-76," he reported. "H-Base, do you copy?"

Tully Gluck was testing the heating system of a tenant's apartment on the seventh floor in the Park Slope neighborhood when the call came through. He bounded down the steps like a mountain goat, hurdled the banister of the front stoop and made tracks for his van. While Joe rode in the elevator several blocks away, Tully was turning the key in the ignition. Nate Wexler was already rolling, but he was way over on Eighteenth Avenue in Boro Park.

F ROM FIVE DIFFERENT directions, Zev, Moish, Joe, Tully and Nate converged on Avenue O and East Tenth Street. These were the men of HATZOLAH. On voluntary call day and night, each ready to drop whatever he was doing, go wherever he was sent, whenever he was needed, these men — along with a cadre of hundreds of other "ordinary" Jews like them — formed a unique corps. All of the Big Apple was their beat.

Copy — receive message **ten-four** — end of transmission **D.O.A.** — dead on arrival **EMT** — emergency medical technician **Smokeys** — highway patrolmen **CPR** — cardio-pulmonary resuscitation **thumper**— automatic CPR device **EKG**— electro-cardiogram **ETA**— estimated time of arrival **IV**— intravenous

Zev, travelling down Ocean Parkway from Avenue X, was the "first responder." Unaware that four of his associates were already en route to the emergency, he called upon every ounce of driving proficiency he possessed in his haste to reach the patient. "Code Blue" meant cardiac arrest: the victim's heart had ceased beating, cutting off the vital supply of oxygen to the brain. After four minutes without oxygen, the irreversible process of deterioration begins: the rapid destruction of brain cells that results in paralysis, loss of memory, loss of sensory function, and, ultimately, brain death — the stage at which the patient is reduced to a "vegetable," kept alive by machines.

The static-crackle of responses coming over his radio was comforting. Now he knew he wasn't alone in his race against the clock. He reached out the window and attached the magnetic red light to the roof of his car, then flipped the siren switch on the dash. Instantly, the siren began to whoop and the "cherry" light to rotate in a concert of urgency, and the traffic divided to allow him passage.

The human brain is an incredibly efficient apparatus. Unlike man-made computers, God's ingenious piece of work is equipped to handle a multitude of problems simultaneously. Thus Zev had no difficulty guiding his car skillfully through the mid-morning traffic while mentally reviewing the medical supplies in the kit at his side and calculating the time elapsed since the emergency call was placed. He'd been doing forty-five when the flow of vehicles entering this major Brooklyn artery had forced him to decelerate to thirty. With the aid of the siren, he was able to spur his little Mustang up to sixty.

Copy — receive message **ten-four** — end of transmission **D.O.A.** — dead on arrival **EMT** — emergency medical technician **Smokeys** — highway patrolmen **CPR** — cardio-pulmonary resuscitation **thumper**— automatic CPR device **EKG**— electro-cardiogram **ETA**— estimated time of arrival **IV**— intravenous

OCEAN PARKWAY, however, was never designed to accommodate vehicles at that speed. A broad, bench-lined thoroughfare with an asphalt divider down its center, it splits the borough roughly along an East-West axis. On either side of the divide, three lanes of traffic flow in both directions, accessed by alphabetically sequenced avenues and paralleled east and west by numerically sequenced streets. The flow of cars and buses entering the heavily used boulevard is constant.

Drivers scattered at the sound of Zev's siren but few were able to pinpoint its source. Inevitably, with some cars merging into the traffic from the right, others pulling over to avoid the speeding siren-sounder, and still others stopping altogether in bewilderment, a massive traffic jam resulted. Undaunted, Zev shifted into reverse and backed away from the wall of honking cars and into the intersection, with no noticeable reduction in speed.

Zev swung right onto Avenue T and burned rubber all the way to East Eighth. At Avenue R, he hooked a left on two wheels in front of the Mirrer Yeshiva, and squealed into another left directly under a Con-Ed cherry-picker, from the crow's-nest of which a yellow-suited electrician was changing the bulb on a sodium-vapor lamp. Zev's unexpected appearance beneath his perch caused him to drop the huge bulb and it crashed to the pavement explosively. The sound convinced a co-worker, emerging from a manhole, that Brooklyn was under nuclear attack. He took a flying leap back down his manhole and slammed the cover over his head.

By this time, Zev was long gone. Ignoring the light at the corner, he braked slightly for a right back onto Ocean

---

Copy — receive message **ten-four** — end of transmission **D.O.A.** — dead on arrival **EMT** — emergency medical technician **Smokeys** — highway patrolmen **CPR** — cardio-pulmonary resuscitation **thumper**— automatic CPR device **EKG**— electro-cardiogram **ETA**— estimated time of arrival **IV**— intravenous

Parkway beyond the traffic jam he'd created. He was only six blocks short of his goal.

11:27:40 Similar stunts were being perpetrated in other parts of Brooklyn. Had the emergency call come through at any other time, up to thirty HATZOLAH men would have been rushing to the scene, wreaking minor havoc with the city's traffic patterns as they sped through the streets. But what's a little havoc when a life is at stake?

ALTHOUGH few HATZOLAH volunteers shared Zev's enthusiastic derring-do, they all — for one reason or another — were equally motivated. As the borough's elderly population increased, the volume of emergency calls to the City hospitals rose and the ability of paramedical rescue teams to reach victims in time diminished. On average, City ambulances arrived on the scene nine minutes after the call. Occasionally it was possible to revive the victim; more often, the patient was wheeled into the hospital under a red blanket: D.O.A.

Zev's next-door neighbor had suffered such a fate twelve years earlier, when Zev himself had been hardly more than a teenager. He had stood by helplessly as the clock ticked that nice woman's life away. With each jerk of the second hand on his watch, Zev's youthful imagination had conjured up the vision of millions of tiny brain cells gasping for breath, collapsing on the floor of the cerebellum, and, finally, stiffening in the classic comic-strip pose of *rigor mortis*.

The woman who had been like an adoptive grandmother to Zev had not made it. There were no more of Bubbe Bella's oatmeal cookies, no more stories "from the old

---

Copy — receive message **ten-four** — end of transmission **D.O.A.** — dead on arrival **EMT** — emergency medical technician **Smokeys** — highway patrolmen **CPR** — cardio-pulmonary resuscitation **thumper**— automatic CPR device **EKG** electro-cardiogram **ETA**— estimated time of arrival **IV**— intravenous

country," no more fresh-baked challah after that. That summer, Zev had taken an EMT course at Lutheran Hospital, not knowing how he would put it to use — until HATZOLAH was formed. And while the City ambulances continued in their failure to meet the rising demand with their nine-minutes-plus response time, HATZOLAH was always on the spot in under two.

Zev made a right onto Ocean Parkway directly into the passing lane alongside the median, sailing across the bows of two lanes of oncoming cars in the process. His own siren was swiftly joined by several others. He glanced at the rear-view mirror, expecting to see a flotilla of his fellow HATZOLAH members, but finding only the looming shapes of the Highway Patrol cruisers. They bore down ominously on his spunky Mustang and Zev shrugged in resignation.

"H-base, I've got three Smokeys on my tail," he reported to the dispatcher at Headquarters, "and they don't look very friendly."

"Ten-four, F-98." There was no time to spare for a driver who was out of commission. The dispatcher's next transmission brought a grimace to Zev's lips. "Attention all FLATBUSH and BORO PARK units responding to the call: F-98 out of action. Units F-76, B-91, F-79, B-83: report your locations."

Z EV RAISED the volume on his radio for the benefit of the trooper now swaggering towards his window. The patrolman hitched his Sam Browne higher on his spreading hips, tilted his hat to the back of his head, and thrust his big face into Zev's car.

Copy — receive message ten-four — end of transmission D.O.A. — dead on arrival EMT — emergency medical technician Smokeys — highway patrolmen CPR — cardio-pulmonary resuscitation thumper— automatic CPR device EKG— electro-cardiogram ETA— estimated time of arrival IV— intravenous

"Cute little cherry light ya got there, fella," he said, breathing into Zev's nostrils. "Ya playin' cops an' robbers or somethin'?"

"Officer, I'm an emergency medical technician, on an urgent call. It's a matter of life and death!"

"D'ja get that, Mike?" the patrolman called to his partner. The second policeman was white-gloving traffic around the captured Mustang. "The little guy's in a big hurry — sez he's goin' to a *'mergency!*"

Zev smiled disarmingly. "Officer, please, I'm on a mission of mercy!"

"Uh-huh," the skeptical cop grunted. "An' I'm Cinderella, on my way to the ball." Then, suddenly tiring of the game and reverting to type, he squared his hat and commanded: "Step out of your vehicle, *sir*. License and registration, *please*." The order was spiked with a generous dollop of sarcasm.

11:27:48 While Zev was being slapped with nine citations for traffic violations, including exceeding the speed limit, failure to stop for a red light, failure to signal, unauthorized use of a revolving light, and constituting a vehicular menace to the general public, Nate arrived on the scene. His drive from a far greater distance had been only slightly less creative than Zev's, but he'd been mercifully unencumbered by either traffic or "Smokeys". He braked to a screeching halt with one wheel up on the sidewalk and jumped out of his car, leaving his door flung open.

Copy — receive message **ten-four** — end of transmission **D.O.A.** — dead on arrival **EMT** — emergency medical technician **Smokeys** — highway patrolmen **CPR** — cardio-pulmonary resuscitation **thumper** — automatic CPR device **EKG** — electro-cardiogram **ETA** — estimated time of arrival **IV** — intravenous

NATE FOUND the victim slumped over the kitchen table. He opened the man's collar and felt for a pulse in his neck. There was none. He eased him off the chair and laid him flat on the floor, preparing to administer cardio-pulmonary resuscitation.

Tully's arrival was no less dramatic. The HATZOLAH team, folk-heroes of the religious community, attracted a crowd of admirers wherever they went. School teachers had long since abandoned hope of controlling their classes when an emergency occurred in the vicinity of their school: the moment a siren was heard, the students bolted from their seats and jammed the windowsills to watch their heroes in action. Tully's car had zipped past a group of school children on a science outing and their teacher — no less prone to hero-worship than his youthful charges — had no trouble keeping pace with his pupils as they raced to join the mob gathered on the sidewalk on Avenue O.

Joe's Austin was ideally sized for sidewalk driving, a tactic that had frequently come in handy when traffic blocked his path. If the Sanitation Department were to give out Purple Hearts, countless Brooklyn trashcans would be thus decorated, having been wounded in action by Joe's front bumper. The patrolmen who spotted "The Sidewalk Streak" — as they called him — were of the friendly variety and, with the best interests of the City's trashcans at heart, graciously provided a police escort.

11:27:59 Just as Nate was checking the victim's pulse a second time, Tully appeared at the door with Joe at his heels, each gripping an equipment bag. Tully broke his open and removed the oxygen unit while Nate checked to see if

---

Copy — receive message **ten-four** — end of transmission **D.O.A.** — dead on arrival **EMT** — emergency medical technician **Smokeys** — highway patrolmen **CPR** — cardio-pulmonary resuscitation **thumper**— automatic CPR device **EKG**— electro-cardiogram **ETA**— estimated time of arrival **IV**— intravenous

the victim's mouth and throat were clear of obstructions.

Joe spoke into his hand-held transmitter: "H-base, units F-76, B-91 and F-79 reporting. Over."

"Go ahead, F-76."

"Patient is a male senior citizen, about seventy-five. Pulse: negative. Administering CPR. Send us a bus with a thumper and notify the medics."

"Ten-four, F-76."

TULLY POSITIONED the oxygen mask over the old man's nose and mouth, adjusting his neck to prevent the tongue from blocking the airway, and Nate straddled the victim's torso. There was no need for any signals to pass between them: each man knew his job. Tully pressed the button on the manual respirator, pumping three blasts of air into the man's lungs, and then began counting. "One-one thousand, two-one thousand, three-one thousand." The count set the cadence for Nate — ninety beats per minute.

With his left hand gripping the back of his right and elbows locked to exert the maximum pressure, Nate pressed the heel of his right hand down on the victim's chest just above the sternum, once for every "-one thousand." By simulating the heart's normal rhythm, they could keep the brain adequately oxygenated to sustain it undamaged. Every five beats, Tully reactivated the respirator.

"My Sidney!" the victim's wife cried. "My Sidney! What are you doing to my Sidney?"

Copy — receive message **ten-four** — end of transmission **D.O.A.** — dead on arrival **EMT** — emergency medical technician **Smokeys** — highway patrolmen **CPR** — cardio-pulmonary resuscitation **thumper** — automatic CPR device **EKG** — electro-cardiogram **ETA** — estimated time of arrival **IV** — intravenous

"It's alright," Joe said, trying to keep her calm. "They know what they're doing. Now what's your husband's full name and does he have a previous history of heart attack?"

"Heart attack!! *Oy vey's mir.* No, no. Just angina, sometimes a little indigestion. Is he having a heart attack? *Oy mein Gott!*"

Joe was afraid they might have another victim on their hands if he didn't get the woman under control. "Missus, please, just relax. Sidney's going to be alright. But you've got to help."

He quickly hooked up the small EKG monitor and attached the leads. Instantly, the machine issued an audio-visual representation of Sidney's inert heart. The uninterrupted "bee-eep" was far from encouraging. He hurried back to the victim's wife.

"...two-one thousand, three-one thousand..."

11:28:45 Moish arrived at last and took in the whole scene at a glance. He nudged Joe aside and positioned himself so as to block the woman's view of the kitchen.

"Are you Mrs. Bulofsky?" he asked, gesturing towards the nameplate below the doorbell.

"Yes, Ida Bulofsky. Is my Sidney going to be alright?" She peered around him nervously.

"Is that B-u-l or B-e-l?" he asked, distracting her from the frightening spectacle behind him.

"B-u-l." She noticed Moish's suit for the first time. The air of officialdom with which it endowed him seemed to steady her.

"Can you tell me what happened to your husband, Mrs. Bulofsky? Did anything like this ever happen before?"

"No, no. Never. He's got angina, see, and he got this pain in his chest so I went to get him his pills and when I come back he's laying there and I called him and called him but he don't answer so I take a look and he's not breathing!"

"When was this, Mrs. Bulofsky?"

"When? How should I know when? When I called you, that's when."

"**W**HAT TIME have we got?" Tully called. While Moish was doing his number on Ida Bulofsky, Joe had taken over for Nate, Nate had replaced Tully on the respirator and Tully, with the stethoscope around his neck, was trying to find a heartbeat.

"I make it just under three minutes," Moish replied, looking at his watch. "How long has he been on CPR?" "Less than a minute."

A siren wailed in the street, and Moish dared to hope. In an instant, though, the sound receded. "H-base," he shouted into his transmitter, "this is B-83. Where's that *farshluggener* bus?!"

"On the way, B-83. ETA 11:34."

Five more minutes! Moish stripped off his jacket and tie and replaced Joe on Sidney Bulofsky's chest. Joe stood up slowly. Patches of perspiration mottled his coveralls; his arms trembled after the exertion of the closed-chest massage.

Copy — receive message **ten-four** — end of transmission **D.O.A.** — dead on arrival **EMT** — emergency medical technician **Smokeys** — highway patrolmen **CPR** — cardio-pulmonary resuscitation **thumper**— automatic CPR device **EKG**— electro-cardiogram **ETA**— estimated time of arrival **IV** intravenous

"I think I got a flutter that time," Tully said tentatively, pressing two fingers to Bulofsky's carotid artery.

Moish gave it everything he had. Broad-shouldered and heavily built, he put his weight and years of experience behind the push that compressed Sidney's heart against his spine. The strongest muscle in the body, the heart can withstand enormous pressure; the ribs, however, cannot. Even when properly administered, CPR occasionally breaks some ribs — a small price to pay for a life. On the third count, Moish felt the gentle cracking beneath his hands as the old man's fragile bones gave way.

"...four-one thousand, five-one thousand..."

11:29:15 The trembling in Joe's extremities had settled down to a tolerable quiver. He turned his attention to Ida Bulofsky. The poor woman reacted to every push on her husband's body with a shudder of her own and all the color had drained from her anguish-pinched face. Joe quickly sent her on an errand to collect all of her husband's medications and assemble them on the hall table.

A minute later she returned, holding the corners of her apron skirt like a sack: Isordil, nitroglycerin, Inderal, antacid tablets. Joe was pleased to note that the effort had brought some color back to her cheeks. Then Sidney vomited.

NATE WHIPPED the oxygen mask off the man's mouth, turned his face to the side to prevent aspiration, and cleared the airway. Tully handed him a fresh respiration unit. Working together like parts of a well-oiled machine, they each performed a separate, critical function, fueled by a unity of purpose. Moish hadn't missed a beat.

"...three-one thousand, four-one thousand..."

11:32:55 The men had all switched positions. In the four minutes, fifty seconds since CPR was initiated, the patient's pulse had registered only two feeble flutters. They had no idea how long a cardiac arrest victim could be sustained by this method, but statistical data on the subject was irrelevant: the men of HATZOLAH were prepared to keep going for as long as was necessary, as long as there was strength in their hands.

"He's fibrillating," Moish exclaimed, reading the EKG monitor. The twitching of the muscle fibers was a good sign, but the muscle itself was still inactive. Another siren wailed down Avenue O, this time followed almost immediately by the sound of heavy footsteps on the stairs. The paramedics had arrived. Nate sent Mrs. Bulofsky off to pack a bag for her husband: she had to be safely out of the way during the next procedure.

The paramedic crouched on the floor and peeled back Bulofsky's shirt. He turned a rheostat to charge up the battery-operated unit and removed the defibrillating paddles — two black-handled rods, each terminating in a metal disk — from his case. Placing the paddles on the dying man's chest, he called "Clear," and everyone stood back. Two hundred volts of electricity slammed through Sidney Bulofsky's motionless form. His body arched and flapped momentarily like a beached trout and Moish searched again for a pulse.

"Hit it again."

Copy — receive message **ten-four** — end of transmission **D.O.A.** — dead on arrival **EMT** — emergency medical technician **Smokeys** — highway patrolmen **CPR** — cardio-pulmonary resuscitation **thumper** — automatic CPR device **EKG** — electro-cardiogram **ETA** — estimated time of arrival **IV** — intravenous

"Okay." He waited for the electric surge to build. "Clear." Another powerful jolt smacked into Sidney's inert heart muscle. There was not a sound in the room as all eyes remained glued to the monitor. Four pairs of lips moved in silent prayer while the men of HATZOLAH awaited the verdict.

The EKG blipped sharp peaks on its screen, and Moish slapped his stethoscope to the patient's chest. "Got it!" he cried.

"All *right!*" the others cheered. "*Baruch Hashem!*"

11:33:40 "Let's get an IV going here," the medic ordered. Nate held the plastic bag of saline solution while Joe inserted an intravenous line in Bulofsky's arm. Tully was tossing the litter of equipment into their bags when the stretcher bearers entered. They strapped the patient securely to the aluminum frame.

Nate carried the IV bag aloft and Joe handled the oxygen respirator as the team maneuvered the stretcher down the narrow stairwell. Tully was the next one out, carrying three equipment bags. With one hand, Moish swept Bulofsky's medicine bottles into his own case, knowing the doctor would require them, and glanced over his shoulder before stepping out the door.

Ida Bulofsky's red-rimmed eyes pleaded with him wordlessly.

"Promise to be good?"

She quickly nodded her assent. "Get your coat, then, and I'll take you to the hospital." She grabbed her purse and coat and Sidney's overnight bag and hurried to join him in

---

Copy — receive message **ten-four** — end of transmission **D.O.A.** — dead on arrival **EMT** — emergency medical technician **Smokeys** — highway patrolmen **CPR** — cardio-pulmonary resuscitation **thumper** — automatic CPR device **EKG** — electro-cardiogram **ETA** — estimated time of arrival **IV** — intravenous

the hall. "Don't worry, Ida," Moish said. "Sid is in good hands, *B'ezer Hashem*."

HE WAS HELPING HER into his car when Zev pulled up at the curb. Vehicles were scattered along the street and sidewalk like Pik-Up Stix dumped at random from their can. The ambulance screamed its way through traffic and Moish gave his friend a broad smile and a hearty thumbs-up sign.

"H-base, F-98 here."

"F-98?!" The dispatcher exclaimed uncharacteristically. "Where *are* you? I thought we'd have to raise bail for you. Over."

"Yeah, well, I turned on the charm and mentioned my uncle the judge who suspended the last cop that stopped me for speeding, so they let me go. I'm at the scene now. Over."

"Report, F-98."

"It looks like my buddies managed without me — this time." He grinned, mentally chalking up another HATZOLAH for Bubbe Bella. "Over and out, H-base."

"Hold it, F-98. Proceed to Coney Island Avenue pizza shop. Choking victim. Do you copy?"

"Ten-four, H-base. I'm on my way..."

Footprints

T WAS YITZCHAK who first noticed something wrong with Naomi. The children in the summer playgroup which she directed were frolicking in the sand box and had slipped out of their sandals to wiggle their toes in the warm sand.

Yitzchak saw that Naomi's toes were unnaturally flexed and that one foot was slightly extended. He wasted no time in bringing the oddity to the attention of the other children and they all gathered around Naomi, placing their bare feet alongside hers. "Look, everybody, look! Why are your toes all bent like that, Naomi? They look so funny!"

Naomi became very self-conscious. The mockery of the four-year-old hurt, perhaps more than it should have, because the flexing of her toes was a recent development which she was unable to control. Until that morning, no one else had noticed it.

For the average nine-year-old, the concept of serious illness is a difficult one to grasp. In his mind, bruises and scrapes, viruses and rashes, all readily remedied by mother's caresses, band-aids, cherry-flavored syrups and time, in that order, constitute "sickness"; disorders, disabilities and diseases are the province of "grown-ups." But for a child as gifted and precocious as Naomi, the severity of the problem was all too apparent.

FOR SEVERAL WEEKS she had been experiencing pain, at first as innocuous as writers' cramp. Naomi did not complain, and made certain to slip out of sight whenever she sensed the onset of the writhing, twisting spasms which racked her body. She was afraid that if she were to tell her parents about the pains, they would not allow her to conduct the playgroup about which she had dreamed the whole year.

Tears welled up in Naomi's eyes and spilled to the sand. "Let's go back now and have something to drink," she said to distract the children, but they were far more interested in staring at her toes.

How much longer will I be able to keep this from Imma and Abba? she wondered. Naomi had planned a variety of activities and programs for the children and felt she had so much to offer them. She hated the thought of having to cancel the playgroup. Such were the worries of a little girl. Her real problems were far, far greater.

Naomi Spira was stricken with a rare, fatal disease with dystonic features, a crippling genetic disease of the nervous system, which occurs primarily among Ashkenazic Jews. Her condition deteriorated rapidly, with the flexing of her toes being followed by a bending of the knees, compelling her to walk on tiptoe. By the time Naomi was ten, she was unable to walk at all. The writhing of her body and the involuntary spastic movements of her limbs were constant.

The Spiras sought medical assistance, but dystonia is a disease for which no cure has been found. Medications did not offer any relief, nor could they control the violent movements which were almost as agonizing to witness as they were to experience. The doctors offered no hope for Naomi's recovery. They advocated institutionalizing her since caring for her physical needs at home was bound to prove burdensome. They hinted that it would not be for very long, in any event, since the disease tended to progress with appalling speed.

The Spiras' means were limited. Zvi Spira learned in a Jerusalem Kollel and Chava was an English teacher in the Beis Yaakov school system, with Naomi — at her young age her prize pupil. Despite their meager resources, the Spiras spared no effort to find a cure, or at least some measure of relief, for their afflicted daughter. However, before long, even they began to accept the inevitability of their only child's demise. Although Chava Spira continued to tend her daughter, to feed Naomi and change her soiled clothing, Chava's face began to bear the fixed expression of despair reserved for the bereaved. She was beyond tears and, tormented by her own helplessness, went about her duties in an almost trance-like state.

"IMMA," NAOMI ASKED one morning, "do you know why people die?" Chava looked up abruptly from her sweeping. Throughout the long months of their daughter's suffering, the Spiras had not allowed themselves to utter that terrible word within Naomi's hearing. "So that life would be precious," the child continued, not waiting for a response. "Something that is yours forever is never precious."

Chava sat down on the edge of Naomi's bed and covered her face with her hands, as much in shame as in sorrow. Naomi's bright little mind, trapped inside a contorted, pathetic body, was as sharp as ever. It was a fact easily forgotten, for the painful, convulsive movements had significantly stifled her natural loquaciousness. In her grief, Chava realized, she had neglected her daughter's own need for solace.

She hugged Naomi gently. "Why should you talk of dying, *motek*?" she asked. "You're not..." but the denial solidified in her throat.

"Imma, what I mean is that I..." A spasm gripped her and only when it passed could she go on. "I don't think Hashem wants us to give up. Because life is so precious, we can't give it up without a fight."

Naomi's words spurred the Spiras out of their inertia. That evening Chava and Zvi talked long into the night, reviewing their options. "Look," Zvi said quietly, "we've seen the specialists in Hadassah and in Tel Hashomer. They all say the same thing. We've read the medical journals ourselves. All we can do now is pray that her suffering not be prolonged."

Chava almost replied harshly, but she saw how the ordeal had taken its toll on her husband. At thirty-five, his beard was already streaked with grey and his eyes were dull and sunken into deep hollows. She softened her tone. "I think we should take her to America. I know," she went on hastily over his protests, "I know it will cost a fortune and that we'll have to borrow the money. And I know the doctors here are wonderful, but none of them could have seen many cases like Naomi's."

Zvi knew his wife was right: they had to explore every possibility of saving Naomi, no matter how heavy the price. He chastised himself for his own lack of faith, cloaked in the guise of *emunah sheleimah*. Perhaps God's chosen messenger resided elsewhere, in a country where the skills with which he was endowed could be employed to benefit greater numbers of sufferers?

Despite the lateness of the hour, Zvi hurried off to consult with his *Rosh Kollel*. The Rav placed a call to a prominent Bnei Brak rabbi and secured the name of a top American specialist. The *Rosh Kollel* also assured Zvi that the money for the trip would be raised and encouraged him warmly.

D R. HOWARD TAUBER, Chief of Neurosurgery at Westchester Medical Center in Westchester County, New York, was considered a pioneer in dystonia research and a man who did not flinch at a challenge. Extensive correspondence, accelerated by cooperative couriers, provided Dr. Tauber with Naomi's medical records in addition to answers to many questions others had failed to ask. Then came the weeks of silence while the surgeon weighed accepting the case and possible courses — if any — of treatment. As the family waited for a reply, the tension in the Spira household rose to a fevered pitch.

When the invitation arrived at last, Chava and Zvi felt another wave of ambivalence sweep over them. Perhaps the trip and the expense would prove unjustified? she argued, suddenly unsure. This time it was Zvi who was firm: they had to try.

Arrangements were made for the Spiras to be hosted by the nearby religious community of New Square because of its proximity to Westchester Medical Center. They knew no one in New Square personally but, armed with the names of several relatives-of-friends who were willing to help, they boarded the plane.

The trip was blessedly uneventful. At Kennedy, the Spiras were met by representatives of the community and transported to New Square, to the home where they would be staying for the duration of their visit. It was a modest row house with a tiny furnished apartment in the basement, complete with an old but serviceable stove, a sink and a working refrigerator. Chava's face lit up at the sight of the miniature kitchen. It would minimize the imposition on their hosts, she thought, if she were able to manage her family's meals on her own.

Chava could not have known that throughout the difficult weeks ahead, she would not once prepare a meal with her own hands. In fact, the volunteer duty roster of the Spiras' host community was so long and comprehensive, that had their stay been extended for six months, or even longer, hospitality would still have been forthcoming. Such is the measure of *gemilus chassadim* in New Square.

T HE DAY AFTER their arrival, the Spiras met Dr. Tauber for the first time. A tall, taciturn, distinguished gentleman in his early fifties, he had little time for the amenities and quickly got down to business. His preliminary examination of Naomi, however, lasted for over an hour, during which time he had the secretary hold all of his calls. The abruptness of his manner was in no way offensive: the Spiras had come to America not to enjoy the doctor's social graces but to benefit from his superior medical talents.

"My initial findings lead me to concur with the diagnosis of dystonia. Naomi will have to be hospitalized for three days of extensive tests after which I will require a week to analyze the results and decide whether or not she is a surgical candidate. I won't burden you with a detailed explanation until that time."

Somewhat bewildered, the Spiras followed a nurse from the Medical Center's administration office and were handed a sheaf of official forms to complete. Their New Square chauffeur-of-the-day came to their rescue, explaining the nature of the unfamiliar documents and helping them to fill in the blanks. Normal hospital admission procedures were telescoped and bypassed for the Spiras' benefit. [Naomi was the only patient at the Medical Center without hospitalization insurance coverage]. She was taken that very day to a private room on the neurology floor.

Barely a minute was wasted. As soon as a nurse's aide had exchanged Naomi's clothes for a hospital gown, Naomi was examined by the resident and two interns; laboratory technicians collected various specimens; a nurse took her temperature and blood pressure; and a series of X-rays was scheduled for that afternoon. It was as though all of Westchester Medical Center was aware of the rapid progression of Naomi's illness and was determined to win the race against time.

While Chava fed her daughter a light dinner — courtesy of New Square's volunteer kosher catering — all the unasked questions flooded her mind. What if Dr. Tauber decided Naomi was *not* a "surgical candidate," as he had put it? Was there any treatment other than surgery? And, for that matter, what *kind* of surgery? What were the prospects for success? What constituted "success"? How risky was the surgery?

Naomi was drowsy from the sleeping pill she'd been given earlier so Chava tucked her in and kissed her good night. The drug seemed to lessen both the intensity and the frequency of the spasms and Chava wondered if it was necessary to subject a child who had already suffered so much, to the trauma of an operation which might possibly make things worse, or even — *chas ve'chalilah* — hasten the end. Could they not simply keep her sedated?

At that moment, Naomi's eyes suddenly opened wide, the dilated pupils almost totally concealing her irises. "I hate this medicine, Imma," she said sleepily. "It doesn't let me think." Chava understood that constant sedation was too cruel to contemplate. It would rob Naomi of the one thing she was still able to control: her mind.

THE DOOR OPENED and Dr. Tauber, dressed in street clothes, entered the room. Zvi looked up from his *sefer Tehillim*. "I'm sorry to intrude," the physician said, "but I owe you an apology. In my eagerness to get things moving today, I neglected to provide you with any useful information, and I'm sure you're terribly concerned." He seemed to have discarded his aloofness along with his hospital whites. Chava was pleased to discover a human being behind the facade of distant professionalism, and both she and her husband warmed to him instantly.

The doctor sat down and crossed his long legs. "Most of the patients who come to me are familiar with my work," he said, looking slightly embarrassed. "There have been several, ahem, mentions of it in the media, but I don't suppose you're up on it." The Spiras nodded their agreement.

"Well, I should like to say, first, that I admire and respect the work of your Israeli doctors. I've met a number of them at international neurological conferences and I think they are outstanding physicians.

"Second, everything you've been told about your daughter's illness is accurate. Dystonia is a crippling, devastating disease. Like Tay-Sachs, it occurs most commonly among Jews of Eastern European descent, and particularly, the very brightest ones — children like Naomi. The spastic convulsions are caused by a sort of short circuit in the nervous system, centered in the brain. The patient suffers a great deal of pain, as the spasms place unnatural strain on the muscles and ligaments. As you've seen, drugs do not significantly reduce the symptoms, unless they induce sleep in the patient. The disease progresses at an unpredictable rate, to the point where the frequency and intensity of the spasms impair breathing.

"Now, theoretically, if we can repair the short circuit, that is, the phenomenon of the brain receiving incorrect messages, we can alleviate the symptoms. I've had some success in this area," again the embarrassed throat-clearing, "by deadening or blocking the brain cells receiving the wrong message. However, the surgery involved is still classified as experimental."

Chava and Zvi looked at one another for a long minute, each trying to read the other's thoughts. "How long..." Chava began in a quavering voice, "how long can she live without the surgery?"

"I would say six months." The Spiras gasped. "But," the doctor hurriedly continued, "even if we do operate — and I can't say for certain yet that surgery is indicated — we may not be able to cure your daughter. And even if the operation is successful, we might relieve the symptoms and thereby prolong her life, but there is no guarantee that the disease will not attack other brain cells later on. Furthermore, although all surgery carries an element of risk, brain surgery has a significant mortality rate. If and when we reach the point of deciding, you will have to weigh that against the certain fatality of the disease itself."

Dr. Tauber gravely shook hands with Zvi and left. Throughout the impromptu consultation, Naomi had slept soundly, and now her parents, physically and emotionally drained, gazed at her sleeping form. All the doubts and fears crowded their minds; there was no room for rational thought. They knew they too should leave, but the effort required to do so was beyond them.

THE MUFFLED hydraulic whoosh of the door startled them. It was the night nurse. "Your driver is here to take you home. Naomi will be fine. We'll look after her," she said with a warm smile. "You two go and get something to eat and a good night's sleep." Her firm hand guided Chava out into the hall and Zvi followed.

In the car the Spiras sat in a stunned silence while the driver — another New Square volunteer — took them "home". A surprise awaited them in the apartment: piping hot stew simmering on a low flame, the beds turned down invitingly, and, leaning against a fresh sponge cake, a note that read: "If you need to talk, we're right upstairs."

The smell of hot food reminded them that they hadn't eaten since early morning, and even then, had only been able to swallow a quick cup of coffee. They ate ravenously, barely tasting the stew as it went down. Later, while Chava filled a kettle for tea, Zvi fell into an exhausted sleep at the table.

Chava knew sleep would not come so easily for her. Fueled by the hearty meal and propelled by nervous energy, she cleared and washed the dishes, scrubbed the pot, and brewed a cup of strong tea for herself. Dr. Tauber's voice echoed loudly in her head: "Experimental... mortality rate... devastating... fatality..." She fingered her hostess' note absently. "... we're right upstairs..."

Chava knocked hesitantly on the big front door. It was opened almost immediately by a large, round woman with the kindest eyes and sweetest smile Chava had ever seen: Rebbetzin Zeinwerth. "I..." Chava began and the Rebbetzin reached out and drew her across the threshold. "I'm so glad you decided to come up!" she said. "Was supper all right?"

"I..." The words refused to come. Her eyes misted over with tears. The Rebbetzin wrapped Chava tenderly in her arms and said, "I know, *mammaleh*, you need to cry." She caressed Chava's shuddering back and crooned to her softly. "I know, yes, *mammaleh*, I know. You feel so helpless." Chava sobbed and held on tight to this woman, a total stranger, who seemed to understand everything. Joined in an embrace of sorrow, the two mothers stood in the front hall as the big clock on the wall slowly ticked away.

"Thank you," Chava whispered, the crying done for now. "I... I can't talk about it yet."

"You just get some sleep now. I'll be right here whenever you need me." Chava looked up into those kind eyes and suddenly the stone that lay on her heart felt lighter.

WHEN THE SPIRAS arrived at the hospital on the morning of the third and final day of tests, they found Naomi's bed empty. In that heart-stopping moment before comprehension replaced irrational fear, Chava learned a rare lesson; she now knew exactly how she would react on the day of her daughter's death. She would not faint, nor would she become hysterical. The emotional storm of the first evening with Rebbetzin Zeinwerth was over and in its wake Chava felt stronger, more able to cope with the trials ahead.

Zvi had been the strong one all along, she thought. From the outset, when Naomi's illness was first diagnosed, his capacity to deal with the situation calmly had exasperated Chava. It was he who had compelled them to see one specialist after the other; it was he whose faith had remained unshaken, while she had railed against a cruel fate. Only after they had exhausted all the local options, had he lapsed into resigned acceptance of their *gezeira*. And when they had both reached their nadir, it was little Naomi who had found the words to rouse them from their stupor and force them to continue waging the battle for her life.

The sound of Naomi's laughter rang through the corridor. An orderly was pushing her wheelchair swiftly along the polished floor, making the clanging and whooping noises of a fire engine. It had been so long since the Spiras had last heard Naomi's infectious giggle! They smiled at one another as if to say, "No matter what the outcome, it will all have been worthwhile if only to hear Naomi laugh again."

In the short time since Naomi's arrival at Westchester Medical Center, she had won the hearts of all the staff members with whom she came in contact. The overworked nurses would pop into her room to say hello as they passed by; orderlies competed for the privilege of reading to her; lab technicians took the time to explain procedures and demonstrate their instruments. All were drawn to the inquisitive, unusually intelligent child whose desire for knowledge was not dimmed by her grave condition.

After Naomi had rested a while, a different orderly arrived to accompany her to the radiology department for a CAT scan. Chava joined them, as much to protect Naomi from what she imagined would be a frightening experience, as from curiosity to see for herself what fearsome procedures were being inflicted upon her child. She was not permitted to enter the room, however, and had to be satisfied with watching through the window of the door.

Naomi was transferred to a table-height conveyer belt and her arms and legs were strapped in place. A technician checked the position of Naomi's head relative to the gigantic doughnut-shaped scanner that dominated the room. Then he secured her head to a styrofoam block with adhesive tape.

OUTSIDE the communicating door, Chava watched as the technician activated the table and Naomi's head disappeared into the scanner's gaping mouth: a white steel behemoth devouring a defenseless child. The huge ring began to rotate silently with abrupt, intermittent movements like the gear of an enormous clock. For every degree of rotation, the CAT scanner made two hundred and forty separate cross-sectional readings. When sorted and analyzed by computer, these would provide a color-keyed representation of Naomi's brain, along with all pertinent data: dimensions, weight, blood flow, etc.

After a few minutes, the scanner halted its rotational movement, and the computer console came alive. Blinking lights flickered on and off and in thirty seconds the computer solved over forty-three thousand equations of tissue-density measurements. The cathode-ray tube on the output console lit up as the first image appeared. The technician hastily adjusted the window width and resolution to give the best image.

The picture was oval with a white border and a granular interior. It was a computer-constructed image of the inside of Naomi's head, positioned as if someone were looking down on her after the top of the skull had been removed. Each image was wiped off the screen by the next one. At the push of a button, the entire file was permanently recorded on a disc.

A nurse appeared at Chava's side. "That's the last of the tests," she said. "You'll be able to take Naomi home now."

"**A**RE YOU ALL RIGHT?" Chava asked anxiously, examining her daughter's face for evidence. There were dark smudges under her eyes and her usually rosy coloring was tinged with grey.

"Of course, Imma," she said impatiently. "This was the most exciting test so far." Her extremities twitched and trembled as she spoke and Chava recognized the harbingers of a full-blown seizure. Naomi's shoulder pivoted forward and her right arm jerked outward. Her left leg kicked away from the wheelchair's footrest.

The nurse grasped Chava's arm comfortingly. "We'll give you a supply of strong muscle relaxants you can administer yourself," she said. "They'll help her get through the next few days more comfortably. And you'll feel better knowing that you have some way to help her when it gets real bad."

Zvi packed up Naomi's belongings while Chava dressed her and combed her hair. The bottle of pills and detailed instructions were waiting for them at the nurses' station and Chava reached for them like a drowning man grabbing hold of a life preserver. "Mrs. Spira," the nurse said gently, "this isn't a cure, or even a temporary solution. Please, use them sparingly."

Chava was alarmed. "Are they... dangerous?"

"Not if you follow the instructions carefully."

"I will," Chava promised. Zvi wheeled Naomi out the door and through the parking lot to the bus stop. They had insisted upon making their own way home, despite the driver's protests, as they were unsure about the time of their departure.

"We may have missed the bus," Zvi said, checking his watch. "It might be an hour before the next one. What do you think?"

"I'm too exhausted to think at all," Chava replied. "I just want to get Naomi home and settled down and then put *myself* to bed. I feel as if I could sleep for a week."

JUST THEN a very elegant car drew to a whispering halt at the curb. It was not the gleaming chromework or the white sidewall tires or the expanse of tinted windows that caught the Spiras' attention, but the absolutely mammoth proportions of the vehicle itself. In Israel, where European compacts constitute the cars of the masses, a moderate-sized American model turns heads. But not even visiting dignitaries would be seen driving along the thoroughfares of Jerusalem in a car of this dimension.

The automatic window slipped smoothly out of sight and the ruddy face of an elderly gentleman appeared at the rear. He tipped his fedora politely and asked, "Can I offer you a lift? It looks like rain." Zvi took one quick glance at his wife's drawn visage and gratefully accepted.

The driver stowed Naomi's wheelchair in the cavernous trunk while the Spiras settled themselves on the wide leather-upholstered seat. "You must be one of Hashem's angels," Naomi told their benefactor. "How else could you have known that my Imma was too tired to wait for the bus to New Square?"

"Perhaps you're right, my dear," he said with a twinkle in his eye. "It just so happens that I myself am headed for — where did you say again? Yes, New Square. That's near Ramapoe," he instructed the driver. "When I saw you at the bus stop, I thought I should do my part for the energy crisis and not travel with an empty car. So here I am and here you are. Now, you must tell me all about yourselves because we have a longish trip and I am an insatiably curious man."

Naomi took it upon herself to be their spokesman. Chava sank wearily into the cushioned seat and allowed herself to drift into a state of pre-slumber but Zvi was fascinated with their anonymous friend. Throughout Naomi's recitation, delivered in her usual halting though eloquent fashion, punctuated by frequent spasms and twitches, the gentleman listened attentively, seemingly oblivious to her debility.

Even Zvi, who had been painfully witnessing his daughter's convulsive movements for more than a year, could not do so without reacting in some way. Although he tried to mask his expressions of pity and restrain any empathetic gestures, both of which irritated Naomi, his fatherly emotions and human sensitivity always got the better of him. Was this stranger, then, inured to suffering — or, in fact, far more attuned than Naomi's own father to the child's need to be treated as a normal person?

The "longish" trip lasted no more than twenty minutes, and the Spiras expressed their effusive thanks as they climbed out of the car. The fedora lifted briefly again and the electrified window hummed up its track. As silently as it had first approached them, the boat-sized vehicle pulled away into the evening traffic, its tires squealing slightly on the damp asphalt. "It looks like he was right about the rain," Zvi said. They hurried inside.

DURING THE week that followed, the Spiras hardly had a moment to themselves, and the difficult waiting period was made nearly tension-free. The neighborhood children dropped by daily to entertain Naomi with puppet shows and stories, and the Spiras' tiny apartment was filled with youthful giggling and boisterousness. Each night another New Square housewife appeared with shopping bags and armloads of cooked food and baked goods, and often stayed for tea and light conversation.

Only when they took their leave did the subject which had brought the Spiras to New Square come up. "We're all praying for you," they would say, or "May the Almighty send Naomi a complete and speedy recovery." Even the youngsters never failed to call a hearty *"refuah sheleimah"* as they waved goodbye.

"It's as if they've undertaken 'the cure of Naomi Spira' as a community project," Zvi remarked, overwhelmed by the genuine concern displayed by the residents of New Square.

"I think most people have difficulty expressing their feelings, especially sympathy. They don't want to hurt you by ignoring your problem and don't know how to handle an emotional outburst that they might inadvertently cause. So usually they avoid contact altogether. This community doesn't seem to have any difficulty whatsoever, thank God. I don't know how we could ever repay their kindness."

The long-awaited phone call came at last and word spread quickly via communal grapevine: Dr. Tauber was prepared to operate. Now it was up to the Spiras to decide. The magnitude of that decision came crashing down on them as all the fears and trepidation that for days had been relegated to the distant background came to the fore. It was Friday and Dr. Tauber required their answer before noon on Sunday.

Their neighbors sensed the Spiras' need to be alone over the weekend and it was a very glum threesome that sat down to the Shabbos meal that Friday night. Naomi tried to lighten the mood with cheerful recollections from her afternoons with the children, but her parents' tight-lipped smiles and grim, preoccupied stares were unaffected by jokes and jests.

"Shabbos is *mayain olam haba,*" she said aloud, "and we have no right to be sad on this day." Zvi and Chava looked at one another across the table. Naomi was right, but the words "*olam haba*" had a special meaning for them at this moment. Her casual use of the term went through their hearts like a knife.

Zvi broke into an exuberant round of *zemiros* then, his eyes squeezed tightly shut to hide his tears and his fist pounding the tabletop hard enough to make the saltshaker dance. Naomi grinned broadly. Once again, the little ten-year-old child had lifted her parents' flagging spirits.

WHEN ZVI RETURNED from shul on Sunday morning, he tiptoed into Naomi's room to make sure she was still asleep. Weighty matters demanded his and Chava's attention and their discussion was not for her ears. Naomi lay so motionless in her bed that Zvi watched for long seconds until he was certain he'd seen the regular rise and fall of the covers that indicated she was breathing.

"I had to give her a pill in the middle of the night," Chava said, setting the table for breakfast. "She was in agony, but she wouldn't cry out. I think she didn't want to disturb us."

"How do you know she needed that medicine, then? The nurse warned us to save it for emergencies."

"I heard a noise so I went to investigate. She was..." Chava swallowed hard and took a deep breath. "She was *davening*. Her pillow was soaked with tears and her lip was bleeding where she had bitten it, trying to hold in the screams." She glared at him angrily. "How much more of an emergency should I have waited for?"

Zvi stared wordlessly at his wife. Since the phone call Friday morning, she had hardly had a bite to eat and he doubted she'd slept very much — if at all — in the past forty-eight hours. Her nerves seemed to be stretched to the limit. How was he going to hold his family together in this crisis? he wondered. What could keep them all from falling apart? Their child's life was slipping away and with it his wife's health and his own sanity.

He waited a moment for her to calm down. "Chava," he said, "I think we should consent to the operation. It's Naomi's only chance."

Chava whirled on him suddenly. "No!" she shouted. "*I will not allow the operation!* I intend to take her home — not with tubes and catheters sticking out of her, not with machines pumping breath into her lungs, not with the smell of hospitals in her nostrils! I'm taking her *home* to die!"

"Chavaleh," he said softly, "and what if she *lives?* What if the operation is a success and Naomi *lives* — not like she is now, but like she *was?*" In the silence that followed, they heard Naomi calling to them. They hurried to her bedside.

"Please, please, listen to me," she begged, her eyes brimming with tears. "I'm not afraid of dying. I'm more afraid of living... the way I am. If Hashem wants to take me, He will whether we're in Yerushalayim or in New Square or in the operating room." Her parents gripped her hands tightly. "I... I want to do the operation. Maybe Dr. Tauber will learn something from it that can help another girl with my problem. Or maybe, if Hashem wants it, maybe... He'll make me well again."

Chava put her head down on her daughter's bed and cried.

"I once heard a story," Naomi said, "about a man who was mourning the death of his beloved wife. While walking on the beach, in his anguish he cried out to the Almighty, 'You promised to walk alongside me in times of trouble, but when I look down I only see one set of footprints.' There was silence and then a voice lovingly called out, 'My dear Yankeleh, what seems to be one pair of footprints is not really you walking alone. It is me carrying you.' Don't worry, Imma, I can see those footprints!"

T HE SPIRAS conveyed their consent to Dr. Tauber by phone and returned Sunday evening to the Medical Center. They stayed with Naomi all night long, *davening* with her and reading to her until she fell asleep, but not another tear was shed. In the morning there was an avalanche of paperwork to attend to: consent forms, release forms, insurance documents. Zvi's hand trembled at the autopsy provision and again when he came to the organ donation clause. He got a firm grip on himself and emphatically denied his consent to both.

Dr. Tauber invited them into his consultation room and slipped a computer disc into the terminal on his desk. Pointing from time to time at the incomprehensible picture that flashed on the screen, he described the surgical procedure and reiterated its experimental nature and possible catastrophic consequences. But only one piece of information succeeded in penetrating the Spira's benumbed consciousness: Naomi was to be awake for the operation.

"She won't feel any pain, I assure you. A local anesthesia will be administered. But she will be aware of everything that's going on. I need her to guide me."

The Spiras had not yet recovered from that shock when Dr. Tauber delivered the next one: "My fee plus that of the anesthesiologist and the rest of the surgical team, in addition to hospital expenses, clinical tests and medicines, is $63,540." The Spiras reeled.

"However," the physician hurriedly continued, "it's been taken care of." He handed them an embossed card with only the words "Best Wishes" inscribed and a winged angel drawn in the corner. "An anonymous benefactor, no doubt."

ZVI AND CHAVA rode with their daughter in the elevator to the operating theater. She looked so small and pale in her oversized hospital gown, imprisoned by the siderails of the stretcher-table. Chava knew she should be saying words of encouragement, but none came. Each time she opened her mouth to speak, her throat closed, and the too-short descent to the Operating Room passed in silence.

The doors split apart to reveal the over-bright fluorescence of the surgical floor. Naomi reached over the rail and grabbed hold of her mother's sleeve. "My *morah* told us once about Reb Simcha Bunim," she said as the orderly wheeled her towards OR8. "When the hour arrived for Reb Simcha Bunim to depart from the world, his wife stood by his bedside and wept. He said to her, 'Be silent; why do you cry? My whole life was only that I might learn how to die.'"

Naomi kissed her parents goodbye. "I love you, Imma. I love you, Abba. I always will."

In the anteroom of OR8, Naomi's hair was shorn and her head was painted with a yellowish-brown disinfectant. The sterile chemical smell seemed exceptionally acrid to her and she wrinkled her nose in disgust. OR8 was a theater used exclusively for brain surgery and fitted with overhead-mounted Zeiss operating microscopes, closed-circuit video systems with recording capabilities, and special OR tables.

A post-operative patient was wheeled past her, his chin held back by one of the orderlies pushing the stretcher and his head a bandaged nightmare. The sight of that patient was enough to illustrate the kind of ordeal she was about to undergo. Her central being would be rudely cracked open and violated — not just a peripheral part of her, such as a foot or an arm, she thought, but her head... where the very core of her *sechel* resided.

The ceiling of the theater was illuminated by two large stainless steel operating room lights shaped like inverted kettle drums with six giant eyes. At the center of the room stood the operating table, at one end of which was mounted a round piece of padding with a hole in the center. Naomi knew immediately that the hole was meant to hold her head.

"GOOD MORNING, NAOMI," said a pleasant male voice with a British accent. Dr. Mohandas Shastri, the Indian anesthesiologist, had soft dark eyes and skin the color of coffee. "Relax now, little one, and I will take away all the pain. There is just one thing you must do for me: you must avoid coughing during the operation. Do you think you can do that, little one?" Naomi smiled bravely and nodded.

Naomi felt a small prick in her left forearm. Looking up, she could see tiny bubbles rising up in a clear bag over her head. Dr. Shastri had begun the IV and then repeated the procedure in her right forearm, threading a long thin plastic tube into her. He then adjusted the table so that it tilted slightly downward.

Several masked faces surrounded her. Some of them belonged to scrub nurses and the others belonged to residents in neurosurgery. Just as two doctors moved away to reexamine the X-rays which lined the back wall, Dr. Tauber walked in. "Shalom!" he said cheerfully to Naomi. "Naomi, you are going to be my assistant. So be strong and be a big girl, and with your help, God will help us both." Naomi grinned.

The pace in the OR quickened. A scrub nurse already gowned and gloved appeared with a steaming tray of instruments which she placed atop a nearby table. Another nurse reached into the jumble of instruments and began to arrange them on a tray. Dr. Shastri wrapped a blood pressure cuff around Naomi's upper right arm. A nurse exposed Naomi's chest and taped on EKG leads and instantly sonar-like beeps could be heard.

Dr. Tauber studied the CAT scans and X-rays and then positioned Naomi's shaven head. Placing his pinky on her nose and his thumb on the top of her head, he drew two lines with a marking pen: the first line from ear to ear over the top of her head, the second line bisecting the first, starting at the middle of the forehead and extending back to the occipital area.

"Turn your head to the left, honey," the surgeon instructed. Naomi felt a finger palpate the ridge of bone that ran back from her right eye toward her right ear. Then she felt the marking pen trace a looping line that began at her right temple and arched upward and backward, ending behind her left ear. The line defined a horseshoe-shaped area with Naomi's ear at its base.

As soon as Dr. Tauber had finished his illustration, Dr. Shastri took over once again. Holding a syringe in his hand he informed Naomi that the hypodermic contained a substance that would make her relax and not feel the work performed on her head.

TIME BECAME DISCONTINUOUS; sounds drifted in and out. Naomi felt herself being turned half on her side with her right shoulder elevated and supported by a pillow. Both of her wrists were bound to a board that jutted out perpendicular to the operating table. Her arms felt very heavy and weren't twitching as they usually did. A leather cinch went around her waist, securing her body.

Naomi felt her head scrubbed and painted again. There were several sharp needles accompanied by fleeting pain before her head was clamped in some sort of vise.

A blue-eyed nurse held Naomi's hand tightly, but that didn't offer any relief from the sudden acute pain she felt above her right ear. It occurred again. "Everything is fine,"

Dr. Shastri said. "I am injecting the local anesthetic. You'll only feel it for a moment."

The pain stopped as suddenly as it had begun and Naomi heard Dr. Tauber breathing directly over her right ear.

"Scalpel," the surgeon said.

Naomi felt pressure like a finger being pressed against her scalp and rotated around the line drawn by the marking pen. She could feel warm fluid on her neck through the layers of surgical drapes all around her head.

"Hemostat," said Dr. Tauber. Naomi could hear sharp metallic snaps. "Raney clips." With each brisk order, Naomi heard the instrument being slapped into the doctor's gloved palm.

The surgeon then made a thumbnail-size, semi-circular incision near the top of her head. He stopped the bleeding around the flap with a bipolar cautery, which works like a soldering iron. Dr. Tauber lifted the tiny tongue of scalp and tissue with a little retractor that held it out of the way. Then, using a drill the size of a fountain pen, he penetrated the skull. The drill stopped automatically when it reached the dura, the brain's semi-transparent protective covering.

Naomi heard the high-pitched whine of a gas-powered motor and felt a sense of pressure and vibration on her head, something like the feeling of a dentist's drill on an anesthetized tooth. But the noise was far more frightening. Naomi knew what it meant: her skull was being opened with a surgical saw, and the smell of scorched bone permeated the gauze drapes over her face. The sound of the saw died and the rhythmic beeping of the cardiac monitor emerged from the sudden stillness.

"Bone forceps," said Dr. Tauber. Naomi heard and felt bone crunching. It sounded very close to her right ear.

"Dural hook and scalpel." With the knife he made a small opening. A pinkish gray mound of naked, pulsating brain could be seen through the hole. "Elevators," said Dr. Tauber.

Naomi felt several more twinges, followed by what sounded like a loud snap. She knew her brain was exposed.

T HE SURGEON'S HANDS moved with economical deliberateness, his prominent eyes behind special magnifying lenses never wavering from his patient. He inserted cottonoid strips between the dura and the brain for protection, and with small scissors opened up the covering over Naomi's brain to the extent of the bony window.

"Let's have the stimulator and EEG leads," he said.

A resident wrestled with the profusion of tiny wires. The circulating nurse took the appropriate leads when the doctors handed them to her and plugged them into electrical consoles. The junior resident carefully placed the wick electrodes in two parallel rows, one along the middle of the temporal lobe and the other above the Sylvian vein. The flexible electrodes with the silver balls went under the brain. The circulating nurse threw a switch and an EEG screen next to the cardiac monitor lit up with bright green blips tracing erratic lines.

Working in concert with the brain waves, Dr. Tauber began the pioneering aspect of the operation: testing the patient's reaction to his stimulus. He started on the right side of the brain. "Naomi, do you feel this? Does this hurt? Try and keep your foot still..."

In a little over an hour Dr. Tauber had finished the right part of the brain and moved over to the left, following the same procedure. When he completed his work there, he told the surgical team that he wanted to go back to the right side to make sure that he had covered everything.

Four hours and thirty-seven minutes after he had begun, Dr. Tauber was convinced that he had done all he could. He peeled off his gloves and stepped away from the table while the resident sutured the flap of skin of Naomi's scalp back in place.

"Mohandas, I want her out for at least twenty-four hours. I want her to be well-rested when I make my check-up."

THE VIGIL at Naomi's bedside was tense and lonely. "At least she survived the operation," Zvi said as he wiped his daughter's brow with damp gauze. Chava moistened Naomi's cracked lips with chips of ice. They realized the simple chores they performed were largely superfluous, but it was a way of occupying themselves during the hours that stretched before them like a road without end.

"Dr. Tauber said to be prepared for anything. Her personality may be altered, her speech could be affected, or there could be no improvement at all in her condition, or — *chas v'shalom* — it could be worse. What do you think?"

"I can't think," Zvi said. He mopped Naomi's forehead again.

Day became night and Chava dozed fitfully in her chair. Zvi was able to recite several chapters of *Tehillim* by heart, he had repeated them so many times. Naomi's head, encased in bandages, was huge, a gigantic white orb with eyes, nose and mouth. Her skin looked almost transparent, with a purplish cast. He tucked an extra blanket around her in case she might be cold.

The sky outside the window was pinking with the rising

sun and still Naomi slept on. The nightshift nurse took her temperature and blood pressure before going off duty. Chava awoke with a start. "There's something for you at the desk, Mrs. Spira. Don't get up — I'll bring it to you."

The thermos of steaming coffee and the package of Rebbetzin Zeinwerth's sponge cake were accompanied by a note: "All of New Square stormed the Gates of Heaven last night and we won't settle for anything less than a complete recovery!"

By midday, Naomi was beginning to revive. She mumbled incoherently and her eyelids fluttered, but she did not fully regain consciousness. A nurse examined her catheter and replaced the intravenous drip with a glucose solution. At one o'clock, Dr. Tauber entered and scanned the notations on her chart. Naomi opened her eyes.

"Hi," she said. "How am I?" Her speech was slow and her words slurred by the sedative. Everyone in the room seemed to be holding their breath. Naomi looked down at her legs and then at her arms, which for so long had been unruly beasts whose will she could not subjugate to her own. They moved now on command and lay still at her behest.

"*Baruch Hashem!*" she cried joyfully. "*Baruch Hashem!*" She kicked her feet and wiggled her toes with sheer delight.

Zvi shook Dr. Tauber's hand enthusiastically. The cool, detached surgeon took a large white handkerchief from his pocket and wiped his eyes with a show of removing a cinder. "Yes, ahem, that's quite... good," was all he could say.

A nurse pushed open the door and noise from the hall poured into the room. "Uh, there are some people here to see Naomi, doctor," she said uncertainly. "Can she receive visitors?"

"How *many* visitors are there, nurse?" The buzz of excitement outside increased in volume as word of Naomi's recovery was passed along.

The nurse glanced over her shoulder. "I would say about — I mean at *least,* three bus loads..."

Boston, Mass. and the Bostoner's Masses

N LESS THAN an hour, the sun would set over Boston, and with the appearance of the first stars of the night of *Shemini Atzeres,* 1946, the *Sukkos* holiday would fade into cherished memory.

A row of old houses stood silhouetted against the darkening sky, looking solemn and vaguely sinister. But in one house the bleak exterior belied the unmistakable warmth of the lights that burned within its windows. It was the home of the Bostoner Rebbe.

While the Rebbe himself, in the *sukkah,* was savoring the parting mitzvos of the holiday, the Rebbetzin was in the kitchen putting the final touches to the *Yom Tov* meal. Her preparations were always something of a mathematical feat: no matter how many guests were expected, she invariably seemed to produce three times the quantity required. And somehow, nothing ever went to waste.

The Rebbe's house was a veritable magnet for guests — those who were invited and those who invited themselves. Some were travellers unable to catch a connecting train or plane; others were strangers who had come to the area for medical treatment at one of Boston's renowned hospitals. And still others simply wanted to participate in a chassidic experience in the heart of New England.

How did they all find their way to the home of the Rebbe? Most had simply heard about him from others who had enjoyed his hospitality. The Bostoner Rebbe's reputation as a host extended nearly as far as his reputation as a charismatic leader.

MEANWHILE, in the harbor at the other end of Boston, preparations of a different sort were being made. The longshoremen on the wharf, securing the thick ropes, cast long shadows as the sun dipped into the horizon and, with its last rays, poured buckets of light on the barges in the adjacent ferry basin. It was 4:05 in the afternoon and the *Thomas Edison* was about to dock at Pier 34.

Huddled aboard the overcrowded vessel were over 400 passengers from all over Europe. Of them, sixty-two were Jews, all survivors of the Nazi inferno. The rest were prospective immigrants who would first have to undergo medical examinations before an immigration official would determine their fate.

For the Jews, the United States would at last provide a haven from the murderous horrors they had endured in Europe. Alas, their relatives and friends would not share their new home. It was too late. And so, together with the haunting memories that were their constant companions, they joined the other passengers passing through the Reception Center, up the central stairs to the Great Hall. They had made it this far and now they were actually on American soil. But were they really home yet?

During the voyage they'd heard disheartening stories of people who had been turned back because of sickness.

Heaven knew, none of them were strong. And after all they had endured, it seemed inconceivable that they would soon be granted the precious gift of a secure existence.

The Jews crowded together in the vast hall, one hundred and sixty feet long and eighty feet wide, with a ceiling so high that every step they took seemed to find an eerie echo way above them. This was the main center for immigrant registration, but all that registered with the disoriented new arrivals was the cacophony of clattering baggage-carts and touting money-changers, and the frightening sight of lines leading in all directions — to ticket offices, food counters and baggage depots. Even more alarming were the immigration officials, hoarsely shouting incomprehensible commands and wearing dark uniforms. For the Jewish immigrants, a uniform — any uniform — represented an army officer. And the sight of an army officer elicited an involuntary shudder.

They stood waiting nervous and confused, monotony accentuated by the sight of the daunting bureaucracy ahead of them. It was an exceptionally busy day, for three other boats — from Liverpool, Piraeus, and Naples — had arrived earlier that morning. The Jews were separated from the others and directed to a side room where they would be checked and deloused. The very idea of such "selections" touched a raw nerve, awakening still-vivid memories of the painfully recent past.

For the delousing process, the men and women were herded into small, separate rooms while uniformed personnel clinically ordered them to strip. Their ragged, filthy garments were then handed over to be sprayed by an attendant sitting on the other side of a window. As though in a trance, the Jews slowly undressed and shuffled toward the window. While they stood around — naked, hungry and shivering — other attendants sprayed them with a foul-smelling substance. Now they were ready to shower.

JEWISH IMMIGRANTS who arrived in New England invariably travelled directly on to New York by train. Rarely, if ever, was there an acquaintance in New England to encourage them to stay. And while many who arrived on Fridays made the mistake of continuing their journey, not realizing that New York was six hours away, those who had arrived at this late hour of *Hoshanna Rabba* knew that no trip before *Yom Tov* was possible.

In fact, the Jews had talked of little else during the voyage, for not one of them knew a soul anywhere near their vessel's destination. And yet, the most devoutly religious among them seemed to be the least concerned with the dilemma. Their apparent indifference was so striking that a group of fellow Jewish passengers had finally approached them and asked how they intended to spend the next two days of *Yom Tov* and the Shabbos which immediately followed them.

"Didn't you see the sign in Yiddish pinned up at the Hamburg port?" asked the oldest one, Abish Gottesman, a stooped, gray-bearded man with a smile of rare warmth.

"What sign?"

"The one about the Bostoner Rebbe."

"Bostoner Rebbe? What's that?"

"A 'Rebbe' is a Rebbe, and Boston is the town he comes from... I guess."

"Where is Boston?"

"I never heard of it before so I imagine it must be in Galicia," Abish ventured. "But that doesn't matter. The notice said that he takes guests and that the food is reliably kosher."

"How will you find him?"

"If there was a sign in *Germany* I'm sure that there will be signs in *America* telling us how to get to him."

"Are you really serious?" mocked Isaac Hertz. Isaac's father had been a tailor, and a pious Jew, but Isaac himself had long since discarded the traditions and was now the self-appointed chief cynic. "You don't even know what city he lives in."

"Don't worry," said Abish. "I saw the sign, and he takes guests and new arrivals."

AND SO NEWS of the Bostoner Rebbe had swept quickly among the Jewish passengers, and in their state of anxiety, the image of the Rebbe was grasped enthusiastically as a sign of promise in the new and strange land they were entering. It did not matter that they had never heard of the town of Boston. It hadn't occurred to a single one that a "Rebbe" could get his title from an American town. All they knew was that the boat was docking at a city in New England, far from New York.

For the last two days of the voyage, the Jews had begun to wonder who this Bostoner Rebbe could be. A man who just picked up Displaced Persons from the piers and gave them food and lodging? A long-lost father who would be there to welcome them? Their imagination was heightened by the tedium of the voyage and the harrowing memories of the world they had left behind. Exhausted and close to despair, they had begun to think of little else but the Bostoner Rebbe. For some, he had taken on the dimensions of a Messianic figure; and even the non-religious among them were intrigued by this mysterious man from an unknown city.

There were, however, a few men on board who had, somewhere in the ashes of Auschwitz, relinquished all their faith and hope. Derisively, they called Abish and his friends the "wise men of Chelm," and accused them cynically of fantasizing about a mysterious "Chassidic Savior" with imagined agents all over Europe soliciting guests to his court.

"Did you hear these learned men?" Isaac Hertz had mocked. "They will end up spending their so-called holiday in the streets!"

And now, in the stark, unfamiliar surroundings of the immigration building, the reality of the delousing and processing procedures did indeed shatter most of the illusions that the Jews had nurtured. As they gathered their meager possessions, the setting sun outside seemed to join in ridiculing their earlier fantasies. And the cynics clearly enjoyed the discomfort of the others, though some of them still appeared to expect the Bostoner Rebbe to emerge somehow from among the throng of officials.

"Maybe your Rebbe has a dark uniform," jeered Isaac, indicating a group of officials, "and plans to use this hall for the *Simchas Torah* celebration."

What could they say? In their pitiful imaginings, they had actually pictured the Rebbe greeting them at the docks and escorting them, all sixty-two of them, into his home. Now they stood outside, blinking in the sun's dying glare. Some children began to cry.

A T THAT MOMENT two young men were walking down through the docks to the immigration building. They walked briskly but their steps were heavy, as though they were reluctantly following instructions. And indeed they were. For Tuvia and Shabsai had instructions from the Bostoner Rebbe.

By the time the immigrants had cleared official

registration and customs formalities, it was just one hour before *Yom Tov.* Those who had placed their frail hopes in the imagined hospitality of the Bostoner Rebbe felt so gullible and dejected that they hardly noticed the sarcastic comments of their cynical companions.

But then something happened that took everyone by surprise. Two chassidim appeared among the crowd of visitors outside the doors of the Arrivals Hall.

"Shalom aleichem, welcome to America, and *gutt Yontiff!* The Bostoner Rebbe would like to invite you for *Yom Tov* and Shabbos," said Tuvia mechanically, prepared for a blanket refusal of his invitation by the group.

All the members of the group froze. They simply could not believe their ears. Even the children stopped wailing for a moment and looked up wide-eyed. Tuvia and Shabsai drew back a few paces, glancing at each other in surprise as if to ask, "Did we say something wrong?" The cynics slipped shamefacedly to the back of the group.

The sound of Abish's voice, quavering but clear broke the silence: "We accept."

"'We?'" The question came simultaneously from both the chassidim and the cynics.

"Yes, *we,*" he said firmly, "the whole group. We thank you very much. We had already decided to accept the Bostoner Rebbe's invitation."

THE CHASSIDIM looked around at the tightly assembled group and saw the nodding heads. Their spokesman was indeed speaking for all of them. It suddenly dawned on Tuvia that somebody had finally accepted an invitation. Somebody? That *sixty* somebodies had accepted. He dashed over to a phone booth to make a call.

"Hello, Rebbe? We found some guests!" he blurted out excitedly. "A whole group of DPs have just got off the boat and they don't want to travel to New York before *Yontiff*."

"*Baruch Hashem!* But you must hurry. There isn't much time."

"But Rebbe, they wo... wo... won't fit in our car! The Rebbe doesn't understand, it's a group of over si... sixty!"

"All the better," replied the Rebbe calmly. "I can see we'll have a very joyful *Simchas Torah*."

"Some of them are not religious."

"Even better."

"Even better?"

"Yes, they need a proper *Yontiff* even more. Now hurry and help them into taxis. I will have someone waiting outside with money for the taxi fare and instructions as to which families will host them. I'll make the arrangements right away."

"But Rebbe, I don't know how to break this to you. We were speaking to the group, and they think, they think that they are all coming to *you!* As if you were expecting them! I told them that I hoped we would be able to place them with different families but they told me, I repeat THEY told me, that the Bostoner Rebbe was waiting for them. They won't go to anyone else. They trust only YOUR *kashrus*."

"*Be'ezer Hashem,*" came the relaxed reply of the Rebbe, "we will think of something."

A S SOON AS he put the phone down, the Bostoner Rebbe made a quick reckoning. It was now forty-five minutes until *Yom Tov* and all of the stores carrying kosher products were closed. Even if the Rebbetzin had enough food stocked in her kitchen, there would certainly not be enough time to cook as much as was needed for three days.

"Hello, a *gutten erev Yontiff*, this is the Bostoner Rebbe speaking..."

"... *She'ayris haplaita!** Of course, we'll do anything, send them right over."

"One last thing — we need food. Please bring over whatever you can spare right away, and don't come in the front entrance. Come around the back and bring the food directly to the kitchen."

Sleeping arrangements also presented a problem. Among the arrivals were families who should be housed together. The irreligious ones needed to be placed with extra care. And all of them had to be close to the Rebbe's house, where they would eat.

But the Rebbe was not unduly troubled. Despite all the problems, and the fact that many homes were already filled with *Yom Tov* guests, the issue at hand dealt with a mitzva of *hachnasas orchim* and so was certain to evoke Divine assistance. The Rebbe also had two factors working to his advantage — his charisma and his *kehilla*.

"Hello, this is the Bostoner Rebbe speaking..." In call after call, the Rebbe made the same appeal, pulling strings like a puppeteer and keeping a ledger of how many beds he had amassed. In less than twenty-five minutes, as the first taxis drove up to the entrance of his home, his work was done.

THE GROUP, exhausted after the seven-day ordeal of their voyage, also bore the indelible scars of a decade-long experience of horror. They were utterly drained and

* Remnants of the Nation, referring to Holocaust survivors.

their tattered clothes hung loose from their shrunken frames.

In the few minutes it took for the group to emerge from the taxis and enter the house, the Rebbe braced himself for the extraordinary variety of temperaments and dispositions that he was about to host for *Yom Tov.* He knew that this group would require particular sensitivity and understanding. The very fact that they had all left the taxis even though his representative had asked them to remain inside so that they could be taken directly to their lodgings, was indication enough of what trouble might be in store. But the Rebbe was wrong.

Those who trooped into his house did not want food or sleep. It was twenty minutes to *Yom Tov,* and they were starving for mitzvos. The Rebbe was *gezegenen zach fun de sukkah* and *dalet minim* (bidding farewell to the *sukkah* and to the *lulav* and *esrog*) when he heard them call, "Where is the *sukkah?*"

The Bostoner Rebbe was inside the *sukkah* waving his *lulav* to and fro in praise and deep supplication. The group had just a few minutes left to fulfill the mitzvos of the holiday and not a second to waste. Cake was hurriedly rushed into the *sukkah* for a blessing of *laishev basukkah* while the guests impatiently waited on line for their turn to bless the *lulav* and *esrog.*

At the same time, a veritable underground railroad was chugging its way into the kitchen. The Rebbe's wife had also been busy on the phone and women were soon bringing *kugels,* chickens, cakes, fruit, desserts, pastry — and whatever else they had in the house. Within minutes, the Rebbetzin's kitchen appeared to be equipped for a year-long siege.

Now, squeezing out of her packed kitchen, the Rebbetzin emerged to meet her guests. A more calm and courteous woman never graced New England. Moving effortlessly through the crowd, she smiled her *"Shalom aleichem"* and "Thank you for coming," lighting a spark of warmth and hope in everyone she greeted.

Noting the relatively humble surroundings, they wondered how she was able to prepare for such a huge crowd.

"I have help," answered the Rebbetzin sweetly, pointing to the steady stream of women coming and going outside the window.

L IKE THE REBBE she was careful not to betray the fact that they had only just found out about the group's arrival. Had the newcomers known of the desperate flurry of activity preceding their arrival, they would surely have felt embarrassed at causing their hosts so much trouble. Instead they smiled in their blissful ignorance — believing that they were doing this Rebbe — who, *nebbach,* lived so far from New York — a favor by joining his court for *Yom Tov.*

The members of the Rebbe's community played their roles with equal elan. In almost every home, the hosts willingly vacated their own bedrooms and gladly suffered discomforts to make room for their guests. They were only too eager to do whatever they could to help the *she'ayris haplaita.* And whatever they gave up was well compensated for with the most moving and memorable *Shemini Atzeres* and *Simchas Torah* of their lives.

The singing that night seemed to resound for miles around. The city of Boston had not seen such celebration since its Tea Party. And the dancing was the dance of victory. The feverish intensity of the celebration continued until the small hours of the morning. Not *mir vellen zey iberlebben,* but *mir hot shoin...* We have not been defeated, we still have our Torah and our faith, we are blessed with fellow Jews who perform mitzvos and good deeds and love each other as themselves.

This lesson was not lost on the non-religious members of the group, all of whom received the same attention and even additional courtesy from the Rebbe. And the skeptics? Their skepticism was quickly melted away by the Rebbe's warmth. They soon forgot themselves and sang and danced no less heartily than the rest. As crazy as it was, it all made sense. Even to the cynical immigrants who had thought they would never see their host, and the cynical young chassidim who had thought they would never greet these guests.

three on salvation

אודך ה' כי אנפת בי ישוב אפך ותנחמני, במה הכתוב מדבר בשני בני אדם
שיצאו לסחורה, ישב לו קוץ לאחד מהן. התחיל מחרף ומגדף. לימים שמע
שטבעה ספינתו של חבירו בים התחיל מודה ומשבח, לכך נאמר : ישוב
אפך ותנחמני.

נדה לא

❀ Two men embarked on a trade expedition, and a
thorn entered the foot of one of them (causing him to
miss his boat). He began to blaspheme, rant and
rave. After a while he learned that his friend's ship
had sunk in the sea, and so he began to give thanks
and praise. Thus is it written, "I will give thanks
unto You, O Lord; for although You were angry
with me, Your anger is turned away, and You
comforted me."

Niddah 31

S.D. 613

IRST, the dead bolt. *Thunk.* Then the mortice. *Clack-chunk.* And last, the multi-lock. *Err-chingg.* Reuben Finegold was home. *Err-chingg. Clack-chunk. Thunk.* The Finegold household was secure for the night. He tiptoed to the hall closet and hung up his hat and jacket. Then he remembered the chain. *Clatter-clatter-ping.*

"That you, Rubie?" Edith called from the living room.

"No, it's Robin Hoodlum, come to rob from the rich and keep it for myself."

"In that case, sir, you've come to the wrong address. My husband's a *melamed* and I'm a retired *balabusta.* The rich Finegolds are on Bedford Avenue." She looked up from her knitting. "Rubie!" she cried in exasperation. "Couldn't you have changed out of those pajamas before you left the 'Y'?"

"I beg your pardon!" her husband replied indignantly. "I'll have you know these are not pajamas. This is my karate outfit and I'm not ashamed if all of East Flatbush sees me."

"I thought you were going to tell me it has some fancy Oriental name."

"It does, but I forgot it. What are you doing up at this hour, anyway?"

"I just wanted to finish this sweater for Rivkeleh. Hey — you got your *gartel!* Mazel tov."

Reuben smiled. "You like?" He rotated slowly under the chandelier, modeling his brand-new, hard-won Yellow Belt, the badge of the aspiring karate expert. "I'm ready for them now, just you wait! *Haii yah!*" He lashed out with his left foot, kicking over the coffee table. Edith calmly got the dustpan and started sweeping up the shards of broken crockery.

"My hero. Another twelve-dollar vase bites the dust. Just do me one small favor, will you? Don't start strutting around Brooklyn like the 'Karate Kid', looking for trouble. You only took that course to learn self-*defense*, remember? Not self-*destruct*. Now go change your clothes and throw those smelly pajamas in the laundry and I'll wash and iron them tomorrow. You can wear them on Purim with a red sash and call yourself 'Borscht Belt.'" She gave the dead vase a decent burial in the kitchen trashcan and put away the broom. "I'll defrost your supper in a couple of minutes."

R EUBEN RIFFLED through the bills and junk mail on the hall table. "Is this all the mail, Mrs. Occupant?" he asked as he joined her in the dinette.

"Well, there was another one of those fright flyers from our friendly neighborhood blockbuster..." She saw the instant fury flare in his eyes. "Now, Rubie, remember your blood pressure!"

"I don't have any blood pressure, Edith. I'm only fifty-two years old and healthy as a horse."

"*K'na hara,* ptui, ptui, ptui. You should live to a hundred and twenty!"

"Thank you. It makes me so mad, this blockbusting, it should be declared a sin. We finally move into a nice house, on a nice street, close to the shul and the buses and the subway, we even got ourselves a tree, for Heaven's sake. Our own tree!"

"That you call a tree? I thought it was a hatrack."

"I know it isn't much, but I always wanted a tree, even if it has to be the kind they put in one of those cages, like an endangered species, which let me tell you a tree is, with all this air pollution. And what happens? One not-so-bright fellow sells his house down the block to a non-Jew."

"Yes. And then the real estate agents' eyeballs turn into dollar signs and they start the scare tactics about increasing crime rates and increasing insurance premiums and declining property values."

"Right. And that gets more and more people to move out until there isn't a single Jewish family left in the whole neighborhood."

"And the only ones that are happy are the real estate guys who make a commission on every sale and again on every purchase."

"What about the Gentiles who move in? Don't you think they're happy to buy a house with its own tree for a cheap price?"

"Why would a Gentile want to live near shuls, yeshivos and a *mikve*?"

"Hah! In the sales brochures those are 'social halls,' 'public schools' and a 'health club.' Those suckers will believe anything. You know, Edith, this is our fifth neighborhood. Fifth! Talk about wandering Jews! I'm sick and tired of moving. I don't care, this time nobody's going to make me leave. Not some greedy blockbuster and not some so-called criminal element that tries to take over."

"What are you, the Lone Ranger? Do you mean to tell me that the guy who has to take a Valium before he has enough nerve to open the door for the Avon lady, is going to take on the blockbusters *and* the local punks singlehanded? I can just see the headlines: 'BORSCHT BELT GETS CREAMED'. Who do you think you're kidding? Did you talk to the fellas in shul? Did you deputize them? Are they going to stay and defend the Alamo?"

"Yeah, yeah. Until their house is burglarized. Or until someone dumps a load of garbage on their front step. Or until somebody sneaks up behind them and says 'boo!' You know what I think? I think those miserable blockbusters are behind all those incidents."

E DITH AND REUBEN had been through this conversation countless times over the past months. They even knew each other's lines and occasionally, for variety, switched roles. Their children, all married and raising their families a safe distance from the old homestead, pleaded with them incessantly to move. They could not believe their father was learning karate. Could you?

But Edith and Reuben knew that what had happened to so many once-peaceful, once-pleasant communities in Brooklyn could happen anywhere. The four-step process of "destabilization" was simple: one sale to a non-Jew > blockbuster mailbox stuffers > more quick sales > rise in crime. "Destabilization" was a euphemism for the death of a Jewish neighborhood.

The Finegolds were no braver than you or I, but they felt that five upheavals in their lives were four too many. This was, after all, America, the Land of the Free — not pre-War

Europe — and that meant that they were free to live where they chose to live. Their lighthearted banter belied the intensity of their resentment and anger.

They were not the only ones who were prepared to fight for what was rightfully theirs. In one neighborhood, the Residents Committee became its own real estate brokerage, buying vacant homes at a fair price and reselling only to Jews. Elsewhere, the homeowners patrolled their own streets in nightly shifts and cooperated with the police in crime prevention and the apprehension of criminals. The Finegolds had gone from door to door, trying to convince the neighbors to do the same. But they had soon discovered that the neighbors would rather leave than fight.

Edith and Reuben were among the first Brooklynites to take a stand against crime and "destabilization." Although their contribution, in the greater scheme of things, was perhaps modest, their efforts did not go unrewarded. The Finegolds are living proof that a good Jew, wherever he may be, never stands alone.

ON THURSDAY NIGHT, they were riding home late on the subway. As the train neared their station, two tough-looking teenagers brandishing "Saturday night specials" sauntered over and accosted an elderly gentleman at the far end of the car.

"Hand it over, ol' man, o' you is dead meat!" The victim turned white as a sheet. He began to tremble so violently he couldn't even get his hand into his pocket to comply with his attackers' polite request.

"Did you see that, Edith?!" Reuben whispered furiously. "They're mugging that helpless old man!"

"Sha! Be quiet or they'll start on us next."

"Let them just try!"

"Move it, mister," the thugs demanded, closing in on their prey. "We ain't got all day."

"Hold it right there, you, you, you... bums!" Reuben shouted, leaping from his seat into a threatening karate stance. "D-d-drop those knives! Now!" His hand traced stiff circles in the air; he jumped up and landed two feet closer to the muggers, the leather soles of his shoes skidding on the littered floor of the train.

Edith shut her eyes tight and began reciting *Tehillim*. Every other eye in the car was riveted to the bearded maniac in the center aisle.

"I'm, I'm, I'm warning you, these hands have been c-c-classified as lethal w-w-weapons," he snarled at the would-be assailants. "I can p-p-paralyze you for life with one blow!"

"*Gott in Himmel!*" Edith muttered, and continued her recitation with greater fervor.

The teenagers stood frozen in their tracks. They looked Reuben up and down, estimating the odds, trying to gauge their chances of overpowering a middle-aged Bruce Lee.

And Reuben looked *them* up and down, from the top of their limp, greasy heads to their cracked leather jackets and down to their — ulp! — hob-nailed boots.

"*Oy vey,*" Reuben groaned inwardly. One ruffian turned to the other and said "Man, dis honkey is bad, an' Ah do mean ba-ad." The second agreed. "Two o' him'd would make just one shadow. He look like he bin do-natin' blood an' fo-got to say 'when'!" They laughed and hooted derisively. Reuben's muscles, such as they were, turned to jelly.

BUT JUST AS his resolve was about to crumble, the doors of the train lurched open and the muggers spun on their hob-nailed heels and fled down the subway platform. No one was more astonished than Reuben himself.

"I did it, Edith!" he shouted triumphantly. She rolled her eyes. He posed heroically, hands on hips, big idiotic smile plastered on his face, awaiting the inevitable applause.

But the only sound he heard was the crackle of newspapers. The entire audience, apathetic New Yorkers every one, had gone back to reading about the dramas and tragedies of the Big Apple, the shocking government scandals, the handicap at Off Track Betting, and Dennis the Menace's thrilling escapades.

"*Haii-yah!*" Reuben cried, shooting his arm out smartly, and banging his knuckles into a pole. No one noticed. "Sit *down*, Rubie, before you *fall* down. The train is moving."

He sat, mopping his streaming face with a handkerchief. His heart was still palpitating wildly. "How do you like that guy, Edith?!" He hooked a thumb in the direction of the almost-muggee. "He's just reading his paper like nothing happened. Didn't even thank his rescuer, can you believe it?"

"Did *you?*" his wife chastised. Reuben opened his mouth to deny the accusation, then the lightbulb in his head lit up.

"Right you are, Edith. That was a *goimel-bencher* if I ever saw one. Did you get a load of those hob-nail boots?" Reuben offered up a silent prayer of thanksgiving and promised to do a more thorough job of it the next day during *shacharis*.

"That hand is swelling up real nice, Superman. Did you dent the pole?"

"Nah." He glanced at it surreptitiously, hoping he had left behind some evidence of his valor, but the pole that had withstood the ravages and punishments meted out by millions of commuters was undamaged. "But I think I broke my hand."

Although a little sympathy at that point would have gone a long way towards mending Reuben's fractured ego, Edith was having visions of her husband in a body cast, the reward for his reckless impetuosity, so she certainly wasn't going to encourage him. "I'll give you a bowl of ice when we get home. You'll be ready for the heavyweight championship by Monday, guaranteed.

"Edith, I think we missed our stop."

MONDAY'S NEWSCAST informed them of two more break-ins on their street and Edith's best friend was mugged right in front of her own house. She was very shaken. "I guess it feels like a greater personal violation if it happens so close to your Polaroid, yet too far to be recorded for posterity," Edith said.

"I have something to show you, Edith," Reuben announced when he came home that night. He opened a square white box to reveal its deadly contents.

"A gun!" Edith gasped. "It looks like a miniature blunderbuss. What does it shoot, cannon balls?"

"No, mace. You shove a cylinder of mace into here," he explained, "aim it at your assailant's face and pull the trigger. The mace will immobilize him for fifteen minutes at least."

"What if I blind somebody, God forbid?"

"Somebody who's sticking a knife in your ribs and stealing your wedding ring you're worrying about blinding?! It's only temporary, anyway."

"No, thanks. You can keep your Colt .45, I'll stick with my

S.D. 613. 'S.D.' for *Siyata d'Shemaya* and '613' for the number of mitzvos I'll have to perform to earn it."

"We'll make an unbeatable team."

THEY WERE RIDING the Canarsie line on Wednesday, heading for Edith's nephew's bar mitzvah, when a young, glassy-eyed Hispanic swaggered through the train. He chinned himself on the overhead bar, whooping wilding and swinging his long legs into several straphangers. He vaulted over an empty seat and landed in the lap of a frail-looking woman.

"That does it!" Reuben shouted, once again leaping from his seat. Edith tugged at his sleeve, but there was no stopping him. "I've had it with these hoodlums! They think they own the trains. They think they can drive decent people out of their own neighborhoods." He raised his voice even louder and the crowd parted to let the nut pass.

"I've had it, Buddy-boy," he roared. "This time *I'm* driving *you* out!" Reuben drew his mace gun from the pocket of his raincoat, sure of the affect it would have on the gangster-in-training.

But the boy was flying too high on PCP to grasp that Reuben had him at a disadvantage. "Iss nobody poolin' thee gon on Chico, man," he sneered menacingly, and out of nowhere a switchblade appeared in his palm. With a flick of his wrist, eight inches of cold steel sprang out towards Reuben's chest, the blade glinting under the subway lights, and suddenly Reuben realized his foolhardiness. A person could get himself killed like this! Perspiration poured down his face, soaking his collar and distorting his vision as his index finger tensed on the trigger. Still, Chico kept coming closer, closer, the knife poised at a gutting angle.

Reuben's heart was pounding in his chest. "I'm w-w-warning you," he snarled, but the snarl came out a croak and Chico grinned with evil satisfaction, sensing that the tables had turned. Reuben's sweaty fist slipped on the gun butt. His life flashed before his eyes.

"*Shema Yisrael,*" he screamed, certain it was all over, "*Hashem Elokeinu, Hashem Echad!*" Chico's eyes went wild.

All at once, the train screeched to a halt. The doors slammed open and two transit patrolmen boarded. Chico threw up his hands and hurled himself at them. "Bost me! Bost me! I geev op! Tha' crasy man, he curse me! He put thee curse on Chico!"

The cops, momentarily stupefied, quickly regained their composure and recited Chico his rights. They looked around the car for witnesses, but all the passengers were busy memorizing editorials or studying the subway map or fixing their make-up. Except for one couple: he was sprawled on his seat, ashen-faced, and she was fanning him with the *Daily News.* The patrolmen shrugged at each other, as if to say: "To each his own," and dragged their willing, babbling captive away.

"I'M HANGING UP my gunbelt for good, Edith," Reuben proclaimed on Sunday, when he had regained the power of speech. He was installing a Fox Lock on the front door.

"*Gott tzu danken,*" she said, eyes heavenward. "What's the matter? You didn't like the view from Boot Hill, Sheriff?"

"Joke if you must, but last night was more than any good Jewish boy from Williamsburg should have to go through."

They had accompanied Reuben's brother and sister-in-law to the airport to catch a late flight for Boston. Yitz and Chanie had walked through the metal detector; Edith had followed. Reuben's mace gun had set off all the alarms and sirens in the terminal.

In a matter of microseconds, he had been surrounded by airport security men and slobbering German shepherds, and whisked away to an interrogation room. For four-and-a-half hours they grilled him and Reuben had had to tell, and retell, and tell again why he'd been carrying a concealed weapon. In the end, it was Edith's S.D. 613 that had facilitated his release.

"Look, fellas," she had argued, "would a terrorist be stupid enough to march through the metal detector with a hunk of iron like that in his pocket? May God grant you such stupid terrorists! Then you could *really* keep the skies friendly."

O N HIS WAY to *shiur* one Tuesday night, Reuben found himself walking alone on a poorly-lit street. Well, not quite alone. The gang whose turf he was trespassing was preparing a proper welcome for their uninvited visitor. They formed a solid wall of tattooed biceps across the sidewalk.

"Gotta match?" asked their fearless leader, obviously not elected because of his superior intelligence or originality of style, thought Reuben. It would be wrong to say that Reuben was undaunted. In fact, Reuben was daunted. *Very* daunted. His karate-toughened right hand had never regained its former strength after the encounter with the Transit Authority's rolling stock and his mace gun was surely resting in the bottom of some airport security man's wife's purse. In short, the only weapon he had was his wits. Where was Edith when he needed her? What would she do in a situation like this?

"Uh, uh, match?" He patted all his pockets, stalling. "No, I'm, I'm afraid I don't. Wait!" he put up his hand defensively, "I know a *story* about a match, if, uh, you boys have the time to hear it. If not, I'll just be on my w..."

"Do we got de time, Boss?"

"Yeah, sure. We got de time. We don' gotta be in soigery or nuttin' for maybe half a hour, yet." The speaker, an oversized specimen with a hideous picture of a woman on his bare chest, a bloody axe implanted in her head and the inscription "Mama" below, guffawed disgustingly. "Let's hear de toikey sing, yeah."

So Reuben began to spin a matchless tale full of excitement, adventure, and — special for this audience — gore. After a few minutes, he made a show of looking at his watch. "Oops! Er, sorry fellas. I'm, uh, late, you know? Be seeing you!" He tried to make a quick getaway.

"Freeze," growled a member of the rank and file, one of the ranker ones. "You finish dat story or I'm gonna stick ya!" Reuben could almost feel the point of the ice pick going into his throat.

The Fearless Leader smacked his subordinate on the forehead. "Stick him an' he won't be *able* to finish de story, pea-brain. Behave yaself an' I'll let ya stick him when he's done." Reuben's Adam's apple bobbled nervously.

"Listen, uh, boys, if you maybe want to, er, walk *with* me," he suggested, in what he hoped was an amiable tone, "I'll, I'll be happy to continue the story." Amazingly, they did. Reuben kept on talking, all the while hoping to see someone he knew — anyone! — who might call the cavalry and rescue him. But the streets were deserted.

Five long blocks later, he stopped. His mind refused to produce even one more chapter. "Uh, boys? Ahem. Er, this is, uh, where I g-g-get off."

Fearless Leader pointed to the one who obviously grew up when meat was cheap. "Animal. He's yours." Reuben looked heavenward for salvation. "S.D., don't fail me now!" he said aloud, and the Brainy Bunch followed his gaze.

In a flash, they dispersed and disappeared, completely camouflaged by the filth of the city. When Reuben dared at last to open his eyes, he discovered that he was standing right below the sign of the local police precinct.

"How do you like that," he mused. "And here all I was praying for was a good ending to the story."

West Side Snatch

I T WAS CLOSE to midnight when the man entered the tall office building on the corner of 38th Street and Broadway. The sidewalks were empty of pedestrians at this hour, the windows of the grimy building dark. All but one on the eighth floor. New York's garment district, by day a turbulent, hustling confusion of trucks and vans, wheeled clothing racks and bargain hunters, was asleep. But the man had business to attend to.

Despite the dashing cut of his trench coat, the rich gloss of his hand-sewn shoes, and the high-priced scent of his cologne, there was something about him that was essentially weak and inexplicably unclean. A little man with a face like a rat. He had a high, thin aquiline nose that ended just above a sparse, drooping moustache. Prominent incisors jutted out between his lips, calling attention to a receding chin. His eyes, small, black, close-set, flickered first left, then right, then left again with a furtiveness inconsonant with the elegant attire — the furtiveness of a small-time hood. Anyone who might dismiss the rat-faced man as insignificant, however, would be wrong. Dead wrong. In an empire peopled by rats, the rat-faced man was king.

His face gleamed white in the lobby fluorescents as he boarded the elevator and depressed the button marked "8". He admired his reflection in the tarnished wall mirror, and told himself that he'd come a long way for the grandson of a European peasant, the son of an immigrant shoemaker. His father had wanted him to carry on the family business, he recalled with amusement. That was precisely what he was engaged in: "Family" business.

He stepped out of the elevator on the eighth floor and walked slowly down the narrow corridor, with his heels clicking across the cracked linoleum. He raised a bony fist but the door opened before he could knock. No greetings were exchanged.

A bulky white envelope changed hands, and a thin, cruel smile appeared on the lips of the rat-faced man, making him look truly grotesque. The envelope fit comfortably into the customized pocket of his trench coat. The door closed. He rode the elevator down to the lobby and climbed into the back seat of the black sedan that waited at the curb.

S ENDER FRIED AWOKE just before sunrise with an eerie sense of foreboding. It was not quite a premonition, not like the one he'd had several years back on the night before the big Diamond Exchange robbery. The mental warning he'd received then had been clear enough to prompt him to empty the steel vault in his office of everything that was not insured and carry the merchandise home on his person.

This tactic was not as risky as one would believe since Sender, despite his affluence, routinely wore a shabby suit and crumple-brimmed hat — to his wife's chagrin — in order to discourage New York's cadre of determined muggers. The stratagem had worked and Sender had arrived home unmolested. His colleagues at the Exchange had been somewhat less fortunate and many had incurred substantial losses. That experience had taught him to trust his intuition.

This morning's presentiment, however, was more subtle and seemed directed at his person, a disquieting sensation that made him want to pull the covers over his head and hide. He glanced at his sleeping wife, Rachel, his partner of more than sixty years and the mother of his four children. If the Almighty did indeed have something unpleasant in store for him today, Sender thought, far better that it take place out of her sight. He rose and dressed quietly, washed in the small bathroom so as not to disturb Rachel, and downed a quick cup of coffee before he left for shul.

With his *tallis* bag tucked under his arm and his overcoat buttoned against the December chill, Sender went out to greet his destiny. He was unable to rid himself of the feeling of impending doom. He thought about the results of the annual check-up he had undergone only a week earlier and the doctor's comment that Sender was amazingly fit for a man of eighty-six, that he had the constitution of someone twenty years his junior. Well, he had always been a great one for walking, neither smoked nor drank, remained active in business and kept his mind agile through Talmud study. Maybe the doctor had given him a dose of *"ayin hara,"* he mused.

He strode along the still, deserted street in this exclusive Manhattan neighborhood of high-rises and condominiums. It would be at least an hour before West End Avenue awoke, and another hour after that before the first doors were opened to haul in the Sunday papers. As he neared the shul, the brisk crystalline clarity of the early Sunday dawn began to wipe the cobwebs from his mind and all at once Sender felt somewhat relieved. He stepped off the sidewalk to cross over to the shul.

He knew his hasty escape from the discomfiting atmosphere of the apartment would cause him to arrive early, preceding by several minutes the trickle of congregants at the morning services, and this pleased him. It was right and proper that an old-timer such as himself should set an example for the "youngsters" and other late-risers. It might turn out to be a fine day after all.

BUT SENDER WAS WRONG on both counts: he would neither precede the others to *minyan*, nor would he have a particularly fine day. Furthermore, he was not, as he assumed, alone on West End Avenue. Had he been less preoccupied, Sender's sharp mind might have registered the unusual presence of a Gristedes supermarket van parked at the curb, inches from where he was crossing the street — unusual because the supermarket was closed on Sundays and the truck had no business being there.

He had taken no more than three steps from the curb when the rolling rear door of the truck flew up with startling speed. Two muscular men in zippered coveralls leaped down and pounced upon Sender like lions on an unsuspecting gazelle. One threw a hairy arm across Sender's chest from behind, the other deftly lifted his legs off the ground and together they heaved him into the truck bay as though he were a side of beef. His *tallis* bag slipped from his hands and fell to the ground. Before a cry of surprise could escape his lips, the rolling door crashed down like the blade of a guillotine. A third accomplice tied a dirty rag over Sender's mouth and the others swiftly and brutally bound him hand and foot.

The brutality and the binding of Sender's wrists and ankles were an unnecessary precaution. It was unlikely that their victim could overwhelm three brawny assailants, or even put up very much resistance, but the kidnappers were savage just the same, displaying technique and expertise that marked them as professionals. And they were. They worked for a man known only as "The Rat."

The unseen driver gunned the truck's motor and the one they called "Vinnie" banged twice on the wall to signal him. Taking advantage of the light traffic, he sped uptown through the city streets but carefully avoided running any red lights. They couldn't risk drawing the attention of some hot-shot cop who might get it into his head to find out why Gristedes was delivering on a Sunday. If they were stopped, the truck's unusual cargo was certain to raise some eyebrows.

WHILE THE TRUCK made its way to its prearranged destination, the one and only clue to Sender's kidnapping was discovered. The embroidered silver initials caught the eye of two joggers coming down West End Avenue. They probably would not have noticed the *tallis* bag had it been lying in the gutter face down; an old, discarded velvet cushion would not have merited a second glance. Although they had no idea what this bag or its contents were, they recognized the lettering as Hebrew and brought it across the street to the synagogue to ask one of the worshippers for an explanation.

The men in shul had no difficulty identifying the *tallis* bag as Sender Fried's. Everyone had wondered where Sender had been that morning, for barring out-of-town vacations, the old man never missed the *minyan*.

"Where did you find this?" a congregant asked with concern.

"Across the street, in the gutter. Is it worth anything?"

"It only has religious value... Tell me, did you notice an elderly gentleman standing next to it, or anywhere in the vicinity?"

"Mister, we haven't seen a living soul for the last seven blocks. Now if that isn't worth anything, I guess we'll be going," he said, jogging in place. "C'mon Jeff, let's move it. We got another mile yet!"

The fellow from the shul phoned Sender's house and woke up Mrs. Fried. She became panicky when she heard what he had to say. "He must be there," she cried. "Sender would not have gone anywhere but to the *minyan!*" Perhaps there had been an accident, she thought, or he'd become confused and was wandering around the neighborhood somewhere. She hung up the phone with a trembling hand and called the police.

"Lady," the officer told her in a disinterested monotone, "we don't check out no skips 'til they been gone twenty-four hours. Department rules. Maybe he's takin' a walk or feedin' the pigeons or somethin'."

"Have any accidents been reported in the area?" she asked, making a valiant effort to keep the note of hysteria from her voice. "No," he informed her, "no accidents and no lost old men either." She thanked him and phoned her son.

Shloime Fried lived in Riverdale. His nearest neighbor was a State Senator whose reelection campaign fund regularly benefited from injections of Fried capital. The Senator obligingly called the Police Commissioner and advised him to mobilize his troops. Political "clout" being a most effective catalyst, within ten minutes a police lieutenant and two patrolmen were knocking at Rachel's door, apologizing for the delay, and the search for Sender Fried was on.

SENDER, BY THIS TIME, was far from West End Avenue. The Gristedes van had pulled up in front of an abandoned tenement on 126th Street and Amsterdam Avenue in Central Harlem. This neighborhood is a part of New York few Whites ever venture into, even in broad daylight, without an armed escort. Sender's captors, however, were unconcerned.

He was hauled out of the truck like a carpet and carried into the dark, empty building. The stench of stale urine and excrement filled his nostrils and made him gag. Rancid garbage was strewn everywhere; eggshells and beer cans crunched beneath the kidnappers' feet as they dragged Sender up the stairs.

Sender had been aware from the outset that these men intended to hold him for ransom; it was a risk that almost any man of substantial means had to face every day of his life. But now he knew their plan was far more nefarious. The fact that they hadn't blindfolded him or made any effort to conceal their own faces from him was the clearest indication that they did not fear being identified.

The Harlem locals he had seen on the street corner had been totally unaffected by the spectacle of an old man trussed up like a chicken for barbequeing, as though the sight were commonplace. Sender was certain they wouldn't dream of reporting the incident to the police. This was not the kind of neighborhood where the residents volunteered *any* information to the authorities.

The kidnappers carried Sender into a vacant apartment and dumped him unceremoniously onto a mound of broken glass. Blood began to flow freely from cuts he sustained in his legs and cheek and above his eye. The pain was excruciating, but he couldn't scream. The two men grinned at him malevolently and left.

Sender trembled violently. From the pile of yellowed newspapers and rotting mattress stuffing in the corner of the room came an ominous rustling sound. He heard one of the kidnappers in the hall say: "Rat said to make the call at eight," and Sender realized with horror what the source of the rustling was. His stomach churned and only by tremendous effort was he able to control the urge to disgorge its scant contents.

His terror was keen. In a city where the demolition of an old condemned building had been known to release hordes of dog-size rats from their subterranean lairs, and where, in certain areas, the rat community is larger than the human one, only good fortune had kept them from Sender's view for over seventy years. Ever since his immigration to America, his life had been blissfully rat-free. There was nothing Sender Fried feared more than rats.

HIS HEART THUMPED WILDLY with the dreaded recollection. In the Polish village of his youth, his family had owned a small dairy farm which supplied milk and cheese to the entire community. Although tending the herd of cows had been Sender's primary responsibility, he was frequently assigned chores in the shed which housed his family's primitive cheese factory.

The cheese shed was a natural attraction for both cats and field mice, but the Fried's cats generally maintained the mouse population at a tolerable level. Sender was a boy of twelve when he came face to face with his first rat and the experience left him with a permanent phobia acute enough to induce an almost cataleptic reaction.

He was just reaching for a bucket that stood on a shelf high above his head when his fingers brushed against the stiff pelt of the huge rodent. In that brief space of time between tactile sensation and intellectual awareness, the world seemed to thud to a halt, and in the silence, the putrid odor of the shed was laced with the feral, carrion reek of rat.

The beast displayed none of the tremulous timidity of the tiny field mice; it aggressively stood its ground, baring sharp teeth and flicking its long, whiplike tail. Sender took one uncertain step backward, tripped over a rake and landed hard on the packed earth floor. The rat sprang at him. He shielded his face and the animal sank its teeth into the flesh of his hand. He flung his arm out and the rat's slimy tail slithered across his cheek, but its teeth held fast.

Suddenly, Sender's older brother appeared. He grabbed a shovel and swung at the beast. The rat, unharmed, released its tenacious grip at last and ran away. Later, they found the litter of dead kittens behind the milk vats, all six of them hideously disemboweled.

Now, in the foul, dilapidated Harlem tenement, Sender stared at the puckered scar on his right hand, breathed the fetor of sodden garbage, and listened to the menacing rustle of newspapers.

Was his long life of philanthropy and humanitarianism to come to such an ignominious end? He cried for his poor wife who would have nothing to bury but a half-chewed carcass — if he were ever found at all.

RACHEL FRIED was now nearly out of her mind with worry. She sat huddled in a wing chair in the corner of her living room, a room no longer recognizable as the comfortable, welcoming parlor where she and Sender had so often entertained guests. The plush blue rug was now a tangle of wires, electronic equipment and black-leather-shod feet; the endtables were laden with overflowing ashtrays and stained coffee cups. Draped across her newly reupholstered sofa were the hats, coats and scarves of half a dozen strangers and the air was thick with their cigarette smoke. The home of Sender and Rachel Fried had become an adjunct of the New York City Police Department.

While his men were setting up and settling in, Lieutenant Connelly had patiently explained the procedure. The sudden disappearance of a wealthy citizen was always presumed to be an abduction for ransom. Inevitably, the kidnappers would telephone to make their demands and the call would be electronically traced. This would enable the police to pinpoint the kidnappers' location and, hopefully, give them a lead as to Sender's whereabouts.

It was generally known that a phone trace required three full minutes to complete, but with their new, sophisticated equipment, the police department had been able to cut the time almost by half. Connelly had instructed Rachel to try to keep the kidnappers on the line as long as possible. There was nothing to do now but wait.

The only clue the police had was Sender's *tallis* bag, and the forensic laboratory, after subjecting it to numerous tests for fingerprints, hair, or particles of fabric, had returned it along with a negative report. A house-to-house search all along West End Avenue had failed to turn up any witnesses. The wiretap on the Fried's telephone, Rachel knew, was their only hope.

MINUTES TICKED BY with agonizing slowness and Rachel's nerves shrieked with the tension. When the phone rang at last, she hurled herself from the chair to answer it, but Connelly signalled her to wait. Recording equipment was switched on, earphones set in place, and a police psychologist rested his hand on the dining room extension. At the nod of his head, they lifted the receivers simultaneously.

"Rachel? It's Thelma Holzberger. Are you going to the Ladies Auxilliary meeting tonight?"

"Thelma, you'll have to excuse me. I... I'm expecting an important call. I'll get back to you later." The false alarm only served to increase the tension. Rachel paced up and down the hall, wringing her hands and glancing repeatedly at her watch. The jangling of the telephone bell startled her. Again she grabbed for it, and again she was halted by Connelly's urgent signal to wait.

"We got yer husband..."

"Let me speak to him!" Rachel cried. "Is he alright?"

"It'll cost ya two hunnert grand t' find out," the voice told her.

"P-please," she begged, "please don't hurt him! I'll give you anything you want!"

"Unmarked bills," the voice continued, ignoring her, "small denominations, packed in a brown suitcase..." The kidnapper quickly detailed the time and place of the ransom drop-off but Rachel's mind went blank. She could think only of Sender.

"... and no cops or the old man gets iced." The phone clicked loudly in her ear.

"Sorry, Chief," the earphoned detective said with a shrug, "they hung up before we could finish the trace. All we got is the last four digits."

"Well, have them run it through the computer anyway," Connelly ordered, "maybe we'll get lucky. And while you're at it, get the tape down to headquarters for a voice print match-up." Every human voice creates a sound-wave pattern as distinct and individual as a fingerprint. If the pattern could be matched with that of one of the tens of thousands of known criminals in the police data bank,

Connelly would at least have somewhere to start his investigation.

A police psychologist listening in on the call believed the perpetrators to be of low intelligence despite the complexity of the ransom delivery instructions they enumerated. In other words, hired thugs. From the inflection of the voice on the phone, the linguistics expert to whom the police gave a recording of the conversation determined that at least one of the kidnappers was not a native American. The detectives exchanged a knowing look. Lieutenant Connelly called the FBI.

A MOLDERING chicken claw lay inches from Sender's face. Any distraction from the rat-rustle was welcome, and Sender contemplated the death of the chicken in relation to his own likely imminent demise. The bird, he thought, had been born to feed God's creatures and by all accounts had served its purpose in life. Had he likewise fulfilled his own earthly mission? In his eighty-six years he had married a good woman, raised a fine family, had the *nachas* of grandchildren, and great-grandchildren who were all *shomrei mitzvos* and lovers of Torah. The Almighty had granted him enormous success in business, yet he had continued to live simply and donated huge sums to many charitable causes.

Sender recited *Viduy* by heart, not knowing when or how his death would come. When he was done, he closed his eyes and thought: "I'm ready, Lord, but must it be in Harlem?"

H ARLEM, perhaps the poorest of New York City's neighborhoods, is noted for its squalor and soaring unemployment rate. It is a high-crime area, where liquor store owners are licensed to carry guns and all of them do. The regional five-and-dime, like many other commercial premises there, is equipped with the most elaborate burglar alarm system available, not that it noticeably discourages the indigenous robbers. Harlem has more than its share of narcotics addicts and financing a drug habit is a costly business. It is not possible to support a $200- to $300-a-day addiction on welfare checks alone; holdups, muggings and break-ins supplement the modest government stipends.

⚘

When the junkie entered the abandoned tenement building to shoot up, Sender saw a tiny ray of hope. Perhaps this place was not meant to be his last stop after all. The door to the apartment in which he lay had been left open and he could hear the intruder quite clearly. At first he thought there were two of them, but then he realized the boy was only talking to himself.

"Shakin' so bad... gonna make me well... man sez dis is first class smack... HOO-EEE!"

Sender waited until he heard the junkie humming happily, then lifted his legs and thumped them against the floor. No reaction. He did it again, not too hard. He didn't want to frighten the boy off.

"Wuzzat?"

Sender thumped his bound feet twice more. He could hear movement in the hall. The junkie wasn't about to miss an opportunity to roll a drunk or rip off some helpless squatter. Sender naively believed that even this high-flying miscreant might be moved to rescue a defenseless old man.

"Wha' we got oursels heya?"

"Mmmf," Sender muttered through the gag.

"Well, well, well, well, WELL. We got us a TUR-key, tha's

wha' we got." Sender looked into the wild eyes of the young addict. The boy's face was cadaverous, deep hollows in his scarred cheeks. Needle marks tracked his skeletal arm and a double-edged knife gleamed in his hand.

"Mmmf," Sender said with feeling and pleaded for mercy with his eyes.

"Ya got som' bread, man? Sho' ya do. Now you give Leroy yer dough an' Leroy gonna lecha die easy, jus' don' fool wi' me."

"Mmmf," Sender said, more emphatically. The boy was too far gone to see that Sender was tied hand and foot. He pressed the point of the knife against Sender's throat and reached for his pocket, but Sender's bound wrists prevented access.

"I TOL' YA NOT TA FOOL WI' LEROY!" the boy screamed, slashing the knife at Sender's face. The old man pulled his head out of the way just in time, but the movement reopened the cut over his eye and blood flowed down his face.

"Man, you tied up!" the junkie noticed at last. He thrust the blade under the bands of rope and cut through them all at once.

"Mmmf!" Sender cried painfully as the circulation rushed back into his numbed fingers. He quickly handed Leroy his wallet and the junkie ran to the window to examine its contents by daylight.

"HOLEE MOLEE, Leroy is struck it rich fo' SHO'!" While the boy counted up his treasure, Sender grabbed a shard of glass and sawed away at the ropes around his ankles. In moments he was free. He rapidly rubbed sensation back into his legs and stood up shakily. His rescuer was still busy counting. Sender made his getaway.

He didn't know what new horrors might be awaiting him on the street; he only knew he had to get as far away as he could as quickly as possible. The kidnappers could return at any time. He hurried down the short flight of stairs and onto the sidewalk, tearing away the gag as he went. Just then, a patrol car cruised by and Sender flagged it down. His ordeal was over.

A T THE AMSTERDAM AVENUE police station, a doctor cleaned and dressed his wounds and a weary, red-faced detective interrogated him. The police were very interested to hear Sender's account of the kidnapping, especially his abductors' reference to someone called "Rat." But Sender refused to answer any more questions until he was permitted to make a phone call.

"Rucheleh?" he said, looking at his watch as he spoke. Incredibly, it was not yet nine A.M. "Maybe you know where my spare *tallis* and *tefillin* are? It's a long story but I... I got tied up and missed the *davening*. If I hurry, I can still catch a *minyan* for *shacharis*."

The Man Who
Missed the Boat

LMA HOYT paced back and forth on the sidewalk opposite 222 Central Park West, shifting the bulky parcel under her arm. In this classy upper Manhattan district, the names on the mansions were synonymous with New York City's famous cultural institutions and foundations — Astor, Guggenheim, Huntington-Hartford, Rockefeller, Vanderbilt — and the smell of 'old money' hovered like a hot-air balloon over the clean, well-kept streets.

Gone were the horse-drawn coaches and sputtering motor cars of a quarter of a century earlier, but the sights of Alma's youth passed before her eyes like flickering images in a nickelodeon. Governesses in long black coats and veiled hats wheeled lace-trimmed baby buggies across the broad avenue and down the flower-bordered lanes of Central Park. Red jacketed riders with high-gloss boots and pale jodhpurs sat astride their chestnut and palomino mounts, clip-clopping along the cobblestones from the stables behind the brownstones towards the Bridle Path. And little boys in short pants and girls in ruffled pinafores licked All-Day Suckers and rolled hoops down the pavement.

It seemed as though a millennium had passed, for the stone gargoyles and griffins that adorned the stately brick facades were blackened with soot now and the once-quiet boulevard was choked with motor cars and clanging trolleys. Alma shifted the package one last time and strode resolutely up the stoop of 222. The heavy door was opened by a pinched-faced woman, a frilly cap on her head and a matching apron over her simple grey dress.

"Yes?" she asked in a condescending tone. Alma's lips quirked at the irony of the circumstances.

"I come to see Miss Sara Straus," she said. The maid eyed her shabby raincoat with disdain and Alma self-consciously patted her fresh permanent.

"*Mrs. Hess* is entertaining. She does not receive peddlers or salespersons." She began to close the door.

"Wait!" Alma cried. "Please... please tell her Alma Hoyt is here an' that I got somethin' belonged to her mother, rest her soul." The maid closed the door wordlessly. A panicky feeling gripped Alma. "What if she don't wanna see me?" she thought, "or if — oh my gosh! — what if she thinks I stole it!" She almost turned to run when the door suddenly swung open.

"ALMA! How delightful to see you again!" It was Miss Sara, looking as lovely as her mother had at her age. "Won't you come in?" Alma allowed herself a small superior glance at the maid as she handed her the raincoat and then followed Miss Sara — "No," she reminded herself, "it's *Miz Hess* now" — into the spacious parlor.

"Hanna, darling," Sara said, addressing the striking, early-middle-aged woman perched on the sofa, a fragile china teacup poised at her lips, "I'd like you to meet Alma

Hoyt. She, ah, worked for my mother — ages ago." Hanna raised a quizzical eyebrow and a cool hand. Alma grasped it tentatively. "Alma, this is my cousin, Mrs. Straus-Brandeis."

"A pleasure, ma'am," said Alma, "you must be Mr. Nathan's daughter. A fine man, Mr. Nathan was. I recollect him comin' here to 222 to visit Mr. Isidor. They was always joshin' with one another, as brothers do, don't you know, or talkin' over business things in Iddich."

Hanna laughed in spite of herself. "I remember. Father often lapsed into Yiddish when it came to financial matters. I think despite his pretensions to progressiveness and modernity, he was afraid someone would give him the 'evil eye.' He really missed Uncle Isidor after he was gone."

"**P**LEASE SIT DOWN, Alma," Sara said, "and join us for a cup of tea."

"Thank you, Miss Sara — I mean, Miz Hess, that's real nice of you, but I won't be disturbin' you an' your company. I... I just wanted to give you this." Alma awkwardly presented the large white box to her hostess.

Sara and her cousin exchanged a puzzled look. "Please, Miz Hess, open it. By rights, it's yours." Sara undid the string and lifted the cover. Inside the box, under a layer of yellowed tissue, was something dark and furry. Sara gasped. She took it out and held it up for Hanna to see: it was a luxuriant, floor-length black sable coat.

"Where... where did you get this?" she stammered. "It's positively gorgeous!" Hanna, whose eye for quality was no less keen, agreed.

Alma toyed nervously with a jacket button. "Your mama give me it on the day she died." Sara looked at her in disbelief. "Now don't you be thinkin' I stole it," Alma said with some heat. "I never took nothin' didn't belong to me in all my life, specially not from a nice lady like Miz Ida was."

"Of course not, Alma. I didn't mean to imply anything of the sort. It's simply the shock of seeing this coat. It quite takes one's breath away. Why, I have an old photograph of my mother wearing it — or one very much like it."

"I know that pikcha, Miz Hess, an' it's this here coat alright. Mr. Isidor give it to her for her birthday that year an' poor Miz Ida, she didn't get to wear it mor'n half a dozen times." Alma found a white handkerchief in her purse and dabbed at her eyes. "The trip was suppose to be a annyversary present — they was always givin' each other fine presents like that."

BOLSTERED with cups of hot tea and *petit fours*, Alma recounted the tale of the fateful voyage of the *S.S. Titanic*, the guaranteed unsinkable ship that went down off the coast of Newfoundland on April 15, 1912.

"That cruise wasn't just for rich folks like your mama an' papa an' their friends, but the First Class deck surely was. The Astors, they was there, an' the Guggenheims, they was in the next cabin from us. An' everyone was havin' a grand old time, until we hit that iceberg."

The allegedly "invincible" ocean liner *Titanic* set sail from Southampton, England, on its trans-Atlantic maiden voyage on the tenth of April, 1912. So convinced had its designers been of its unsinkability that lifeboats for only 1,178 had been installed, although the passengers and crew numbered 2,207. With a double-armored bottom and sixteen watertight compartments, it was deemed invulnerable even if four compartments were flooded. The three-hundred-foot gash inflicted by the iceberg inundated five.

"Your papa, he booked one of them 'posh' suites, with two bedrooms an' a dressin' room an' a bathroom with gold-plated faucets. That there posh cabin even had a little room Miz Ida give me, but Henry, Mr. Isidor's valet, he stayed in third class with most the other servants.

"Well, the steward, he come round to our cabin an' I was just helpin' Miz Ida get ready for bed an' he says all the ladies was to dress up real warm an' line up on the deck to get into the lifeboats. Mr. Isidor, he gets real mad — I never seen him lose his temper before — an' he yells at the steward for not havin' enough lifeboats for all the passengers.

"Pretty soon, Miz Ida, she gets him calmed down, sayin' it's not the steward's fault, young man was white as a sheet, knowin' he wasn't gettin' on no lifeboat neither. Then she says, 'Isidor, we had lotsa happy years together an' if you're gonna go down with the ship, well, I will too, 'cause life without you wouldn't be worth livin'.' Then Miz Ida, she give me her coat. 'Here,' she says, 'it'll be right cold out there in the lifeboat an' I won't be needin' this no more anyways.'"

S ARA STARTED TO CRY and Hanna put a solicitous arm around her cousin's shoulder. "I *am* sorry Miss Sara. I wasn't meanin' to come 'round here an' distress you."

"No, no, Alma," Sara said, composing herself, "it's quite alright. Really. I was only a child when it happened. Such a terrible tragedy. I've actually been on the verge of a good cry all day long. Today's the twenty-fifth anniversary of the sinking of the *Titanic,* you know, and Saturday, by the Jewish calendar, is my parents' *yahrzeit.*"

"Well, 'course I know it. When I seen the headlines in the papers this mornin', it all came back to me. That's how I be recollectin' about the coat, you see. I come down with the penny-monia out there in the middle of the ocean an' when I come back to New York, I just gone straight to my Ma's place up to the Bronx. I wasn't hardly mor'n a girl neither an' that sinkin' was surely one awful thing.

"My Ma was puttin' me to bed an' feedin' me hot soup an' the like an' I was mostly out of my head better part of a week with the fever. When I was feelin' a mite more myself, I come back here to be givin' the coat back an' collectin' my things, but the house was locked up tighter'n a Gramma School on the Fourth of Joo-ly. I come back again some weeks after an' this here new maid be handin' me my old clothes an' stuff 'round to the back door, along with a right nice check from the bank an' a note from some lawya-fella thankin' me for my years of service an' such.

"Well, I wasn't gonna be givin' no new maid no fur coat nohow, not when she be tellin' me ain't none of the family to home, so I come back to my Ma's an' packed it up, nice as you please, just like you seen it now, an' I never give it a thought these twenny-fi' years.

"Ma, she's long gone now an' I been livin' there in her place all these years. An' like I said, when I seen the headlines I all of a sudden thought about the coat sittin' up on the shelf in the big closet underneath the old winter blankets an' such. I'm sure sorry to have took so long to be returnin' it an' if it pleases you, Miss Sara, I'll be goin' now." She rose to leave.

"Don't hurry off, Alma, please. Hanna and I were just talking about the *Titanic*. Did you know Hanna's parents were meant to be on the ship too?"

"You don't say! Mr. Nate an' the missus? Lord sure was

watchin' over them that day, Miz Brandeis, if you don't mind my sayin' so."

"That He was, Alma. Why don't you have another cup of tea? I was just going to tell Sara about it, although I should think she's heard the story more than once. It's rather a pleasant change to have a fresh audience." Sara rang for a fresh pot and soon the maid replenished the cake tray as well. With a wistful expression on her almost unlined face, Hanna began her story.

I N THE SPRING of 1912, Nathan and Isidor Straus and their wives were visiting Palestine for the first time. Reputed to be among the greatest philanthropists in America, the Straus brothers were given a VIP's welcome in the money-starved Holy Land and the red-carpet treatment wherever they went. They toured agricultural settlements such as Zichron Yaakov and Dugania, where Jewish farmers battled the caprices of nature to eke a subsistence out of the recalcitrant soil. They saw the infant metropolis of Tel Aviv emerging from the sand dunes outside Jaffa. But nowhere was Nathan Straus more impressed than in the Holy City of Jerusalem.

There he found thousands of devout Jews dedicating their lives to the study of Torah and living in abject poverty such as he had never seen. His guides were anxious for Straus to view historical sights and tourist attractions which were the pride of Jerusalem, but Nathan insisted on visiting the "real" city within the walls, the habitations and institutions of the impoverished residents.

The destitute masses rent his heart. Large families crowded into crumbling, one-room hovels, yeshivas housed in squalid shacks, *cheder* children huddled on bare stone floors, and synagogues that bespoke the privation and penury of their congregants, all brought tears to his eyes. Like a man possessed, he trudged day after day down the narrow, winding alleys around the Damascus Gate, through Battei Machse, along Rechov Hayehudim.

"Mother told me that she and Uncle Isidor and Aunt Ida had become more and more frantic with Father's behavior with each passing day. The four of them were supposed to sail from Palestine to England and join their friends and business associates there on what had been billed 'the trans-Atlantic voyage of a lifetime.' Ironic, wouldn't you say? There was even a big business deal they'd been hoping to close on board the *Titanic* — I think it was with Jake Astor.

"But all of their pleading and cajoling for Father to call a halt to his expeditions fell on deaf ears. He simply could not tear himself away from the Old City. In the end, Sara's parents gave up and left for England on their own, and Father barely found the time to say 'good-bye' to them. He would return each evening to the hotel room looking pale and haggard — Mother said it was as though he could feel the suffering of the Jerusalemites on his own flesh."

NATHAN STRAUS was no stranger to poverty. He himself had been raised amidst struggle and indigence in Talbottom, Georgia, and it was there that the seeds of his unique style of philanthropy first germinated. As a young man, he had seen self-respecting workingmen transformed into pitiful beggars by economic conditions beyond their control and he had seen how handouts robbed the needy of their dignity.

During the American financial panic of 1893, Straus established food distribution centers where large quantities of foodstuffs were not given away for free, but sold for pennies. The long lines that formed at the doors to the centers were comprised of honest, hard-working citizens, proud to be able to *buy* the necessities to feed their families — instead of the defeated, down-on-their-luck, shamefaced idlers reduced to begging for crusts.

"Father saw the desperate need in Jerusalem," Hanna continued, "but it wasn't until he returned home that he devised a way to respond to it. You see, *there* it wasn't a question of large numbers of unemployed workers; if that had been the case, why, he would have initiated projects to employ them.

"But these men were engaged full-time in the study of Torah, and the women were raising enormous families, so they couldn't be expected to be wage-earners too — even if their modesty would have allowed them to work outside the home. It was apparent that some creative thinking was called for."

MOSES MONTEFIORE had earlier attempted to initiate a work/study program wherein religious youths could acquire a vocation while continuing their studies, but this program was met with vigorous opposition. Nathan Straus, however, a somewhat secular Jew affiliated with the Reform movement in New York, grasped the essential fact that the study of Torah was an end unto itself and that this was the chosen vocation of many Jerusalemites, despite the absence of financial reward.

While Nathan Straus continued his researches, the *Titanic* set sail from England without him, and five days later, the unsinkable vessel sank, taking with it more than 1,500 passengers and crewmen. Among the victims were his brother Isidor and Isidor's wife, Ida.

"Throughout the *shiva*," Hanna went on, her voice thickened by emotion, "Father was consoled by one thought: that God had spared him for a reason. He knew his fascination with and concern for the starving Jews of Jerusalem had been the only thing that had stood between him and a watery grave. It would have been a simple matter to allocate funds and be done with it, but an incident Father had witnessed in the Old City made him hesitant to do so.

"An elderly pauper, bent nearly in half beneath the pack he carried and wearing the most unspeakable rags, passed my father's contingent on *Shaar HaShamayim* Street.* Father quickly offered the unfortunate fellow a few coins, although he hadn't asked for alms, and the fellow, without a word of thanks, turned on his heel and handed the money to a cripple limping down a passage. Father remarked on this unusual behavior and one of his escorts pointed to a street sign and said, 'Stranger things have happened at the Gates of Heaven.' Father was positively speechless.

"The incident was still fresh in his mind and it gave him an insight into the character of these uncommon people. First, the unhesitating acceptance of charity, without any expression of gratitude or even a hint of the embarrassment he'd seen on the breadlines in Georgia. To my father this meant that, unlike strike-bound coal miners, the needy Jerusalemites could accept his generosity and still maintain their self-respect, because for them it would be similar to the old European way of wealthy townspeople supporting Torah scholars. In a way, it was expected.

"Second — and here was the real conflict — Father wanted to be certain that precisely those individuals whose daily sacrifices for their holy calling were so great, would benefit directly from his philanthropy. But these people were so pious and saintly that, after accepting his money, they were likely to turn around and give it away to anyone they considered less fortunate than themselves. Well, that ruled out direct donations."

* Gates of Heaven Street.

THE STRAUS SOUP KITCHEN in the Battei Warsaw district of Meah Shearim and the network of food distribution centers Nathan Straus founded changed the face of the Yishuv*. Countless impoverished Jerusalemites of that era owed their very existence to his benevolence, and thousands were enabled to continue in their dedicated pursuit of Torah study, relieved, in part, of the burden of sustaining their families.

However, even this enormous contribution could not solve the problems attendant to the deplorable living conditions of the Old City. Crowding, inadequate sanitation and abominable refuse disposal gave rise to rampant disease. In 1914, the Nathan Straus Medical Center, the Pasteur Institute and several child health-welfare facilities opened, providing modern medical care to Jerusalem's residents and removing one more major stumbling block from the path of learning.

Hanna sipped her tea thoughtfully. "When Father passed on and his Will was read, the list of institutions to be endowed seemed interminable. I was astonished by the sums designated for Palestine — they amounted to nearly two-thirds of his fortune, a fact which made me particularly curious to see for myself what Father's money had achieved.

"We were in Palestine just this past summer, and I must say the trip was inspiring. I was received like visiting royalty! In the Old City people flocked around me — great rabbis and Talmudic scholars, elderly mothers of ten, even twelve children — to recount 'Nathan Straus stories,' to tell me how Father had saved them or their parents, and so on.

"Can you imagine — about ten years ago they named a

---

* Early settlement of Jews in *Eretz Yisrael*.

whole town for him: Netanya. The word also means, 'God gave.' Oh, Father must have thought that tremendously appropriate. Through those poor people of Jerusalem, God gave him his life and, in return, my father gave *them* the means to go on with *their* lives.

"The most rewarding thing, of course, was to see that his wonderful philanthropy lives on, even now — after his death. And all because he missed the boat."

"WELL, MIZ HANNA, like I was sayin', Mr. Nathan and Mr. Isidor was two boys would make any mama proud to've birthed them. An' I was surely proud to've knowed them both."

Sara lifted the fabulous fur coat off the sofa. "I'd like you to keep this, Alma. I know Mother would have wanted you to have it."

Alma's face creased with embarrassment. "That's right kind of you, Miss Sara, but you make me ashamed 'cause I wasn't tellin' the truth, exactly. All this talk of people like saints is put me to shame, that's for sure." Sara was nonplussed.

"You see, there's no way I'd be forgettin' I had that there coat all these years. There was times I near as pawned it just to put bread on the table. But every time I'd be takin' it down, I'd be rememberin' your good mama an' how kind she was, not just to me, but to every one, an' that there coat was just about all I had left of her. An' every time, well, somethin' come up — a job just when I was needin' it or somethin' and I didn't have to pawn it after all."

"What made you bring it to me now, Alma, after you've cherished it for twenty-five years?"

Alma dug into her simulated leather handbag and drew

out a sheaf of papers. "Your papa, he give me a present some months before he died, for Hannukie, an' he told me, 'Alma, you hold onto this here thing an' you'll never be wantin' for nothin',' an' that I did." Sara unfolded the large, ornately engraved document. It was a stock certificate for one hundred preferred shares of R.H. Macy, Inc., one of the Straus brothers' vast holdings. The cousins burst out laughing like schoolgirls.

"It seems them stocks been payin' nice divvied-ends a long time now, only they didn't know where to be sendin' them 'cause my address is listed as bein' 222, see? Well, they finally found me up there on the Grand Concourse, an' now I got me enough to retire on an' take care my sister over in Detroit. She's got the arther-ritis somethin' awful."

"I'm sure you'll be able to put a warm coat like this to good use in Michigan, Alma," Sara said with a twinkle in her eye. "I'll tell you what: I'll *sell* you the coat — for one dollar."

three on serendipity

יעלה זו אכזרית על בניה בשעה שכורעת ללדת עולה לראש ההר כדי
שיפול ממנה וימות, ואני מזמין להנשר שמקבלו בכנפיו ומניחו לפניה,
ואלמלי מקדים רגע אחד או מאחר רגע אחד מיד מת.
בבא בתרא טז

  ❀ This wild goat is heartless towards her young.
When she crouches to deliver, she ascends to the top
of a mountain so that the young shall fall down and
be killed, and I prepare an eagle to catch it in his
wings and set it before her, and if he were one second
too soon or too late it would be killed.

Bava Basra 16

Goldie and the Red Rope Riddle

S O MUCH MAIL you get, Goldie!" Clara Bitensky exclaimed when they met one morning at the mailbox. "You must be one popular lady!"

"Lissen, Clara. Ven you get by mine years, dere's not a lotta pipple ken lift ah pen, how dey gonna write you a whole letta?" She fanned herself with the batch of envelopes she'd retrieved from her box. "You see dese? Mostly gahbich." The ones she referred to as "gahbich" were bills, stock reports and bank statements, and these she normally accumulated unopened for thirty days, then dumped the entire lot on Mrs. Fink's son, the tax accountant.

"Bot *dese* —" she held up a dozen or so assorted pieces of mail of various description "— *dese* are mine *life!*" An avid correspondent, Goldie routinely exchanged letters with old friends all over the world, but during the war years, all that had changed. Mail service to and from Europe had come to a virtual standstill.

More troubling to Goldie — a gregarious widow who lived vicariously through the letters of her cronies — was the fact that even her stateside correspondence frequently went unanswered or, even worse, was returned by a surviving relative of the addressee. For a person afflicted with acute yentitis, it was as though her favorite soap opera had been dropped by its sponsors just when the story was getting interesting.

Being severed from the regular stream of news and tidbits was at first devastating, but Goldie had soon found a way to remedy the situation. She had begun to scrutinize the many "Personal" notices which appeared in the *Baltimore Jewish Times* — her local newspaper — and to respond to those that particularly piqued her interest.

"Do they all answer you?" Clara asked, incredulous.

"Mebbe ten partzent." Clara tried to calculate on her fingers the number of notices her friend had to have answered in order to generate such a response, but soon gave up in despair.

"Pliz excuse me, Clara dahlink. I gotta go voik on mine project." Projects attracted Goldie like a mountain draws climbers, demanding her attention simply by virtue of their being there. Her zest for living was not lessened by her having passed her sixtieth birthday and her enthusiastic way of jumping in with both feet was not noticeably diminished by those feet being orthopedically shod.

O VER A CUP of fresh coffee ("viddout sugar — I gotta vatch mine figger!") Goldie opened and read each letter aloud, with only her canary, Faigaleh, for an audience. The morning's selection was somewhat less than satisfying. Mr. Hutzler, against her advice, had decided to marry his secretary; Stella's husband had returned from the ETO shellshocked; and Mitzie had given birth to octuplets!

"I don' beliff it! Mitzie is ah ket?!" Mrs. Klotzberg had written long rambling missives rhapsodizing about her "darling children," about Herbie and Morris and Mitzie and Francine, about their "quarreling" or being "moody" or "throwing tantrums." When she had announced Mitzie's marriage to Herbie, Goldie was at first shocked but later assumed that one or the other of them was a foster or adopted child. Then there had been Mitzie's pregnancy, her increased testiness and ill humor, etc., etc. And now: "eight tiny, fluffy(!) babies — four of them calicoes, like their mother!"

Goldie tore up the letter in disgust. "An old lady who tinks kets is like kids is cuckoo — right, Faigaleh?" Faigaleh chirped her accord.

Sifting through the letters, Goldie selected the worthy ones and proceeded to answer them. At one point, her pen-friends had numbered 27, but she had found it difficult to keep track of all their triumphs and travails. With the number down to a more manageable twelve, the job was completed by noon.

Phase Two of Goldie's current project involved replacing the rejects, like Mrs. Klotzberg and her cats. She turned her attention to the day's classifieds. Immediately, she spotted a small display ad printed in boldface:

> **RAHAB:**
>
> **READY RED ROPE**
>
> (signed) **DAVID SHIELD**

"**V**AT'S DIS?" she wondered. The wording of the ad was obscure, as though the advertiser had phrased it so that only "RAHAB" would understand its meaning. "It looks like ah mistry, Faigaleh!" And there were few things Goldie loved more than a mystery. She rose from the davenport, scattering all the stationery and writing paraphernalia from her lap across the Persian rug, and began pacing and pondering.

"It's signed 'DAVID SHIELD' — dat's easy. I got dat right avay. 'DAVID SHIELD' mins 'Moggen Dovid.'" To Goldie that was evidence that the author was Jewish. True, few of the *Baltimore Jewish Times*'s advertisers were *not*, but that was neither here nor there.

"Who's dis 'RAHAB'? Must be none udder den 'Rachav,' dat *shiktza* fun Yehoshua!" The biblical Rachav, mistress of Jericho Inn, had kindly sheltered Joshua's spies, and when Jericho was subsequently destroyed, Rachav's kindness was rewarded: she lowered a red line out her window, thus indicating her location, and her life and home were spared.

"Aha!" Goldie shouted triumphantly. "Dat's der 'RED ROPE' — ah signel! 'DAVID SHIELD' ah Joosh boy, vants dis *shiktza* 'RAHAB' to make him a signel!" Her round face glowed with pleasure at the cleverness of her deductions; laugh crinkles radiated from the corners of her bright blue eyes. She poked a pudgy finger between the bars of Faigaleh's cage for the canary to nip at affectionately.

"So, my leedle *tzippaleh,* vat you tink? Vat's ah good Joosh boychick makink ah signel mit ah *shiktza?*" All of a sudden, realization dawned and her good cheer disappeared. "*Oy vey's mir!* He vants to *merry* her. Surely, she told herself, either or both sets of parents were opposed to the marriage, necessitating their resorting to subterfuge.

"He's goink to elop mit her!" Faigaleh hopped excitedly from her perch to the feeder tray and back. "No qvestion abot it!" Goldie cried. "I gotta make ah stop to dis!"

SHE SAT DOWN again on the davenport and, with her brow knitted in concentration, began to compose her own ad in response to that of "DAVID SHIELD." After several minutes and many crossings-out and emendations, she carried the text over to the birdcage and read it aloud:

"'To der Joosh boy, whoeffer you are: Vat you need mit ah red rope anyvay? If you are needink ah signel to find your gerl, you must be vun lost boychick! Leaf it to me, I'll fix you op mit ah nice Joosh gerl. Tell me vere to meetchoo an' I'll brink ah whole elbum uff pikches you should choose from.' How's dat, Faigaleh?"

"Cheep, cheep!" Faigaleh chirped.

"You're right, *tzippaleh*. It von't be cheap. I gotta cut ah lotta voids." She checked the advertising rates. Ten words were the absolute maximum she could allow herself, and she immediately set to the task of blue-penciling the text. At last, she sat back with a satisfied sigh, then proudly declaimed her ad:

"'DAVID SHIELD: RED ROPE? LOST! FIX MATE. WHERE? PIX.'" She signed it "RAHAB" to attract the "Joosh boychick's" attention and hurried over to the offices of the *Baltimore Jewish Times* to place it in time for the weekend edition.

IN A SPARSELY-FURNISHED loft on Lombard Street, three pairs of eyes scanned the Personal Column for a response to the ad they had placed the previous week. The three, agents of the Haganah,* were engaged in a vital and, of necessity, secret mission: the rescue of thousands of Jewish displaced persons from war-ravaged Europe and the

* Underground military force created by the Jewish Agency to defend and secure Jewish interests in Palestine and abroad.

resettlement of these homeless masses in Palestine.

The mission was perforce clandestine because the British Mandatory Government of Palestine had declared such immigration illegal. During 1946 and 1947, the British turned back one refugee ship after another, determined to prevent the arrival of "reinforcements" for the Jewish populace.

Once a grateful, even subservient lot, the Jews of Palestine had become increasingly bold in their efforts to oust the King's installations. They had carried out numerous retaliatory missions against the occupying forces, captured and executed British soldiers, and, in June of 1946, had blown up the King David Hotel — mandatory headquarters — with heavy losses of British, Arab, and even Jewish life. Despite their repudiation by enemies and brethren alike, these underground cells were sworn to continue their violent activities as long as the White Paper [the document issued by the British government setting a quota on Jewish immigrants into Palestine at 75,000, to be followed by a total moratorium] remained in force, or until the occupation of Palestine ended.

But White Paper or no, the "underground railroad" which transported the immigrants had resumed its pre-war activities in the post-war era. The Haganah, headquartered in Paris, posted emissaries to Mediterranean, Dalmatian and American ports to hire vessels — ranging from small fishing schooners to converted icebreakers — and to arrange the illicit sailings.

With little sympathy for British colonial policy and even less for the White Paper, the French, Italian and Yugoslav governments did not interfere with these sailings; in fact, they occasionally provided support. But U.S. government policy differed radically. All sailings out of Baltimore, therefore, had to be carried out under a veil of secrecy.

THREE WEEKS earlier, the agents in the Lombard Street loft had dispatched Shaike to make the necessary arrangements for the next boatload of DPs. Shaike was to scout out the docks and contract a small cargo vessel to make the Baltimore-Yugoslavia-Palestine run, but after identifying such a vessel — *La Riata Roja,* under Argentinian registration — and making the initial approach, Shaike Rechavam had disappeared. In the interim, the agents had been obliged to relocate from North Avenue and had no way of reestablishing contact with "Rahab" other than through the Personal Columns, a medium routinely employed in such cases.

Word had been received that the "shipment" from Yugoslavia was nearly assembled and now the matter of arranging transport became imperative. Shaike was their link to *La Riata Roja* — the "Red Rope" — and now that they were ready for it, their man had become a "missing link."

"Here it is!" Mottie shouted. "'DAVID SHIELD: RED ROPE? LOST! FIX MATE. WHERE? PIX. RAHAB.'"

"It must mean that Shaike's deal for the *Riata Roja* fell through," Arnie ventured. "See that — 'RED ROPE? LOST!' Obviously, he needs to bribe the First Mate."

"Makes sense," Jack concurred. "That would explain 'FIX MATE.' Now, he must want to set up a meeting somewhere so that we can transfer the funds for the bribe to him."

"Right!" said Mottie. "We'll have to notify him 'WHERE' and bring the 'PIX' — that must mean the bribe money: U.S. dollars have pictures of American presidents on them."

"I'm way ahead of you," Arnie said. "I've already composed the text of our ad. Here it is: 'RAHAB: 3-2-70-400/5-20-6-40-200/1630 GOOD DAY. DAVID SHIELD.'"

COMPLETELY DISREGARDING the mail delivery, Goldie reached for Friday's *Jewish Times* with more than her usual alacrity and rushed up the short flight of stairs to her apartment, thinking that it had been a long time since she'd had such excitement — and so much fun. Turning straight to the classifieds, she had no difficulty finding the one she sought.

"Vat, voids is not goot enough — now ve gotta use nombers?" The canary tapped a staccato rhythm on her cuttlebone. "You tink it's mebbe like Morris Cote, Faigaleh? Dot, dot, desh?" Goldie shrugged her shoulders in resignation. "Vell, den, der jiggle is op. Vat em I knowink from cotes? De only cote I know from is *Gematria*."*

Faigaleh chirped encouragingly. "You're right, *tzippaleh*. I got sometink bettah to do? Nah. So now ve'll see if mine boychick is makink *Gematria* today."

The numerical sequence "DAVID SHIELD" had composed quickly decoded to ג־ב־ע־ת ה־כ־ו־מ־ר - *Givat Hakomer,* and Goldie spread a street map of Baltimore on the kitchen table, looking for anything that might be defined as "Priest's Mountain." But the only "mountain" she could find was Mt. Washington and that could not be right. There were several "Heights," but not "Priest's;" there was Emory Hills and Chestnut Hill and suddenly, there was Druid Hill Park!

"Dat's it! It lays on mine mind ah 'drood' is ah goyische priest, fun der Stone Age." Webster's confirmed that the "drood" that lay in her mind was indeed a Celtic priest — "Nu, so it's Stone*henge,* same difference.

---

* A homiletical interpretation of scriptural passages based on the numerical value of letters in the Hebrew alphabet, e.g. א =1, ב =2, י =10. From the Greek, gamma treia i.e. γ =3

"Hokay. So mine fella vants I should meet him in Druid Hill Park, but ven?" She pondered another moment. "Ach, it's clear like mine nose: '1630' — dat's four-tirdy in de efternoon. 'GOOD DAY' — dat's gotta be Choosday, der tird day — יום שהוכפל בו כי טוב. Easy like pies!"

A T 4:42 ON TUESDAY afternoon, Mottie was sitting on a cold bench in Druid Hill Park, puffing on his hands. The sky looked threatening and the temperature had dipped well below normal for November, but he had drawn the short straw so he had to wait for Shaike. The wind cut right through him, making him yearn even more for the sunny beaches of Tel Aviv. He glanced around surreptitiously. An elderly lady toting a swollen shopping bag reminded Mottie of his grandmother back on a farm in Nahariya; she constituted the only life form Mottie had encountered in thirty-two minutes. There was still no sign of Shaike.

Goldie had been *shlepping* around the park for the better part of an hour and in all that time had met just one birdwatcher, three dogwalkers, two pigeon-feeders and a handful of squirrels doing some last-minute shopping before the onset of serious winter. She knew the young man warming his wind-reddened hands had to be "DAVID SHIELD," since none of the others conformed to the image she'd mentally constructed. "Tenks God, dere's not menny pipple valkink in dis vedder — it's cold like cucumbehs."

With a spring in her step, she approached the bench and said: "You are David Shield, uff course." Mottie's head spun in her direction, a thunderstruck expression on his youthful face. "I know, I know, you vere expectink dat gerl-fren and instead vat comes? Ah nold lady mit pikches. But, like I said in mine ad — farget de *shiktza!*" Mottie's throat emitted a strangled sound. "I got plenny nice Joosh gerls right here," she added, tapping the oversized album in her hand. Mottie's eyes bulged as though he'd seen an apparition.

"Lissen, Duvidel — you don' mind I call you Duvidel?" The strangle became a gargle. "Goot. Lissen. Doze *behaimes, yemach shemam vezichram,* haff spent de lest fife years *shechting* our pipple like dey vas sheeps. Ve lost ah tird fun our pipple, ah tird! Six millions! How ken ah Joosh boy even tink abot merryink ah *shiktza* — when ve need more Joosh childrens now? Shem on you!"

"Gaaagh."

"Here. You see dis byooty? Dis is Mrs. Finkel's grendutter fun next door. So, she's not such a byooty, nu. Bot *inside,* dat's vere she's got byooty. And dis *zeeskeit* — " Goldie introduced a brunette with what appeared to be a large potato in her mouth, "— she plays on der piano like Moe Tzart, I'm tellink you. Fife hundret tuller, mebbe, to fix up de nose. And vat abot dis..."

MOTTIE WAS TREMBLING badly. He reached into his pocket for his Luckies and the pack somehow came out upside down, spilling cigarettes all over the pavement. In an old nondescript DeSoto parked across the street, behind a pair of high-power binoculars, Arnie was witnessing the spectacle on the bench with growing concern.

"Jack! There's the signal! Mottie dropped his cigarette — he must be in trouble. Let's go!" They leaped from the car and dashed to their companion's aid.

"Hallo," Goldie greeted them, "you are Duvidel's frens? I'm Goldie Sokolow, nice to meetchoo." They looked at Mottie questioningly, but all he could offer in lieu of an explanation was that same strangled gag. Over hot milk and cinnamon buns which Goldie respectively decanted and dispensed from her shopping bag, the entire matter was soon straightened out. Sort of.

"So vat's mit all dis clocks and deggers?" she asked, not unreasonably. The agents exchanged a sheepish glance. "Aha, I see. You big boychicks are playink spy rinks!"

"No, no," Jack insisted. "We're only afraid our plans will be upset by some anti-Semitic bureaucrat and then what would become of the DPs? As it is, we're behind schedule and we've lost our connection for hiring the *Riata Roja...*"

"Dis is ah problem? Nah." She dismissed it as niggling. "Dis is chicken's feet." She opened her trusty photo album and pointed to a mousy, fair-haired young lady with a receding chin. "Shaindel's fodder's ah tailor."

They waited for her to continue and when she did not, Arnie asked, "So?"

"Yeah, he sews. It so heppens, he sews ah new uniform far Keptain Sanchez, fun dat boat, how you call it? *Rita Roacha.* Soitenly Shaindel's fodder vill be heppy to help out — specially far ah future son-in-law..."

And so it was that Goldie Sokolow became a secret agent for the Haganah — well, not *so* secret since she *had* to tell Faigaleh, of course — and the unsung heroine of over seven hundred Yugoslavian refugees.

Mrs. Serendipity
Sets Sail

OLDIE SOKOLOW was the mistress of happenstance. Excelling at happenstance, it may be argued, is rather like excelling at a blood test; since both involve factors beyond human control, mastering them as one masters a craft would be an impossibility. Nonetheless, given Goldie's unerring knack for being in the right place at the right time, even a cynic would have to admit that happenstance was her obedient servant.

The confluence of circumstances which led to her initial involvement with the Haganah is a prime example. "You know vat dose boychicks call me, Faigaleh?" she asked her constant companion. "'Meesis Ser-en-dip-i-ty.' It mins ah poisen vat finds good tinks by chence." Since Goldie had joined the ranks of covert volunteers, Faigaleh, her tone-deaf canary, had become the only one in whom she could confide. ["Loose leaps sink sheeps," she had told the bird, "an' I'm not goink to make enny loose leaps!"]

"Chence-shmence!" she derided. "*Ve* know nottink heppens by chence, yes *tzippaleh?* Efrytink goes accordink mit der Mester Plen."

Few things in this world could have given her more pleasure than being a part of the remarkable rescue enterprise in which the Haganah was secretly engaged: transporting Jewish DPs from post-war Europe to Palestine. And few of the Haganah's American volunteers could have offered them the invaluable aid which Goldie so ably provided, with her vast network of contacts and acquaintances, her six decades of life experience and innate resourcefulness, and her spiritual and corporeal sustenance. Goldie's participation in the mission was indeed mutually serendipitous.

S HE WAS A "natural" for undercover work. Who would suspect a maternal, arthritic sexagenarian of clandestine activity? Her elan and aplomb elicited cooperation from the very authorities empowered to police and curtail the activities of her cohorts. She could still make her now-faded blue eyes twinkle innocently, and many a uniformed civil servant was taken in by the harmless old lady of grandmotherly proportions who hung around Lombard Street in the dock area. She became a familiar figure to all the port workers, dispensing cheery words and homemade buns which she withdrew from one of the oversized shopping bags she always toted. Eccentric, they thought, but a welcome sight, with those apple-round cheeks and almost wrinkle-free skin. When "Grannie" showed up, even the most hardened longshoreman raised a work-worn hand to wave hello. No one imagined what those innocuous-looking shopping bags contained.

For days before a sailing, Goldie would cook and bake enough Kosher, nutritious food to sustain a small army. Neither the Jewish crew nor the DPs that comprised the passengers had need to worry about meals during the voyage.

Widowed many years earlier, childless, and having lost all the rest of her family to the Nazi inferno, Goldie adopted all those in her charge; they were her "grenchildrens" and she saw to their nourishment no less than any biological grandmother would. Loaves of bread, jars of preserves, whole roasts and turkeys were among the countless pounds of foodstuffs Goldie brought down to the docks, day after day, in her shopping bags, and she personally saw to their lading.

One fateful evening, Goldie was busily loading the latest vessel — a large converted scow named the *Padawer* — when happenstance, like opportunity, knocked on her door. "Vat ah mess!" she exclaimed when she noticed that the scow was littered with empty bottles, old magazines and other detritus of sailors too long in drydock. The sight was appalling: even a "landlubber" knew a littered deck was a hazard that could cause a fatal accident.

She dropped what she was doing to tidy up the ship. How many times had she admonished the crew to take along volumes of *Tehillim* and other sacred paraphernalia which might help boost their merit account and protect them on so dangerous a mission. Goldie tried to be something of a *mashgiach ruchani,* but her "grenchildrens" were very far from accepting her *mussar.*

No matter. She had a feeling, almost a premonition, that one day their work would bring her and them into close proximity for extended periods of time; then Goldie would mount a relentless attack on their Jewish souls, with the aim of rehabilitating them. Considering her track record and her irresistible style, the likelihood of success was high.

GOLDIE'S PURGE of the boat resulted in her taking far longer than usual to stock it. Her perception of the passage of time was also slightly distorted by the roaring din of the boat's newly-installed engines. And while she busied herself below, the captain received a coded message and ordered the crew to weigh anchor at once.

Had he spared a moment to think of Goldie, he most certainly would have thought her long-since gone. In fact, he did not think about her, or about anything but the voyage ahead. Sailings were determined by a single consideration: security. Whenever they stood the greatest chance of leaving undetected, they left — no matter what. The British had threatened to blow up any ship entering Palestine's territorial waters and carrying "illegals," and it was no empty threat. If the *Padawer*'s cover were "blown," the British would be alerted and would surely arrange a "warm" welcome for the new immigrants.

That is how it happened that when the *Padawer* cast off, Goldie was still below deck dividing the foodstuffs into dairy and meat compartments. By the time she climbed up on deck, they were already three miles out of Baltimore.

The boat, with its Panamanian registration and flying the two-star, four-quadrant flag of that country, maintained its disguise as an ordinary cargo ship by heading towards South America, sailing south along the American coast until it could shake the port pilot. At the mouth of Chesapeake Bay, it would change course eastward towards the Azores and begin its perilous journey across the Atlantic.

T HE CREWMEN, fully aware that the boat beneath their feet was only borderline seaworthy, were incredulous at the sight of their sixty-year-old stowaway, and more than a little concerned for her safety. But Goldie, as always, was unruffled. She understood from their facial expressions that there was no possibility of going back to let her off.

"Vell, boychicks," she declared triumphantly, "dis is de big upperchunity ve haff all been lookink for! Just tink about how menny mitzvos ve ken make on dis voyage." With every word she uttered, enumerating her *mussar*-dispensing intentions for the trip, her audience drew further and further away like well-dressed spectators at a mud-wrestling match hoping to avoid being splattered.

Goldie chased after the Captain, who had strode off to brood in solitude, and asked, "Kep, do you haff mebbe a vay of contactink de shore? I just rillized dat somevone is goink to haff to vater mine plants an' feed mine dahlink Faigaleh vile I'm avay. An' since I'm goink to *Eretz Yisruel,* dat means I vill be avay far qvite ah long trip!" The Captain's face seemed to reflect an incipient ulcer.

"Hold on there, Goldie," he interrupted, attempting to pour cold water on her rising enthusiasm. "Who's talking about *Eretz Yisrael?* We'll be able to let you off in the Azores in another two weeks or so."

"Vhy, Keptain, vat's de metteh? I'm goink to go mit you all de vay an' help you run de Britich blockade. You know, I alvays vanted to go to *Eretz Yisruel,* an' just tink: now I got ah nall-expenses-paid trip. I'm so excited. Don' look so mizrable. Lissen, I got mebbe vone, two mitzvos to mine credit, an' by de time I'm troo mit you, mebbe you vill too, an' maybe den de Bik Chief uf Staffs in Heaven vill lend His hend too."

"Goldie, listen here. You know that I and all of the other men on board would love to share your company, but these are dangerous seas. And if the ocean doesn't get us, the British have their big guns trained on Haifa bay — they're blowing illegal refugee ships out of the water!"

Goldie decided to shelve her appeal for a while, and in the meantime, to devote her energies entirely to the spiritual welfare of the crew. Her reluctant "grenchildrens" were less than enthusiastic about their confinement with her, but as the trip wore on, they cleaned up their language in her presence and even started to recite blessings — at her humorous but persistent urging — before partaking of the food she served.

As the boat approached the Azores — where the *Padawer* was to refuel en route to Italy to pick up DPs — the argument over Goldie resumed. The twenty-one crewmen were solidly united against one extraordinarily tenacious old lady named Goldie Sokolow. Well, she had faced worse odds before... and won.

The First Mate came up with the idea of duping Goldie into getting off at Italy by convincing her that her services were vitally needed there. "Goldie," the Captain said with a gleeful smile, "I have good news. We just received an urgent request over the radio for someone like you to help them out in Italy. You know what the survivors went through over there, and there are a lot of people who have lost their faith in God after the camps. You're just what they need. All you have to do is just what you've been doing to us, er, *for* us for the last few weeks, and before you know it, they'll all be enrolling in yeshiva."

"That's right," the entire crew chimed in. "Goldie, you'll be a smash!" said the First Mate. "We can picture the headlines in the *Baltimore Jewish Times:* 'American Rebbetzin wows Rome; European Jewry Swoons'. What an opportunity! Who could even think of *Eretz Yisrael* when a chance like this drops into your lap?"

But Goldie didn't fall for the ruse. "Nah," she said, casting their arguments aside with a flick of her hand, "I tole you de Bik Chief uf Staffs put me on dis boat far ah reason, an' vhere He puts Goldie, Goldie stays." A disarming dimple appeared on her cheek. "You tink dat just because I em old I em useless but de *Toireh* teaches different. Ah poisen desoives respeck not because uf der age but because uf de visdom dat comes mit der age. You vill see vat ah nesset *old Goldie* vill be durink de hard part uf dis trip."

To the Captain's thinking no asset could outweigh the presence of a sixty-year-old liability on a mission that required clockwork precision. The embarkation of the DPs would have to be carried out smoothly and swiftly. If the boat could not anchor close enough to shore for the refugees to board it across long planks, a wire would have to be strung from the ship to the dock; the DPs, in groups of forty or so would then board large rubber rescue dinghies and pull their lifeboats to the ship by way of the wire. A motor launch would also tow several dinghies over at one shot, and thus the transport of over a thousand passengers could be accomplished in under two hours. The carefully timed operation had to proceed without a hitch or else the *Padawer* would not be underway before dawn.

The pre-dawn sailing was crucial. While the various European governments were willing to turn a blind eye to the mass emigration of DPs, they could not afford to incur the wrath of the British and a daylight departure would have revealed their complicity. But even if all went well during the transfer operation, the *Padawer* still had to evade the British Mediterranean Fleet, the RAF Mediterranean Patrol, and the Palestine Coastal Water Blockade.

"I'm sorry, Goldie, but your continuing with us to Palestine is out of the question," the Captain said firmly.

Goldie began to cry. "It's not enough de Britich von't let us into our homelend, but mine own grenchildrens are also goink to keep me out?" She pulled a lace handkerchief from her sleeve and mopped her streaming eyes. Several crew members rolled their eyes heavenward in a helpless gesture of submission; the rest glared accusingly at the Captain.

The odds had suddenly shifted in her favor. Goldie peeked over the edge of white lace and murmured, "Dis may be mine lest chence..." That was the clincher.

THE LOADING OPERATION proceeded rapidly and Goldie was on deck to welcome the 1,100 refugees aboard. The "illegals", shaken by their recent harrowing experience, seemed not to register the fact that a plump, white-haired figure straight out of a storybook occupied a place on the receiving line. Greeting them with blessings in Yiddish and Hebrew, Goldie distributed warm blankets, a little nosh, and plenty of cheer.

During the next four days, Goldie became well-acquainted with each and every one of the DPs. Even the most silent and sullen among them — those whose war experiences had been so horrid that they had sealed that part of their minds as if behind a brick wall — opened up to Goldie and poured their hearts out. They cried, and she wiped their tears. They shouted angry words at a God who they imagined had abandoned His people to such a fate, and she spoke soothingly of redemption and hope. By the fifth day, almost all of the passengers had joined Goldie's afternoon songfest-cum-*mussar shiur*. "*Chasdei Hashem ki lo samnu*" they sang, and each word struck a personal chord.

That Thursday afternoon, however, was to be the last of their pleasurable sessions on the *Padawer* although when the youthful *chazzan* belted out the first notes of "*Yiboneh HaMikdash*" in his mellifluous tenor voice, none of them knew.

He was only twenty-five, perhaps twenty-eight, but when he sang his eyes glistened and his brow creased. All who gazed upon his countenance and sat mesmerized by his heart-piercing voice knew that the young *chazzan* had seen more suffering than any twenty-five-year-old should ever need to see.

The voice broke sharply in mid-note. For one fleeting moment the crowd on the deck remained transfixed. Then they, too, heard the sound.

The Captain immediately ordered everyone below deck, but of course it was hopeless. A Naval Academy drill team could not have made it down those narrow ladders from a rolling deck in the three brief minutes they had before the patrol plane flew overhead.

The Captain knew to expect the worst. The plane continued to circle and soon two destroyer escorts were sighted on the horizon.

THE APPEARANCE of the British fleet ships etched painfully sharp lines on the faces of the crewmen. The Captain climbed down into the hold to apprise the passengers of the situation. It was far too hot and there was no longer any point in their remaining below: the "cargo vessel" had been identified. The Captain returned to the deck, lowered the Panamanian flag and hoisted in its place one bearing the word DROR [Freedom] in bold blue letters on a white field.

When the refugees emerged from the bowels of the ship and spotted the escorts, they fell silent. Even the youngsters, who normally chattered incessantly, became still, and a pall of terror descended on the decrepit scow.

The decks and armor of the towering destroyers gleamed smugly in the bright sun at the helpless, overcrowded immigrant boat. Sandwiched between those menacing Goliaths, the DROR defiantly continued on its course until it reached Palestine's territorial waters.

It was then that Goldie approached the Captain. "I vish to spick to der leader," she said, and the Captain for the first time lost his patience. "Which leader do you mean?" he retorted with some disdain, "The Prime Minister, Secretary Bevin, or will the Admiral of the British Fleet do?"

At that moment, a launch carrying a well-armed boarding party was rapidly nearing the DROR. The radio operator handed the Captain instructions just received from land: the DROR was to offer no resistance; the safety of the passengers — including many women and children — was paramount. The Captain reluctantly concurred.

WHEN THE BRITISH party boarded, Goldie elbowed her way through the crowd until she stood face to face with the English officer. Then, to the utter astonishment of the Captain and all assembled, she quietly removed her gold-rimmed spectacles and began polishing the lenses with the white lace handkerchief she always kept tucked up her sleeve, her eyes riveting his.

Seconds ticked away but no one moved. She replaced her glasses and then, drawing herself up to her full height of four feet, ten inches, she declared: "I just wanted to see for myself the officers of the invincible British Navy, the proudest Navy in the world, who require two destroyers and scores of crewmen to overpower an unarmed cargo boat filled with homeless war victims. The Almighty has a special place for brave little sailors such as you." Goldie's endearing accent had disappeared, to be replaced by one of which any Park Avenue matron would have been proud.

The jaw of the British naval officer dropped with an almost audible "thunk." Speechless, he slowly holstered his pistol. In the same moment, as though bolstered by Goldie's audacity, the engines of the DROR thudded to a halt, and the mood of the passengers shifted ever-so-subtly. Their silence was no longer one of despair and defeat, but of pride and defiance. The boarding party withdrew.

The DROR, wallowing on the rough sea, was unable — or unwilling — to get its engines going and the British were obliged to perform the distasteful task of piloting the scow to shore. With every bump, the sailors peered down in disgust at the ugly scrapes the filthy refugee boat made on their gleaming hull — and the passengers of the DROR cheered.

As soon as the boat was in clear sight of land, Goldie hurled herself overboard. The British rescue operation was duly recorded for posterity, to the delight of the reporters assembled on the dock, and to the utter consternation of her rescuers.

Goldie had indeed proved to be an asset. The following day's world press would surely carry the story of a sixty-year-old lady challenging British destroyers and throwing herself into the sea rather than be captured alive. Of course, she had had no such suicidal intentions ["Ekshully, mine pocketbook fell in de vater," she later told a friend, "mit mine fency-shmency *siddur* inside. I should let dat drown?! Farget it."] but it was such stories about the heartless British monsters that destroyed the goodwill upon which the British mandate rested.

GOLDIE AND THE other 1,100 passengers were able to step on the holy soil for but a few brief minutes; they were quickly transferred onto deplorable British troop ships which carried them to Cyprus. There they were quartered in squalid, primitive detention camps surrounded by barbed wire, and deliberately deprived of water. It was hoped that the blazing Mediterranean sun would discourage further illegal crossings.

The British, however, had not taken Goldie's spirit into account. The number of escapes from the camps steadily increased and although few were successful, the rate of recidivism was intolerably high. Goldie, who had defied the guns of the British navy, had given the DPs a taste of real freedom, and they thirsted for more.

Under British policy, no more than 750 legal immigrants per month could enter Palestine, "legal" being loosely defined as those whose immigration papers were in order, those who were sponsored by a relative, those who could afford a bribe, and a few DPs — all of this subject to British whim. Because of her age, or perhaps her U.S. citizenship, or more likely because of the effect she seemed to have on the detainees, the authorities thought it best to move Goldie quickly. Thus she found herself among the first group to leave the Cyprus detention camp.

On board the boat to the Holy Land, she struck up a conversation with a well-dressed gentleman. This man turned out to be a high official of the nascent Jewish Agency, returning after an extended mission in Europe. They had several hours to kill and during that time he managed to extract from her the highlights of her recent adventures. Needless to say, he was astounded, but at the same time, concerned for her well-being. Although she was apparently a formidable lady who had handled herself admirably in the most difficult circumstances, she was appallingly ignorant of the present situation in Palestine.

"Where will you be staying when we reach Palestine?" he asked uneasily. "Are you, er, employed? Do you have a sponsor?"

"Goldie Sokolow voiks for only von boss: de Bik Chief uf Staffs in Heaven." Her accent, which conveniently ebbed and flowed with the tide of contingency, had returned. "He giffs me mine orders. Right dis minute I'm expectink ah nurgent message."

"Perhaps you have a relative in Palestine?" he asked hopefully.

"It lays in mine head I got a nephew in *Eretz Yisruel* — der son from der bruddeh from mine Motke, he should rest in pizz. He moved dere menny years ago, but I neffer heard from him. Only de Bik Chief knows if he is eefen alife."

"So then where will you be going?" the Agency man persisted. "These are very difficult times now. The British impose a curfew almost every night."

"Like I tole you before, don' vorry, de Bik Chief vill help."

T HE MAN WAS becoming frustrated with this obstinate old woman. "Mrs. Sokolow," he said with more heat than he'd intended, "I am afraid that you don't realize you are adopting an untenable position. Where are you going to stay at least on the night that you get off this boat?"

"Younk men," Goldie said with her typical equanimity, "I neffer vas minning in de first plece to come to *Eretz Yisruel* so uf course I don' know vhere I em stayink. De Bik Chief brought me here. I am sure He made me a reservation in some nice fency hotel." The man gave up at last in total exasperation.

When the boat docked in Haifa, the press was on hand to interview the Jewish Agency official. "Can you tell us sir," the first reporter asked as he stepped down the gangplank, "was your mission successful?" The young fellow was personable, and polite. On impulse, the Agency man decided to cooperate.

"I'm afraid that I'm much too tired from the trip to answer any of your questions now. However, if you'll come to my office in Tel Aviv tomorrow, I will be happy to grant you an interview. What is your name?"

"Sokolow, sir. For the Palestine Post."

The official halted in mid-stride.

"Sokolow?! Do you have any relatives in America?"

"Why, yes, I... I guess so," he stammered, taken by surprise. "An aunt, er, the widow of my father's older brother."

"Stay right here and don't move!" the Agency man commanded, then turned on his heel and hurried back towards Goldie.

"Officer Sokolow," he said, a sardonic smile twitching at the corners of his mouth, "your new orders have just arrived from the Bik Chief..."

Goldie and the
Providential Prosecution

ASHA CLAPPED a calloused hand to his balding pate and exclaimed: "Are you hearing this? 'OVERSEAS POSTAL RATES UP TODAY'!" It was a sunny morning in Tel Aviv, the first of April, 1966, and the four of them were warmly ensconced on their favorite bench across from the Municipal Building. By mutual agreement, they communicated in broken English, in deference to Frieda, a recent immigrant from Chicago, who — unlike her companions — was monolingual. All together, Frieda, Sasha, Fritz and Goldie spoke a total of thirteen languages with varying degrees of competence, and had seen nearly three centuries of war, poverty, travail and now — at last — tranquil retirement.

Their backgrounds and personalities differed widely, yet they were bound by a common lifestyle and a shared need for companionship. Frieda Kaplan was a grandmother several times over, an incorrigible knitter of vile-colored sweaters of peculiar proportion — all of which she deemed artistic masterpieces and none of which were.

Fritz Pfeiffer was an erstwhile mechanical engineer from Hamburg who since the war had taken to designing espionage gadgets which had all thus far proved nonfunctional or impractical. Only a week earlier, Fritz had arrived in a cloud of smoke and Goldie — ever the quick thinker — had doused him with a thermos of tea. She needn't have worried, though. It had only been a "Pfeiffer Fume-Faker" — an encapsulated smoke bomb designed to discharge when the gelatinous coating was heated and melted. Unfortunately, when Fritz had slipped this new gadget into his jacket pocket, he hadn't taken into account the fact that the melting point of the capsule was 98.6°F.

Notwithstanding numerous disappointments and despite his having been laughed out of the patent office a total of two hundred and thirty-seven times, Fritz appeared at the Municipal Building bench each morning, briefcase and pockets bulging with plans, schematic drawings and prototypes, ready for any *Shin-Bet* or CIA recruiter who might turn up.

GOLDIE SOKOLOW, who'd lost none of her exuberance since her inadvertent immigration several years earlier, was far too polite and kindhearted to disabuse her bench partners of their respective self-deceptions, but neither Frieda nor Fritz had any such compunction. With sharp tongues in both their heads, they frequently went at one another with vituperative exchanges such as:

"You making another gorilla-baby cardigan?"

"At least *it* won't explode if a button pops off!"

"In that *miessa meshunehdigge* color, it might be better off if it did!"

Mikhail Alexandrovich Papashvili, or Sasha, for short, was a shell-shocked veteran of the Bolshevik Revolution who reeked of garlic and was rumored to have sustained a long-distance chess match for over eleven years with a partner in Scotland he'd never met. Sasha was understandably distressed by the new postal rates as all their moves ("Queen's knight to king's bishop, check") were transmitted by mail. However, since he read *all* the headlines to his companions *every* day, each recitation accompanied by the same brow-smacking gesture of anguish, it was impossible to know for certain if his distress was genuine.

Furthermore, it was often impossible to comprehend the headlines at all as his Russian-accented rendering added a "kh" to almost every word ("Are*kh* *kh*you *kh*hearing this? '*KH*OVERSEAS POSTAL *KH*RATES *KH*UP TODAY'!"). This being his sole contribution to the general conversation (a sort of "stream-of-unconsciousness monologue," Fritz called it) his companions usually acknowledged his declamations with a noncommittal "mmn hmn."

"'*KH*U THANT DENIES VISITS TO *KH*ARABS'!" Sasha quoted.

"So, Frieda," Goldie asked the knitter pleasantly, "your Shirley is comink to visit far der summa?"

"I certainly hope so, dear," Frieda replied, "that is if my son-in-law-Harry-the-orthodontist can take off a few weeks from his highly-successful-practice."

Goldie wondered why it was necessary for Frieda, who had only one son-in-law, to always refer to him as "Harry-the-orthodontist" and to his business as a "highly-successful-practice." For some time, Goldie had believed him to be of Greek descent — "Harry Theothodontis" — with a condition known as "Hialeah's Excess Full Praxis," something akin to hiatus hernia, but neither assumption had been borne out by later remarks.

" '*SYKHRIANS KHATTACK KHHULA PATKHROL*'!" Sasha cried.

"My Morton had an asthma attack last night," said Frieda, clicking her needles rhythmically. As often occurred, Sasha's incongruous interjections had acted as a mnemonic. "It was the most pathetic sight, let me tell you!"

"Mmph," Fritz snorted. "I bet you didn't drop a single stitch the whole time."

"Why don't you play a tune on 'Pfeiffer's Poison Piccolo'? That should keep your mouth shut."

"I wouldn't try to compete with your Number 10 castanets."

Goldie tried to deflect the next riposte. "So how is he fillink today?"

They both looked at her quizzically. "Who?"

"Your Morton, der husbent mit estma."

"Oh, *him*," said Frieda, remembering. "How should I know? He left early this morning to go on a nature hike. I hope he took his heavy sweater..."

"Was that the puce one with the camel hump in the back or the mustard-chartreuse checkered number?"

" '*KHYEMENITES CLAIM "STOLEN" CHILDKHREN KHALIVE*'!" Sasha interjected and for once the verbal skirmishing ceased in mid-thrust. Disoriented by the sudden silence, Sasha jerked his gaze from the tabloid and said, "*Kh*Huh? *Kh*Huh?" in stupefaction.

"SASH, YOU MIND I see dat plizz?" Goldie asked. He held the paper to his chest possessively. "Come on, Sasha, I giff it right beck, don' vorry." Sasha surrendered his precious periodical, looking hopelessly lost without it.

"Here, Frieda, you are readink der best Enklich fun all uf us," she said, handing over the newspaper.

Frieda was obviously flattered. She preened and basked in the compliment, then shot Fritz a snide smirk, cleared her throat, and began to read.

"'Dozens of Yemenites who immigrated between 1949 and 1951 claim that during their stay in the Transit Camps (*ma'abarot*) they were compelled to place their youngsters and newborns in the communal nursery. Later on, when they visited their children, the mothers were informed that the babies had taken ill and had been transferred to hospital.

"'The mothers were all in agreement that news of their babies' illnesses had come as a shock. "Only the night before," said Mrs. Miriam Sharaby, "when I went to nurse my daughter, she appeared to be in the best of health." Her eyes filled with tears as she added: "How could a baby born on holy soil be anything but healthy?"

"'Although the families were quartered in different temporary housing facilities for varying periods of time, their experiences were strikingly similar. Bracha Gamliel of the Rosh Ha'ayin camp related the following: "The people in charge of the nursery at first would not tell me where my son was, only that he was in hospital. I became hysterical. Finally they revealed the name of the hospital. My oldest daughter and I hitchhiked to the hospital to see the baby but there we were told that he had died."

"'Subsequent investigations revealed numerous discrepancies. The burial plot indicated as the site of her son's interment turned out to be nonexistent; the attending physician who had issued the death certificate was not registered in the hospital's staff roster.

"'Bracha Gamliel, Miriam Sharaby and over thirty other Yemenite mothers refuse to believe their children are deceased.'"

"Tsk, tsk, tsk, tsk, tsk," Goldie clucked sympathetically. Her eyes glistened with shared emotion. "I don' know vat's voise — to know der kit is det, or not to know vone vay or ah nudder."

"I T'S ALL JUST a bureaucratic mishmash," Fritz derided. "So they didn't write down the right place they buried the kids. Big deal. So the hospital records are a mess — this is news? It doesn't mean the kids are alive, or that they were stolen, or that there was any kind of conspiracy."

"Shem on you, Fritz," Goldie chastised him. "You should know betta. If de kitz vas tiny bebbies, so, sure, dey mebbe buried dem in ah nunmarked grev. Bot if dey vas olter — some uf dem vas two years, eefen four years — der mamas an' papas gotta know vhere is de grev."

"Of course," Frieda agreed, more than pleased to have an ally against her perpetual adversary. "But there were so many of them — you think they all died? It had to be a plot to steal the babies. They figured these women would never notice one more or one less when they had so many. Then they gave the babies to childless couples — or sold them!"

"Frieda, dahlink, it's not nice you should say 'dey' like det whole govemend vas bed. After all, der govemend safed ah lots pipple. Bot in efery berrel dere's vone, two bleck sheeps. If dere vas soch ah conspiritzy, mebbe ah coupl'a bleck sheeps vas in it."

They tossed Goldie's idea around a little while longer, but came to no conclusion. Fritz remained adamantly skeptical of the entire affair. "Ach, you two old yentas are making a mountain out of a molehill," he gibed. "The whole business is just a figment of overactive imaginations."

"Arekh khyou khhearing?" Sasha announced. "'BONN PAYMENTS KHACCOKHRD KHENDS'!"

"I bought a new washer on payments," Frieda remarked. "Very easy terms. It even heats the water by itself."

"Wonderful," Fritz said sarcastically. "Now if you wash that horse blanket you're making in hot water, maybe it'll shrink down to human size..."

THE FOURSOME LUNCHED on cream cheese and olive sandwiches and sweet tea which Goldie doled out from her voluminous shopping bag ("It's *mezoines* bret — I becked it mineself.") and lingered on the bench until an unseasonably cool breeze began to blow.

"Plizz excuse me, lady an' gentlesman. I kent stend ah *tzuk* in mine *kraitz*." She bid her bench friends "Shalom" and headed for her apartment on Rechov Ruth, just off Dizengoff Circle. Faigaleh's replacement, Faigaleh II, was due for an airing in any case — that is, the cage would be suspended from a hook on the balcony for several hours while Goldie took her afternoon nap. Unlike his tone-deaf predecessor and namesake, Faigaleh was a warbler of some note, and a very contrary-minded one at that. Only when he was certain his mistress was asleep did he burst into song, hence the need to put the canary out during "siesta" hour.

WITH THOUGHTS OF Faigalehs I and II flitting through her mind and snatches of the morning's rambling conversation competing for her attention, Goldie was more than normally preoccupied when she stepped off the curb. A rusty-blue pockmarked "tender" swerved sharply and screeched to a halt mere inches from her Dr. Scholl's lace-ups, and as it did so, a cream and tan Mercedes plowed into its rear end.

The swarthy van driver jumped out screaming unintelligibly in fluent polyglot. "*Ya chamor!*"* he bellowed at Goldie, at the driver of the Mercedes, at his van's posterior and at the street at large. He slammed his palms down on the accordion-pleated, sprung hood of the Mercedes and shouted, "*Ayn lechah breksim?! Harasta li bek-ex!*"**

Goldie stood frozen like Lot's wife, visions of her own plump body pleated like the hood numbing her senses. The passenger door of the van creaked open and out hopped a tiny, middle-aged woman, with a colorful scarf wrapped around her head. She scurried to Goldie's side on slippered feet, chattering incessantly in a gutteral tongue, and to Goldie's added astonishment, grasped her hand and kissed it. Still chattering and making signs heavenward, she lifted the hem of Goldie's skirt and kissed that too as one might kiss a Torah mantle.

All the while, Goldie remained transfixed. The woman who Goldie reasoned was the driver's mother, scuttled over to the Mercedes and repeated her performance with the shaky teenager behind the wheel. Trembling, and with tears pouring from her eyes, the girl-driver placed her hands on her sun-tanned cheeks and shook her head from side to side in dismay.

*Fool! **Don't you know how to stop? You've destroyed my back-axle!

Goldie roused herself from her stupor and poked her head through the passenger-side window of the Mercedes. "You spick Enklich, dahlink?"

The teenager turned towards her, shock and terror vying for first place in her eyes. "Ditchoo got a beng?" Goldie asked solicitously. "You vant I should call ah docteh?"

"N-no, no calling doctor," the girl stammered in high-school English almost as atrocious as Goldie's. "I-I not hurt. But auto — is bad, very bad. My parents... my parents be so angry!" A fresh wave of tears burst the floodgates.

"Vat for you cryink abot ah hunk uf teen? Tenks God you got your helt!"

T HE DRIVER and his mother were still carrying on, he handling the ranting and gesticulating, she the osculating. Soon a clutch of rubberneckers had gathered and, in typical Israeli fashion, enthusiastically joined the fray. Traffic in Dizengoff Circle came to a standstill as scores of drivers piled out of their vehicles. There was much vociferous dispute over where to place the blame, the estimated cost of the repair, and, in particular, the best way to disengage the locked bumpers without inflicting even greater damage.

Six beefy bystanders had already lifted the Mercedes clear of the tender-fender and were about to march the cream leviathan backwards along the asphalt when two of Tel Aviv's Finest appeared on the scene.

"Alright, drop that car!" one of the officers demanded and the sextet of human hydraulic elevators promptly complied. The Mercedes came down with a crash that made its driver swoon into Goldie's welcoming arms.

The second patrolman was engaged in a shoving/shouting match with the van driver, whose mother was kissing anything that moved, and Goldie seized the opportunity to slip away to a quieter piece of sidewalk with her semi-conscious charge in tow. She sat the teenager down on the curb and, with a lace handkerchief, dusted off a square of pavement for herself.

"Vat's your name, dahlink?"

"Z-Zehava. Zehava Perlmutter."

"Dat's nice, I em also Zehava, bot you ken call me Goldie. Now tell me efreytink."

Through tears and hiccups, Zehava reported that her parents were abroad and that they had denied her permission to drive the Mercedes in their absence. She had disobeyed their orders. "They will to kill me! They will to kill me!"

"Sha! Don' talk nontzense. I em sure your perentz luff you an' perentz vat luffs der kitz don' keel dem. Mebbe dell scream etchoo, mebbe brek ah coupl'a bones — I'm just choking!"

"It is not joke! They *will* be breaking for sure my bones!"

"Nah," Goldie tried again. "Pipple is not brekkink der bones fun der own blud. Dat fella dere — she pointed at the van driver who was still going strong — dat fella dere dey mide brek der bones from, bot not der own blud."

"That is what... oh, is no important." Zehava fell silent, her shoulders slumped in despair.

The swift-thinking patrolman (who had ordered the release of the Mercedes) finished collecting all the loose car parts into an upturned hubcap and began taking down everyone's particulars on a grimy notepad. From her curbside perch, Goldie could see the van driver being handcuffed and shoved into the back seat of a police cruiser. His hands immobilized, he had become speechless, but his mother had turned ever more voluble.

"Excuse me, dahlink. I gotta do mine tzivic dooty..."

I N THE COURTROOM a week later, Goldie found herself seated next to Mrs. Tanami, of the colored scarf and carpet slippers. Alongside this tiny, fine-boned woman, Goldie, barely scraping four feet, eleven inches in her wedgies, felt like an Amazon. Mrs. Tanami had apparently resigned from active osculation and was conscientiously shredding her straw purse while reciting a *sotto voce* litany of tribulation. Although Goldie's comprehension of Hebrew was fairly extensive, her fluency was limited to *"ken," "lo,"* and *"kamah,"** and these she tried to insert appropriately into Mrs. Tanami's soliloquy.

"God is Great," the woman chanted without irony. "First my Moshe breaks his hip in '51 and has to walk with a cane, then my Avraham gets dysentery in the *ma'abara*..."

"*Lo!*" whispered Goldie in feigned disbelief.

"*Ken!*" Mrs. Tanami rebutted. "Then my Mazal she disappears, then my Batya marries that no good..."

"*Lo!*" exclaimed Goldie.

"*Ken!*" the woman confirmed. "But God is Great and they get divorced. And then Rachamim refuses to finish high school..."

"*Ken?*" Goldie interposed.

"*Lo!*" Mrs. Tanami reiterated. "And then my Tzion goes to America and drives a taxi..."

"*Kamah?*" Goldie tried for variety.

"A lot, but God is Great, he comes home every summer.

* Yes, no, and how much?

Then my Herzl buys the van to deliver eggs from the moshav, and he has an accident with that pretty little girl and now he goes to jail!"

"Lo!" Goldie summed up emphatically and turned her attention to the court proceedings. Zehava was pale under her coffee-colored tan, her wavy hair pulled back tightly from her face. Above prominent cheekbones, her dark eyes swam with tears. Goldie waggled her fingers encouragingly at the girl but received only a wan smile in response.

A TALL, DISTINGUISHED, fair-skinned gentlemen of fifty or so was giving testimony. It was Zehava's father, returned from abroad. "... and the beige Mercedes is registered in your name, sir?" he was asked.

"That is correct," Mr. Perlmutter replied.

"Would you tell the court, please, where you were at the time of the accident?"

"Yes. My wife Berta — " He indicated a pleasant-faced redhead in the observers' gallery. " — and I were vacationing in..."

Goldie looked around the crowded courtroom. She recognized the faces of the car-lifting sextet, the police officers and several of the Dizengoff rubberneckers. "Poor leedle Zehavaleh," she thought. "She's only a tin-etcher — ah kit — bot mebbe she'll learn fun dis ah lessin to lissen ven papa sez no is no."

Herzl was called to the witness stand, unhandcuffed now and consequently garrulous. His testimony invoked all of the parties to the collision, Goldie herself included, and the audience obediently followed his pointing finger like spectators at a doubles tennis championship: Goldie — Zehava — Herzl — Mrs. Tanami — Zehava — Herzl —

Zehava — Goldie — Mrs. Tanami — Herzl.

The affect was dizzying, but the twinkle in Goldie's blue eyes signified anything but confusion. She could hardly contain herself until she was called upon to testify. At last, it was her turn.

"**J**UTCH, YOUR HONNER, you vould mind ve not spick Hibrew?" Lower court sessions in Israel were never noted for exaggerated formality and her request was easily granted.

"That will be fine, Mrs. Sokolow. What language would you prefer?"

She stared at him with wonderment. "Vhy, Enklich, uf course. I spick ah verra goot Enklich."

"Er, yes. Of course."

"I ken esk mebbe ah few qvustiuns, Jutch? Jusl lo shuckle mine memry ah leedle. I em not soch ah sprink chicken, already."

"Very well, Mrs. Sokolow."

"Tenks, Jutch. Zehavaleh, dahlink, how olt are you?"

The girl looked up at Goldie in surpise. "I-I have seventeen years," she answered.

"Goot. An' how come you don' got no broken bones?"

The judge fairly leaped over his bench. "Mrs. Sokolow! I must protest..."

"It's hokay, Jutch. I vill vidraw de qvestion. Herzl, I hear you got ah lot sistehs an' bruddehs, *kineh hara*. Yes?"

The question was translated for Herzl's benefit and it was his turn to look surprised. "Six," he replied through an

interpreter, "*bli ayin hara* may the Almighty bless them."
He hesitated a moment and again the judge interrupted.

"Mrs. Sokolow, I fail to see the relevance of these
questions. If you cannot demonstrate their relevance, I shall
be compelled to call a halt to your cross-examination."

"Plizz, Jutch, your honner. It is mine folt ve're all siddink
here today instead of mebbe svimmink in der helt clop fun
Kink Doovid Hottel. If I vas not so bizzy tinkink about mine
Faigaleh, I vas mebbe vatchink vhere I vas goink."

"Faigaleh is your daughter, then?"

Goldie peered at the judge through her bifocals as though
examining him for signs of latent dementia.

"Faigaleh," she enunciated patiently, as one would
instruct a slightly backward child, "is mine dahlink canerry.
Ah boit. You know — 'tvit, tvit'?"

The spectators laughed uproariously and the judge
banged his gavel with more force than he'd intended. "Mrs.
Sokolow, I still fail..."

"Plizz, ah few more minutes and you vill succeed. Ven I
came to *Eretz Yisruel,* I had to liff mine dahlink Faigaleh
home in Ball-tee-more — it's a lonk story, I'll tell you mebbe
vone day you come to mine house far ah *gluz tay.*"

"Please, Mrs. Sokolow..."

"Hokay. Ven Clara mine neighborkeh told Faigaleh I vas
not comink beck, mine leedle *tzippaleh* dropt det fun griff.
So I vent an' bought ah nudder boit, vone dat looks just like
mine Faigaleh..."

In spite of himself, the magistrate had become absorbed
in her verbal meanderings. "Excuse me, Mrs. Sokolow, but
don't all canaries look alike, more or less?"

"Dat's de point. Faigaleh Nomber Vone vas yella mit ah bleck byooty mark right here — " She pointed to her throat. " — an' Faigaleh Nomber Two is also got ah bleck byooty mark on der trote. Dat's how I em knowink dey vas sisteh an' bruddeh. Just like Herzl mit Zehavaleh.

T HE COURTROOM became utterly silent. All eyes shifted from plaintiff to defendant and back again. A low-gauge rumble surged from the crowd of spectators, rising quickly in volume to a roar as the members of the audience translated the proceedings to one another in countless tongues.

"Order! Order in the court!" The gavel-head went flying across the room, wrenched from its handle by the force of impact with the gavel-rest, and struck the bailiff a stunning blow. No one paid him the slightest attention.

"Order! Order in the court!" The judge shouted ineffectually, tapping on his bench with the decapitated gavel-handle. Goldie imperturbably polished her eyeglass lenses with a snowy handkerchief.

It took a full ten minutes to restore a semblance of order and another hour after that for Goldie to clarify the convoluted thought process which had led to her astounding conclusion. She explained that her first clue had been Zehava's terror at her parents' anticipated reaction to the damaged Mercedes. It had aroused Goldie's suspicions that Zehava was not the Perlmutters' "blud" relative. The extraordinary dissimilarity of her coloring and features with those of her "parents" had been all the confirmation Goldie had needed.

"On de udder hent," Goldie continued, "pud ah mustach on Zehavaleh an' she mit Herzl is tvins!" The gallery gasped in unison. Indeed, the resemblance was uncanny.

"Mr. Perlmutter," the magistrate said, addressing Zehava's father, "is it true that Zehava is adopted?"

Dov Perlmutter's fair skin had turned an unhealthy, mottled grey. "Y-yes, your honor," he stammered. "We-we adopted her when she was a baby. But we were told she was an orphan!"

His wife suddenly found her voice. She rose from her seat and cried, "What is all this idiocy! Zehava is our legally adopted child and we have always been good parents to her. I resent the implication that because we're not her biological mother and father we would have reacted to her disobedience any differently — or more violently — than natural parents would."

"Uf course, Meesis Perlmoota. I em verra sorry. I did not min soch ah tink. It vas just ah clue vat made me tink who Zehavaleh rilly vas." At this juncture the judge lost all hope of regaining command of his courtroom. Clearly, the gavel had passed to the lady in the elastic stockings.

"Dis kit Zehavaleh is rilly Mazal Tanami, der sisteh fun Herzl vat disappeared fun der Trensit Kemp in ninetin-hundret-an'-fiftivone!" The tumult in the room became deafening.

"I don't believe a word of this!" Mrs. Perlmutter railed. "How could you determine from a handful of jumbled facts that she's in any way related to these people!? It's all speculation and conjecture, and utter nonsense!"

THROUGHOUT THIS EXCHANGE, Zehava and Herzl stared at each other across the room, their deep-chocolate eyes locked in seemingly telepathic communication.

"Mrs. Sokolow," the judge interposed, "despite the truly

striking resemblance between the plaintiff and the defendant, you must admit the likelihood of Zehava Perlmutter being Herzl Tanami's long-lost sister is infinitesimal. Are you asking this court to believe that by the most incredible coincidence the Tanamis have been reunited?"

"Dit I say cointzidentz? Nah. It was *bashert,* it vas *min haShomayim...*"

"I can't stand another second of this!" Mrs. Perlmutter shrieked. "It's ridiculous, I tell you..."

"Sit down, Berta," her husband instructed in a defeated voice. "I-I think the lady is right." Again a collective gasp rose from the audience.

"Your honor," Perlmutter continued, "when the social worker gave Zehava to me, the baby was wearing a silver bracelet."

"Yes?" the judge encouraged.

"The name 'Mazal' was etched in the metal."

A LL EYES TURNED to the bracelet which encircled Herzl's wrist, a bracelet not unlike the one Perlmutter had described. It, too, bore the name of its wearer.

"And where is this bracelet now, sir?"

"I-I threw it away." Perlmutter touched a trembling hand to his forehead. "I wanted to eliminate any trace of her past, so that she would be ours and ours alone."

"That is understandable, Mr. Perlmutter," the judge said gently, "but when she reaches majority in a few months' time, Zehava will be entitled to know all the facts concerning her parentage." Perlmutter nodded mutely. "She will not necessarily choose to abandon you and your wife in favor of her natural family, you know. But regardless of her decision, you are morally bound to provide her with the information."

"I understand, your honor."

Mrs. Tanami was virtually jumping out of her skin with ignorance of the goings-on. At last, a spectator explained and the woman flew from her seat with a jubilant cry. She bestowed a multitude of moist kisses on all and sundry, and then ululated joyfully from atop the witness stand. Goldie rested her swollen ankles on a vacant chair, a blissful smile on her lips.

"Veydl I tell Fritz," she chuckled to herself. "I'll show dat Meester *Vays-Alles* dat 'Meesis Serendipity' is neffer makink Montana fun mole's heels!"

three encounters

אמר רב יהודה אמר רב: מעשה בבנו ובבתו של ר' ישמעאל בן אלישע שנשבו לשני אדונים. לימים נזדווגו שניהם במקום אחד. זה אומר יש לי עבד שאין כיופיו בכל העולם, וזה אומר יש לי שפחה שאין בכל העולם כולו כיופיה. אמרו בוא ונשיאם זה לזה ונחלק בוולדות. הכניסם לחדר. זה ישב בקרן זוית זה, וזו ישבה בקרן זוית זה. זה אומר אני כהן בן כהנים גדולים אשא שפחה? וזאת אומרת אני כהנת בת כהנים גדולים אנשא לעבד? ובכו כל הלילה. כיון שעלה עמוד השחר הכירו זה את זה ונפלו זה על זה וגעו בבכיה...

גיטין מח

❀ Rav Yehuda said in the name of Rav: it is related that the son and daughter of Rav Yishmael ben Elisha were carried off (with the Exile) and sold to two masters. Some time later, the two masters met, and, one commented, "I own the most beautiful slave in the world." Responded the other, "I own the most beautiful bondswoman in the world." "Let us marry them to one another and share the children." They placed them in the same room but the boy sat in one corner, and the girl in another. Said the slave, "I am a priest descended from High Priests, and I shall marry a bondswoman?" She said, "I am a priestess descended from High Priests, and I shall marry a slave?" So they passed all the night in tears. When the day dawned they recognized each other and fell on one another's neck and cried bitter tears...

Gittin 58

Remuneration

THEY WERE SIPPING coffee in an outdoor cafe and swapping stories to pass the time. It was winter, not a busy season for Israeli tour guides, even though the temperature was well into the sixties and the gentle November sun smiled bravely between the clouds. Unofficially, it was Chaim's turn. This time, they would not be disappointed. He had been saving and savoring his story for months, waiting for just the right opportunity to tell it.

"My friends and colleagues," he began, "the story I am about to relate will, I think, amaze you. You might even have trouble believing it, but please be assured that every word is true." He allowed the usual volley of good-natured hectoring to subside. *All* their stories began with the same affirmation of veracity.

"In the first week of September, I received a phone call from the director of a large Jerusalem-based firm, a fellow who throws a lot of business my way. He asked me to meet a very important guest of his company at the airport and to give the visitor a condensed tour of the countryside on the way to Jerusalem. Since I had no other irons in the fire at the time, I agreed.

"Well, I arrived at Ben Gurion and who should walk out of the terminal? None other than Marvyn — with a 'y,' no less — Gold, the quintessential American tourist. You all know the type."

"Sky blue silk cowboy shirt?" a comrade volunteered.

"Designer jeans, one size too small, in contrasting color?" contributed another.

"Paisley ascot?" ventured a third.

"Diamond encrusted gold rings on his pinkies?"

"Espadrilles and clocked sox." They were at their cynical best now, warming to the subject. There was no stopping them.

"About a quart of aftershave?"

"Platinum watch, a sapphire where the '12' should be."

"Hair brushed forward from the back and over the bald spot? Hair spray!"

"Aviator sunglasses. With mirrored lenses?"

CHAIM PUT UP his hands to halt the tide of graphic descriptions. "Yes! Yes to all of you. I think you've got the picture. But you forgot a most vital element, one on which, you might say, this story hinges, for if not for that element, so inseparable from our image of the ostentatious American tourist, the story might very well have ended with my driving Marvyn-with-a-'y' Gold uneventfully from B.G. to the King David Hotel."

The guides pondered a moment, each conjuring up in his

mind the revolting vision of Marvyn Gold and mentally examining him from head to toe.

"Tsk, tsk. I'm surprised at you, gentlemen. How could you forget the big, fat, stinking..."

"Cigar!" they chimed in, in unison.

"Right. Well, Marvyn Gold climbs into the back seat of my sedan, leaving his matched set of monogrammed luggage on the sidewalk for me to stow in the trunk by myself, which I proceed to do, fortunately without incident. I get the car started and old Marvyn slips off his espadrilles, hauls his legs up on the seat and leans his elaborate hairdo against the rear window. 'Well, Boy,' he says to me in a childish imitation of LBJ, 'where y'all takin' me?' I mumble a response of sorts, it doesn't matter what, but it satisfies him and he goes back to blowing smoke rings and filling the cab with noxious fumes.

"By now, I can hardly breathe and even though I'm not much of a smoker, I take out a cigarette to light up, purely in self-defense. 'Lemme git that fer ya,' Marvyn-"

"... -with-a-'y'..." they chorused.

"... says, and he leans over the front seat and flicks his fancy..."

"... Dunhill!" they supplied.

"Right. And that's when I see something that makes me start to tremble so badly that I can't control the wheel. I pull over to the shoulder of the road, trying to get my breathing under control and Marvyn says, 'What's the trouble, Boy? Ya look like ya seen a ghost!' He reaches over to light my cigarette again, as it has gone out, and then I get a better look at his arm. My eyes did not deceive me."

"Ach, big deal, so he had a number. Half the people in this country have numbers." The fraternity became derisive.

"Patience, gentlemen. *I'm* telling this story. 'Excuse me, Mr. Gold,' I say, 'but I couldn't help noticing the number tattooed on your arm.'

"**M**ARVYN IS QUIET for a moment and then he says, 'You've probably been thinking I'm a big, gaudy American slob with fancy clothes and luggage and Cuban cigars and an oversized gut packed with rich Grade-A American food. Well, son, I paid my dues. In Auschwitz, believe me, I didn't have any clothes to speak of, whatever luggage I came with was confiscated, there wasn't enough food to fill the gut of a mouse, and the stench was *not* from five-dollar cigars.'

" 'Yes, sir,' I say, and ask if he has any family, any relations who also survived the Holocaust. 'Not to my knowledge,' he replies. 'My brother and two sisters, my parents, my aunts, uncles and cousins all perished.' By this time, he has dropped the phoney drawl and we are speaking normally. He tells me he tried tracing his relations after the War, but had no success.

"Then he gets a little misty-eyed and takes out a handkerchief as white as the snow on Mt. Hermon to wipe his tears and says, 'My older brother, Sollie, stood on line ahead of me when we were processed at the camp. That was the last I ever saw of him. The rest of my family had been taken to Buchenwald and to Bergen-Belsen. None of them made it. But, as you can see, son, I've put all that behind me and made a new life for myself.'

"I ask if he would mind taking a small detour from the planned itinerary. Marvyn has no objection, although he is curious, but I clam up and step on the gas."

Chaim sensed it was time for a hiatus, a pause to build up the excitement. He ordered another round of coffee and cake for his companions and waited until it was served before he went on.

"**M**Y FRIENDS, I have been a part of this informal fraternity for several years now and every one of you has always known me as I am today: a religious man in his thirties, married, couple of kids, soft-spoken and easygoing. But ten years ago, I was a different person altogether.

"When I first came to Israel my name was Charlie and I came for the same reason that thousands of other young tourists make their way here every year: I had finished college, had no job and was looking for an Experience, capital 'E.'

"I was one of that easily identifiable horde of youngsters who trek the length and breadth of this Land bowed beneath the weight of backpacks and bedrolls the size of telephone booths, wearing high-topped hiking boots, cut-off jeans and little else. When the wanderlust was more or less satisfied and the money was more or less gone, I joined my fellow travellers in a kibbutz-volunteer program, which, as you know, entails employing youthful tourists in the various kibbutzim to do menial jobs disdained by the kibbutz members, in exchange for room and board.

"I was sent to Ramat HaPri, a kibbutz overlooking the northern bank of Lake Tiberias that was established by early settlers of Palestine. The founders were socialists, Europeans who had immigrated before World War II, leaving behind most of their families along with most of their Judaism, and Ramat HaPri was an ideological reflection of their collective character. In short, a typical, irreligious, leftist commune.

"It's only fair to add that after the War the kibbutz

absorbed a number of survivors, what we called Muselmanner — the walking zombies who had suffered such unspeakable tortures at the hands of the Nazis, may their names be forever eradicated, that their scarred and disfigured bodies were no worse than their scarred and disfigured minds. It was virtually impossible to establish contact with the Muselmanner; they seemed capable of communicating only among themselves, with those who had shared their appalling experiences. They did the most menial of the menial kibbutz jobs.

"I WAS ASSIGNED to the fruit processing plant. There, unmarketable and surplus produce was first ground to pulp and then converted to juices, fruit extracts and concentrates. Each morning trucks and vans would arrive laden with produce and my job was to unload the fruit into the wide hopper of an enormous grinding machine, a task made-to-order for volunteers as it was immeasurably boring and occasionally dangerous.

"One particular morning, when I was already losing my taste for the 'exciting' kibbutz ambience and could not bring myself to ingest even one more bowl of watery kibbutz gruel, I started work while my 'comrades' were still breakfasting. I backed a tractor-load of apples to the grinding shed, turned on the big motor, and climbed up on the mound of fruit. With a large shovel, I began scooping up apples and dumping them into the hopper.

"What happened next was to change my life forever. My sandals, still damp from walking across the dew-covered field, slipped on the pile of apples and I went plummeting into the hopper. My fall was broken by the large quantity of produce already in the chute, but the grinder blades were rotating continuously, making quick work of the apples that stood between me and a hideous death.

"I screamed. I cried for help at the top of my lungs. But the roar of the grinder drowned out my cries. I scrambled on the shifting pile but could find no purchase on the smooth sloping sides of the chute. I continued to slide inexorably closer to the mauling grinder blades and in moments my foot was trapped between its voracious jaws. I shrieked, as much with the agony of it as with the terrible knowledge that my insignificant, meaningless life was about to reach a gruesome end. I closed my eyes and, for the first time ever, prayed. 'Oh, God,' I sobbed, 'let me not die. I need time to do something worthwhile with my life!'

"Suddenly, a strange thing appeared before my eyes. By this time I was hysterical, and probably suffering from shock, and I imagined that I was already dead and that a Heavenly civil servant was handing me my celestial identification number, inscribed on a piece of human flesh. The human flesh was in fact the arm of my savior. I grabbed it and it hauled me to safety. I had time only to observe that the arm was attached to Zalman, the Muselman who swept up the wood shavings in the kibbutz carpentry shop, and then I passed out."

Chaim's audience was rapt, their cold cups of coffee long-forgotten on the cafe table. The last flies of winter gorged themselves on the untouched cake wedges.

"I'LL SPARE YOU the details of my painful recovery but suffice it to say that my leg was amputated at the knee and I was fitted with a prosthetic limb. Throughout the lengthy rehabilitation period I had ample time to rethink my future, my existence on this earth, my gift of life. I never returned to Ramat HaPri but enrolled instead in a yeshiva in Jerusalem where I studied for four years. Charlie became

Chaim, appropriately enough, and I decided to settle here permanently.

"When the day arrived for me to exchange my tourist visa for citizenship papers, I was astonished to discover that the I.D. number I was issued ended in the very same four digits as my 'celestial' I.D. number, the number on Zalman's arm! The breath went right out of me and I almost fainted on the floor in the clerk's office at the Ministry of the Interior.

"I decided to take a taxi home and I dragged myself weakly up the stairs to the new apartment my wife and I had recently purchased. After I had revived sufficiently to be aware of my surroundings, I noticed that the telephone we had ordered many months earlier had finally been installed.

"The first four digits of the phone number were identical to the last ones on my new I.D.! This was one coincidence too many — I dared not ignore it.

"I seized the instrument in my hand and called the kibbutz. The connection was very poor. I shouted into the phone that I wanted to speak to Zalman from the carpentry shop. Minutes passed before I heard his voice on the other end. 'Zalman, it's Charlie,' I yelled, 'the fellow you saved from the grinder! I...I...' I didn't know what to say. What do you say to the man who brought you back from the dead? 'Thank you,' I said simply, feeling utterly foolish. He just grunted and broke the connection.

"All of this happened years ago, and while I never forgot Zalman — how could I, with his number in my back pocket and on my telephone dial, and this plastic leg as a constant reminder? — I must admit that I never found a way to repay him. Until Marvyn Gold, my despicable tourist, leaned over the front seat of my cab to light my cigarette.

"SO NOW, we are back in my car, making a U-turn in the middle of the highway and all the cars around me are honking like mad and Marvyn is bombarding me with questions. I keep my hands on the wheel at ten-to-two, the only way I can hold them steady, and my eyes on the road and my lips sealed. I drive for two hours straight to Ramat HaPri, and do not stop until I reach the door of the carpentry shop. I jump out and rush into the shop, praying that Zalman is still there, that he is still alive.

"And there he is, still sweeping up wood shavings, exactly as I left him, as if time stood still. He looks me up and down, tugs my pants leg up, nods in vague recognition, and goes back to his sweeping. I run outside and take all of Marvyn's luggage out of the trunk and pile it up right there in the mud. Marvyn is carrying on, shouting, 'What do you think you're doing, Boy?' but I cannot speak. My tongue is glued to my palate, my throat closed. I open the back door and start yanking Marvyn out, but he's fighting me, raising a ruckus, and a small crowd of kibbutzniks begins to form. Then Zalman comes to the door of the carpentry shop, leaning on his broom handle.

"Curiosity gets the better of Marvyn and he stops struggling. I pull him over to Zalman and stretch out his arm with the fancy gold watch and the chunky jeweled rings and lay it alongside Zalman's, the piece of human flesh inscribed with my celestial serial number. A186041 and A186042.

"For long seconds they stand there, my American tourist in his espadrilles and designer jeans, and my savior in baggy work pants and muddy sandals. 'Sollie?' Marvyn says at last, 'is that you?' And the tears are rolling down Zalman's scarred and wrinkled face. 'Mendel?' he says in a cracked voice, 'you're not dead?'

"I leave them like that and go back to my car and drive home to Jerusalem, smiling and crying the whole way."

THE TOUR GUIDES, tough Sabras to a man, were uncomfortable with the prickling sensation behind their eyes, the lump of emotion that lodged in their throats. The November sun was low in the sky and the early evening chill blew up and down the quiet street.

"So, Chaim," one of them chided, trying to retrieve the jocular mood of before, "you finally landed a wealthy American tourist and you didn't even get a big tip!"

"You're mistaken, Ofer," Chaim replied. "Marvyn Gold enabled me to repay the greatest debt I ever owed. I never felt richer in my whole life."

Revenge

R. GISELLA PERL rushed into the labor room in Mt. Sinai Hospital. The patient, a woman past her childbearing prime, lay listless on the bed, a large oxygen mask over her face. "It's only the thirty-second week, Doctor," the nurse reported, "and the mother's in bad condition. She was in one of those awful camps, I think. She has a number on her arm."

The doctor looked up sharply. "So have I," she said gruffly as she felt for the patient's pulse. "Who is her physician?"

"Dr. Marcus, but he's on vacation."

"We will do a section," Dr. Perl announced, scanning the patient's chart. "Has the mother been told it might be necessary?"

"Yes, doctor," the nurse replied. "We'll start prepping her now."

"Wait!" Dr. Perl noticed for the first time the beautifully embroidered kerchief that was wrapped around the patient's head. She ran her fingers over the delicate stitching and the patient's eyes fluttered open. Doctor and patient stared at one another in stunned recognition.

"Gisi!" the woman exclaimed weakly, her voice muffled by the mask. "Is it really you?"

Dr. Perl nodded mutely, her eyes glistening with unshed tears. The patient drifted back into unconsciousness.

"God!" Gisella Perl cried aloud, "God, grant me a life for a life!"

While she donned a sterile cap and gown and scrubbed her hands with antiseptic soap, Gisella relived the terrors of her past and the occasion of her earlier encounter with the patient. Only three years had passed and yet the circumstances were so different it might have been a century ago. She pushed the bitter memories aside quickly and then, with her head held high, strode into the operating theater to seek revenge in the only way she knew.

⁂

THE WHISTLE BLEW, the dogs began to howl and the train doors opened with an ear-splitting crash. Another transport had arrived at Auschwitz.

The dark night was aglow with yellow billows of fire that spewed from huge smokestacks, sharp red tongues of flame licking the sky. Clouds of ash from the crematoria hung over the camp and the air was redolent with the nauseating smell of burning flesh, the flesh of thousands of Europe's Jews. A woman went mad on the spot, emitting a hackle-raising shriek that resembled nothing human. The single pistol shot that silenced her scream was followed by the dull thud of her falling body, and a dreadful silence fell over the new arrivals.

"Everyone out!" The shouted order was accompanied by a hail of kicks, lashes, clubbings and curses. An S.S. detachment, armed with instruments of death, brutally separated the men from their wives, the parents from their children, the old from the young. Then, suddenly, the prisoners were standing before the "master" himself, the master of the Kingdom of Death.

He waited for them as he had waited for so many others, a seductively handsome man exuding the fragrance of expensive cologne and fancy soap. He waited with arms folded and a cruel smile on his bloodless lips: Josef Mengele — the man whose orders no one disobeyed.

With a flick of his manicured fingers, Dr. Mengele began his "selections:" three-quarters of the group — the very old and the very young — to the "left" and death; the others, to the "right," to the living death of the Auschwitz concentration camp.

A young Hungarian gynecologist was among those sentenced to life. Soon after her arrival, Mengele instructed her to set up an infirmary in Camp C for ailing women prisoners. The idea of a clinic was another grisly Nazi joke. There were no medications, no bandages, no beds or water. Nonetheless, Gisella Perl employed the pathetic facilities placed at her disposal and did everything in her power to save the lives of her fellow Jews.

A N ORDER WAS GIVEN for all pregnant women in Camp C to come forward* to be transported to a different camp where conditions were better, rations larger, and the work load lighter. Group after group of pregnant women left Camp C. Even Gisella believed that it was to the women's advantage to volunteer to leave.

* Most inmates suffered from the characteristic bloating of severe malnutrition. Numerous pregnancies, therefore, went undetected and only those women who voluntarily admitted their condition were transferred.

But to her horror, she soon discovered that pregnancy meant a gruesome — instant — death for the expectant mothers. They were to pay with their own lives, and with the lives of their unborn, for the "sin" of bearing a Jewish child.

There was no other special camp for pregnant women. Instead, the group from Camp C was surrounded by a gang of S.S. men and women who amused themselves by giving the prisoners a savage taste of hell before throwing them — alive — into the crematoria. The "less fortunate" were spared for Dr. Mengele's sport, for his barbaric, hideous experiments which included kicking the mothers' stomachs to see how long they took to abort. In other cases, he personally performed vivisection on the mothers and their fetuses.

Gisella turned her horror into courage. From that moment, she vowed, there would be no more pregnancies in her section of the camp, no more candidates for the brutal sport of the S.S. officers or Dr. Mengele's vile experiments. After witnessing with her own eyes the torture meted out to her sisters, "Gisi," as the inmates called her, ran back to Camp C and went from block to block revealing to her fellow inmates what she had seen. And then, Dr. Gisella Perl, a devoutly religious woman, whose peacetime job and chief delight had been the care of expectant mothers and the safe delivery of their babies, became an abortionist. That irony of ironies could only have happened in the nightmare called Auschwitz.

Every night, under the cover of darkness, in the rat-infested filth of the open-pit latrines, Gisi induced abortions in order to save the women from experimentation and certain death. With neither water for cleansing nor surgical instruments, she delivered the fetuses, and then swore the women to secrecy and sent them back to their barracks. Whenever possible, she had the mothers admitted into her "hospital" under the pretext of pneumonia — the only diagnosis which did not automatically mandate immediate death in the crematoria.

Always hurried, and in constant mortal fear that she would be caught and made to suffer the full intensity of the depraved Dr. Mengele's fury, she carried out her abominable act three, even four times a night. And each time she felt as though it were her own baby that she was killing. As she knelt down to perform the abortion amidst the filth and human excrement which covered the floor of the latrine, she prayed to God to help her save the life of the mother.

The Almighty showed his approval of her work, for every one of the women miraculously recovered — women in their fourth, fifth, sixth, seventh, eighth, and even ninth month of pregnancy. And they were able to continue working, a fact which saved their lives — for a short while, at least.

OF THE WOMEN she aborted, some were from her hometown in Hungary, women who had been her patients before the war. Her very first delivery in Camp C was of a woman who — a millennium before, it seemed — had made her living embroidering beautiful baby clothing. Coming from an impoverished family, she had worked at her trade until late at night, dreaming about the baby she herself would one day bear.

Then she married. But month after month, year after year, the couple's most ardent wish had remained unfulfilled. Eventually, the woman had turned to Dr. Perl, and six months before the Nazis invaded Hungary, the treatment had borne results. "I will give you the most exquisite present," the overjoyed expectant mother had promised Dr. Perl.

At every appointment she had repeated her pledge, but in the end it was Dr. Perl who gave *her* a present — the gift of life. In the ninth month of the woman's long-awaited pregnancy, beside the cesspools of Auschwitz, Gisella Perl delivered the embroiderer's baby boy.

She held the warm, tiny infant in her hands, and sent the mother back to her barracks. Then she kissed his smooth face, caressed his soft hair, and placed the silent newborn among the latest group of corpses — those which had been laid out that night. Had the baby been discovered alive, the mother, Dr. Perl and all of the other pregnant women whom Gisella still hoped to save would have been doomed.

&

A T 8:32 P.M., on Tuesday, March 28, 1948 in the gleaming white fluorescence of Mt. Sinai's sterile operating theater, Gisella repeated her private prayer. Moments later, utilizing the most advanced surgical instruments, she delivered the embroiderer's second child, as smooth and soft as the first had been, and as perfectly formed. She placed the squalling infant in his mother's arms.

"Oh, Gisi! He's beautiful," the new mother whispered in awe. "A gift from God."

"He's more than that, my dear," Gisella said. "He is God's revenge."

AUTHOR'S NOTE: Today, Gisella Perl lives in Israel and is affiliated with Shaare Zedek Hospital in Jerusalem, where the pediatrics department bears her name. She has personally delivered over three thousand Jewish babies. "They are my answer to Josef Mengele," Gisi asserts, "each one a life for a life."

Full Circle

LIKE A STATUE hewn from marble, Samson stood at the foot of his father's grave in the Warsaw cemetery. This was the culmination of a journey that had begun in England, taking him back first to Osweikim for a tour of the death camp that had been his "home" four decades earlier, and then to Warsaw, the city of his youth. It was a tour that had been intended to serve as a rite of exorcism to banish once and for all the ghosts that dogged his footsteps.

The trembling fit which had seized him when he'd passed through those notorious iron gates, and the palpitations he'd suffered during the dreadful train ride from the city, had been no worse than the terrors that had plagued his sleep for countless nights-without end. As he'd trudged around the bleak, deserted compound, his mind had become a turmoil of anguished memories: clanging iron doors and rattling chains, snapping whips and the sizzle of the electrified fencing; gaunt, skeletal faces crowding around him; moans, screams, barking dogs and the stutter of machine gun fire.

The horrid visions which he had so long suppressed had become stifling, and although a fresh summer breeze had been blowing, Samson had felt as though he were sealed in an airless crate. He'd gasped for breath and the Auschwitz stench had struck him full force, an odor that a millennium of rains could not wash away. It emanated from the very soil of the place — soil from which nothing live or healthy would ever emerge.

Samson's father had died before the war and was, therefore, the only one in his family to have received a decent burial. Samson had paid for a new monument to replace the crumbling one marking his father's resting place, and he'd had the names of his mother, Manya, his brothers, Modche and Yankeleh, and his sister, Miraleh, added. They had all perished — in Buchenwald, Maidanek and Treblinka — and this one grave, by default, would have to serve them all.

When he had turned his back for the last time on the barbed-wire fence of Auschwitz, he'd been almost looking forward to visiting the Warsaw cemetery and seeing the new monument. There, he had hoped, thoughts of happier times — when his family had been whole and living in relative tranquility — would dispel the awesome sights and sounds that raged in his head. But he was wrong. He had come full circle, back to the cradle of his earliest recollection, and still he had not found peace.

But it was not the terrible memories that made the blood freeze in his veins as he stood by his father's grave. It was the stone marker. Someone had desecrated it. With a thick stripe of black paint, Modche's name had been deleted and Samson's own name, Shimshon, had been written in by hand.

&

"**I**'M TELLING YOU," Jackie insisted, "they're just a couple of crazy tourists." The taxi dispatcher had called him on the radio and asked him to report to the office, but

Jackie had the cab way over in Machane Yehuda, in the midst of the teeming Thursday afternoon marketing crowd, and it would cost him a good half hour to get back to the taxi stand in Rechavia.

"Look, Jackie," the dispatcher said, "I don't care *who* they are. All I know is they won't get off *my* back until they can climb on *yours*. And they won't take 'no' for an answer. What'd you do — gouge a double fare out of them?"

"Nah. They think I look like someone they know in Geneva," he said into the mike as he wove his way through the back streets behind Jerusalem's open-air market. "They nearly drove me nuts yesterday with their questions. I must have told them a hundred times all my relatives are dead. It's just that I got such an ordinary face that I'm always reminding someone of somebody else."

"Listen, Jackie. Do me a favor: humor them," the dispatcher groaned audibly. "This place is swarming with Swiss cuckoos!"

As Jackie came down Ramban Street and neared the taxi station, he saw what the dispatcher meant. Several tweed-suited couples were milling around the sidewalk, most of the men wearing the distinctive Tyrolean hat that pointed to their Alpine origins, and the women shod in sensible walking shoes. All of them wore name tags with the emblem of their Geneva-based Jewish tour company. They clustered around the cab when he pulled into the curb, chattering excitedly in their native French:

"*Ça doit être lui! Ça doit être lui!*"

❧

THE NIGHT BEFORE, Rabbi Mordecai Poliansky had received a troubling phone call. After an emotionally draining, long-delayed visit to the country of his birth, he

and his wife were summering in Lugano and his office at the
Adas Yisrael synagogue had referred the long-distance
operator to his rented chalet on the lake. He had always
known the Weills — who had placed the call from Israel —
to be very level-headed people, but they had seemed
anything but that on the phone.

"I thank you for your concern, *Monsieur* Weill," the rabbi
had said, "but I assure you I have no brothers in Jerusalem
or anywhere else. My family was wiped out in the camps."

Madame Weill had gotten on the line then. She was very
apologetic for having stirred up painful memories, yet she
persisted in interrogating him: Did his brother have blue
eyes? Did he part his hair on the left?

"Yes, *oui, Madame* Weill," he had replied, with more
patience in his tone than he'd felt, "My brother Yankeleh
had blue eyes. And yes, when he was ten years old, his hair
was parted on the left. However, when I last saw him," he'd
added, covering the catch in his throat with a feigned cough,
"his head was shaven." His little brother's eyes, the rabbi
had not added, were then no longer the bright blue of April
skies and bluebirds, but the faded grey of despair. "But
surely, *Madame* Weill, there are many people with blue
eyes and a left-hand part, and plenty of them, I dare say, are
named Poliansky." His words had not dampened the lady's
enthusiasm.

"*Je vous prie, Madame* Weill," he'd concluded, "forget
this nonsense and enjoy your trip. *Au revoir.*"

The conversation kept returning to Rabbi Poliansky's
mind all the next day. He gazed out the window at the
majestic mountain that towered over the quiet Swiss town
and thought of the snow of Buchenwald. Never white like
Alpine snow, it had seemed to be already mingled with
Jewish ashes as it fell from the heavens, and it had lain on
the ground like a dingy, soiled shroud, a silent witness to the

heinous crimes perpetrated by an inhuman race. The rabbi placed his hand on the vast pane of glass and felt again the relentless, pervasive cold of Buchenwald.

&

SAMSON STRETCHED out his hand and touched the black stripe with a shaky finger. The paint was still tacky. He ran from the gravesite to the custodian's booth and demanded to see the guest registry.

"I am sorry, sir," the custodian said, not sounding very sorry at all. "We have no such registry."

"Now, look here," Sam shouted, still winded from his run, "someone has desecrated my family's tombstone and I insist you find the culprit!"

The fuss he was making attracted the attention of the cemetery guard and the two Poles held a hasty conference. Samson could contain himself no longer. "You dare to call yourself a guard and yet you allow a vandal to damage a grave — right under your nose?!"

The guard produced a slip of paper from his uniform pocket. "There was a fellow here yesterday, I think — or was it the day before? He wanted some paint. Well, since I am not authorized to give anyone paint without a proper requisition form, I had to improvise and make him sign for it."

"Let me see that!" Samson ordered. The guard shrugged and relinquished the dog-eared scrap. The name fairly leaped off the paper before Samson's eyes: *Mordecai Poliansky.*

"Who-who was that man?" Samson spluttered in fury. "Who dared to forge the name of my sainted brother?!"

Again the guard shrugged with Slavic indifference. "All I

know is that he wanted some paint so I told him to si..."

Sam's breathing became labored. His head felt as though it were filled with helium and floating inches above his neck. "Wh-what did this man look like?" he asked.

"Look like? Oh, very distinguished, yes." The guard scratched his stubbly chin and squinted, pondering. "Well, I think he had a small beard and..." He looked straight at Samson. "Why, he looked just like you!"

Samson Poliansky collapsed on the ground in a dead faint.

☙

"**O**KAY, LADY," Jackie said, well past the point of exasperation, "so the rabbi of your congregation looks like me. So what? Look, I appreciate what you're trying to do, but count me out, you got it? I've been this route before and believe me, it goes nowhere. It goes in circles.

"After the war, I found myself here in Jerusalem. I was just a kid, see. On my own. *Nobody* hounded that Red Cross office like Jackie Poliansky, let me tell you. I went over those survivors lists until I thought my eyes would pop out. I shined shoes and ran errands to earn stamp money and I sent letters to every single 'Poliansky' they had there. You know what I got for my troubles? A big fat zero, that's what. Oh, yeah. And writer's cramp.

"For ten years, finding a family member somewhere in the world was my big obsession. I had this plan: I was going to use my reparations money to travel all over until I located a surviving relative. But when the money came through, I said to myself: 'Jackie, boy, that dough stinks. It stinks from blood. If you touch it and let those animals buy themselves a clean conscience, you'll stink, too.' All right, so I'm an idiot.

That's me — Jackie the jerk. I refused the reparations."

He sighed deeply and sipped his coffee. The Swiss "cuckoos" had invited him to lunch at their hotel and, well, he hadn't eaten yet, so why not? "Life in this country is a little too fast-paced for a guy to stick to an obsession for very long, if you know what I mean. *Hakol oveir, chabibi** — that's a local motto. Over here, you sort of get sidetracked. War, inflation, that kind of thing. I got married, raised a family of my own — I got two boys in yeshiva, one in Army Officers Training School, and my daughter's expecting. Not bad for a jerk, huh?

"A couple of years back, I told my wife, Edna, if I win the lottery, I'm gonna get hold of all the phonebooks in the world and call every 'Poliansky' I can find. You know what? I won the lottery. Not the big one, of course, just a couple of thousand. Phonebooks? No way. I bought Edna a new mixer.

"You gotta live for *now*, know what I mean? Not for *then*. *Then* is gone. *Now* is here. So, with all due respect, if you people want to go on digging up the past, be my guest. Just count me out. I'm finished running in circles."

$$\text{\&}$$

RABBI POLIANSKY was unable to rid himself of the melancholy that had enveloped him. It was unfair, he knew, to subject his wife to his gloominess and irritability during what was meant to be a vacation, but he could not stop himself from thinking about the Weills' phone call. Then the telephone rang again. It was his secretary.

"Excusez moi, Monsieur le Rabbin," Madame Dreyfus

* "Everything passes, my friend." Roughly equivalent to "Time heals all wounds."

apologized. "I'm sorry to disturb you, but a cable arrived that I thought might require an urgent reply."

"Yes?" The rabbi was puzzled. "Please read it to me."

Bien sur, Monsieur le Rabbin. Of course. It says: '*IF YOU ARE MY BROTHER MODCHE PLEASE CONTACT ME.*' "

The use of the familial diminutive of his name made shivers run up and down Mordecai Poliansky's spine. No one had called him 'Modche' in over forty years. It was the second major shock he'd suffered in less than a week — first the grave marker and now this telegram from a total stranger. There are few things more unsettling than seeing one's own name engraved on a tombstone, he thought, but to receive such a message so close to that unpleasant experience was even more disconcerting.

"*Merci beaucoup, Madame* Dreyfus," the rabbi said at last, "but it is nothing to concern yourself about. The Weills are behind this. They've unearthed some poor fellow in Jerusalem they claim is my brother Yankeleh. But it is all a hoax. I was informed that Yankeleh, from whom I was separated at Buchenwald, was murdered by the Nazis shortly before Maidanek was liberated, may the Almighty avenge his death."

"*Si je peux vous corriger, Monsieur le Rabbin,*" the secretary said in a bewildered voice, " but the cable is from *London,* not Jerusalem, and it is signed 'Shimshe'."

The instrument slipped from the rabbi's hand and clattered against the parquet floor.

❦

THE REUNION was set for Wednesday morning, the 26th of September, at Ben Gurion Airport. A friend of Jackie's from the army reserves got him past airport security and Jackie paced up and down the floor of the arrivals building, nervously jingling the change in his pocket. Would he be able to recognize his brothers, he wondered, after all these years? Or would this turn out to be just another disappointment after all? He didn't know if he could endure that, so when the British Airways passengers began to flow into the hall, he positioned himself near the exit and scanned their faces from a safe distance.

Samson stood at the luggage carousel waiting for his suitcases, his pulse racing. The flight was no more than a blurred memory. He'd been quivering with excitement and anxiety from the moment he'd stepped on the plane.

As he reached out to grab a passing valise, his furled umbrella fell from his hand and the noise it made when it struck the stone tiles reverberated loudly in the vast hall. Samson stooped to retrieve it, frowning apologetically to his fellow passengers as one might after creating a minor disturbance in a library. His glance fell on a tall, dark-suited gentleman standing across the carousel from where he stood. A Swissair tag dangled from his attache case.

The man was staring at him.

"Shimshe!!" Modche cried, hurling his attache case to the ground. "Shimshe — it's really you!" The brothers ran towards each other around the carousel, oblivious of the crowd, the luggage carts, the whining children. They threw their arms around one another and suddenly, Yankeleh flew to their side from across the hall, to join the circle of their passionate, fraternal embrace.

The crowd in the hall grew silent at the spectacle of three grown men — who, but for the varying number of grey hairs in their respective heads, might have been identical triplets — laughing, crying, kissing, and carrying on like schoolboys. In the silence, Modche, with tears pouring from his eyes, intoned a most heartfelt "*Baruch Mechayeh Hameisim!*" and the crowd cheered.

It was *erev* Rosh Hashanah 5745, more than four decades since each Poliansky had first recited the *Kaddish* for his two dead brothers.

three on nobility

רבי מאיר אומר : כל העוסק בתורה לשמה, זוכה לדברים הרבה ; ולא עוד,
אלא שכל העולם כלו כדי הוא לו. נקרא רֵעַ, אהוב, אוהב את המקום,
אוהב את הבריות, משמח את המקום, משמח את הבריות ; ומלבשתו
ענוה ויראה, ומכשרתו להיות צדיק וחסיד וישר ונאמן, ומרחקתו מן
החטא, ומקרבתו לידי זכות ; ונהנין ממנו עצה ותושיה, בינה וגבורה,
שנאמר "לי עצה ותושיה אני בינה לי גבורה" ; ונותנת לו מלכות וממשלה
וחקור דין ; ומגלין לו רזי תורה, ונעשה כמעין המתגבר וכנהר שאינו
פוסק ; והוי צנוע, וארך רוח, ומוחל על עלבונו, ומגדלתו ומרוממתו על כל
המעשים.

אבות ו:א

   ❀ *Rabbi Meir says: One who is occupied with*
Torah for its own sake merits many things; moreover,
such a person is sufficient reason for the continued
existence of the entire world; such a person is called
friend, beloved, lover of God, lover of humankind, a
bringer of joy to God, a bringer of joy to humankind;
the Torah clothes such a person in humility and awe,
and enables that person to be righteous, pious,
upright and faithful; the Torah keeps that person far
from sin and brings that person to virtue.

Avos 6:1

A Tithe in Time

N THE EARLY 1940s, the first modern *mikve* in New York opened its doors to a grateful community. Constructed in a converted brownstone where East Broadway meets Grand Street on New York's famous Lower East Side, it replaced the dilapidated Ridge Street facility that was housed in a building adjacent to a livery stable. Cart horses and horse-drawn wagons were quartered at the stable, and visits to Ridge Street were accompanied by sights and sounds distinctly antithetical to the concepts of sanctity and purification which *"mikve"* embodies. The new facility, therefore, was a welcome addition to the thriving neighborhood.

Since before the turn of the century, the Lower East Side had been a haven for Jews from Eastern Europe. As world wars and civil strife devastated countries across the globe, more and more refugees flooded America's shores and many settled in the area closest to their port of entry. Family and friends from the "old country" awaited their arrival there and the infrastructure of a Jewish existence — including basic needs such as shuls, yeshivos and kosher food stores — was already firmly established. Three-quarters of all Jewish immigrants lived — at least for a time — on the Lower East Side, crowded into decrepit tenements along with Italian, Irish, Polish, Chinese and Russian refugees who found themselves in similarly impoverished circumstances. The Lower East Side teemed with humanity and bustled with commerce.

"My son, the doctor" is a phrase born on the streets of New York. It was there that the destitute Jews found employment of every description — from sewing lace handkerchiefs in the "sweat shops" of Center Street, to peddling rags and used clothing from push-carts — working fourteen to eighteen hours a day in order to send their sons to college. Only through secular education, they thought, could their children hope to rise above the squalor. Thus, the offspring of the greatest European talmudic scholars and the scions of noted chassidic dynasties evolved into a class of American professionals and businessmen. While many did not abandon religious practice in the process, the yeshiva and Torah study were no longer the focus of their activity.

BEFORE WORLD WAR II, several philanthropists poured huge sums of money into the renewal of the decaying slum neighborhood, erecting housing developments, parks and community centers, and the slum, if not eradicated, was at least pushed back and contained. Since the most urgent need was for decent housing, none of the religious institutions benefited from the philanthropy, and certainly not the old *mikve*. While it did not fall into disuse, the area in which it was located became more hazardous than ever. Anyone who ventured there after dark did so in peril for his life: the slum that had been pushed back ended on Ridge Street.

The construction of the new *mikve* was financed by a

long-term mortgage of $25,000, a veritable fortune at the time, and the mortgager was a businessman who operated the facility as a private enterprise for seventeen years. Its new location made it both central to the sizable new housing projects inhabited almost exclusively by Jews, and accessible by pedestrian and vehicular traffic.

Its presence served to rejuvenate the neighborhood, body and soul. Young families who would have relocated uptown or to the suburbs, chose to remain on the Lower East Side. The pleasant atmosphere and decor of the new *mikve* and its convenient location encouraged countless residents to avail themselves of the facility, including many who had disdained and avoided the Ridge Street building.

In 1957, events took an unforeseen turn. Pete's House, an adjunct of the Grand Street Settlement foundation for underprivileged youth, set its sights on the *mikve* building, the rear wall of which abutted its gymnasium. The directors of the Grand Street Settlement viewed the *mikve* premises as ideally suited for the expansion of the Pete's House gym and approached the mortgage holder with an offer he could not refuse. Word of the pending sale spread throughout the community and reached Rabbi Moshe Feinstein, the *Rosh Yeshiva* of Mesivta Tiferes Yerushalayim (M.T.J.).

HAVING RESIDED on the Lower East Side since his emigration from Russia in 1936, HaGaon Reb Moshe was a familiar figure on Grand Street, although few could put a name to that distinguished face. Short in stature and with a luxuriant white beard and lively, twinkling eyes, the *Rosh Yeshiva* could often be seen in the company of his learned sons and *talmidim*, striding majestically from his Grand Street apartment to his rabbinical school at the far end of East Broadway. Partly because of his great humility and partly because of the preeminence of Reb Aharon

Kotler *zt"l*, Reb Moshe was not then a well-known personality outside of the tight Yeshiva circle. Nonetheless, he was a highly-respected Torah scholar and educator.

When Reb Moshe learned of the impending disaster, he realized that immediate and drastic action was called for. It did not require genius to predict what would happen to the level of observance in the neighborhood, and, ultimately, to the Jewish character of the community itself, if the *mikve* were to fall.

His initial approach to the mortgager met with failure; repeated appeals to the man's religious convictions and conscience fell on deaf ears. As a source of revenue, the facility had not turned out to be the "gold mine" the man had hoped it would, and the opportunity to unload it for a tidy sum was too tempting to pass up. There was no question of building another *mikve*: property values in New York had skyrocketed and the cost would have been prohibitive. The only hope, then, was to raise the funds to meet the price that Pete's House had offered and for the community itself to assume responsibility for the operation of the facility. This hope, however, was somewhat divorced from reality.

Thousands of Jews of every stripe called the Lower East Side their home but scattered as they were among a dozen apartment complexes and hundreds of *shtieblach*, any thought of uniting them behind a cause (the significance of which eluded many of them) constituted little more than a pipe dream. Never before had they amalgamated for any purpose — certainly not a religious one — and it was unlikely that any attempt to bring them together would meet with success. Reb Moshe, however, was not dismayed. The cause was too vital to be dismissed — so vital, in fact, that it took precedence over many of his myriad obligations.

In addition to the enormous responsibilities he bore as

Rosh Yeshiva of Mesivta Tiferes Yerushalayim, where he delivered a daily *daf shiur*, and personally examined all of the *smicha* candidates, every available moment of his time was accounted for by his personal learning schedule. He began his day at four in the morning and from then until he retired late at night, Reb Moshe was actively engaged in Torah study and in recording his *chiddushim* and *piskei halacha*. His telephone, always close at hand, rang incessantly with *klal Yisrael* on the line, and the *Rosh Yeshiva* had difficulty finding the time for the *dinei Torah* and occasional *gittin* which he hosted in his house every afternoon. Despite all this, he allocated countless hours to this project and proved to be a tireless campaigner when it came to a cause of such importance as the *mikve*.

RECOGNIZING THE NEED to conduct matters in a businesslike fashion, he called a meeting of local merchants and prominent businessmen and asked them to join him in this effort. Few could deny his impassioned appeal for their cooperation, but for a neighborhood that was, at best, lower-middle class, the sum of money required was beyond their limited means. Wealthy people did not live on the Lower East Side.

A committee to save the *mikve* was formed and like any wise board chairman or chief executive who surrounds himself with an advisory panel of experts, Reb Moshe chose some of the more successful business people as committee members. The *Rosh Yeshiva* himself sat at the helm. The task they had undertaken seemed overwhelming but Reb Moshe set an example that was impossible not to follow. At the end of exhausting work days, the committee members made time to attend frequent hours-long plenary meetings and campaign strategy sessions. The *Rosh Yeshiva* said,

"Just as we are enjoined to set aside a tithe of our income for charity, so are we obliged to allocate a tithe of our time and energy for our community." The committee did that — and more.

At the meetings, not a moment of awkwardness or discomfort passed for the committee members, several of whom were awed by the presence of the brilliant scholar. Reb Moshe always deferred to their greater commercial expertise and acumen, and treated them as equals, calling them "my esteemed friend" and "my honored colleague." No task — regardless of its triviality — was too demeaning, for the *Rosh Yeshiva* endowed the committee's endeavors with an aura of spirituality. Saving the *mikve* became a holy mission.

NOTICES WERE distributed to all the yeshivas and *shtieblach* and posted in stores and shops, followed by a door-to-door fund-raising effort. Night after night, fair weather or foul, these dignified committee members personally knocked on every door in the neighborhood, begging donations. Had every Jew on the Lower East Side been willing to contribute five dollars, enough money could have been raised to buy the *mikve and* Pete's House, and even put a down payment on the Grand Street Settlement to boot. But this was not meant to be.

A pathetic pile of bills and coins was dumped each week on the *Rosh Yeshiva's* desk and the committee members were losing heart. Their disappointment in their fellow residents knew no bounds. People who would have unhesitatingly purchased a box of *treife* Girl Scout cookies — only to throw it in the trash upon the little uniformed salesgirl's departure — dropped nickels and dimes into the *mikve*-solicitors' waiting hands, or closed the door in their faces. More extreme tactics were required.

Armed only with the force of his charismatic personality, Reb Moshe *himself* went out door-knocking. But his activities bore little more fruit than those of his "esteemed colleagues". Men of means rooted around in their pockets for loose change to hand to the illustrious "*meshulach*" and the *Rosh Yeshiva* learned on his own flesh the indignities his co-workers had suffered. His efforts, however, were not in vain.

The very fact that the *Rosh Yeshiva* would so demean himself for this cause served to drive home its salience, galvanizing the community at last, and the fund-raising campaign was given a much-needed boost. The campaign chest began to swell as contributions poured in, some from the most surprising quarters.

Encouraged by this development and by Reb Moshe's unswerving faith of optimism, the committee took a bold step. Since there was no possibility of raising the *entire* sum in time to meet the mortgage holder's deadline, they borrowed the remainder from "*Gemach*" funds and from private parties — and *personally* signed for the loans. If their fund-raising efforts were to fail, the committee members themselves would be burdened with awesome debts.

T HREE YEARS after this holy mission was undertaken, the *mikve* mortgage was ceremoniously burned at a gala dinner and responsibility for operating the facility passed to the community at large. To this day, it stands in the heart of the Lower East Side, renovated, refurbished and ready to serve the flourishing neighborhood.

The moment Reb Moshe Feinstein shouldered the burden of saving the *mikve* he ceased to be "merely" a *Rosh*

Yeshiva and became instead a *Rosh Kehilla,* and the *kehilla* came first to know, and then to love and honor, the diminutive giant who dwelled in their midst.

An Ordinary Jew from New York

HOW DOES ONE become *Gadol HaDor* — the most highly-respected contemporary rabbinic authority? Is a competition of some sort staged, perhaps one judged by a council of Talmudic sages? Or does one — after meeting certain criteria — simply declare oneself a *gadol*? Can an ordinary Jew achieve such stature and universal acclaim? A *New York Times* [May 5, 1975] interviewer received the following reply from a gentleman who has often referred to himself as "an ordinary Jew from New York":

"Well, it begins with one person asking a question and receiving an answer he can live with, which is yet in perfect consonance with *halacha*. He tells his friends, I suppose, and they, too, bring their questions and they, too, receive viable, halachically sound answers. And so it goes. In time, one becomes accepted."

This "ordinary Jew from New York" has won international fame and adulation for his outstanding scholarship, brilliant insights and incisive commentaries. He has learned *Shas* over two hundred times and knows by heart all of the major commentaries on *Shulchan Aruch*;

has written seven impressive volumes of responsa as well as novellae on Talmud; and serves as *Rosh Yeshiva* of Mesivta Tiferes Yerushlayim and as member of the Council of Torah Sages of Agudath Israel of America. His vast achievements have earned him the respect of Jew and Gentile in every part of the civilized world.

But perhaps more than any Torah luminary in our generation, Rabbi Moshe Feinstein has won the heart of his people.

Had the interviewer asked the *Gaon* why he is so well-loved, Reb Moshe might have answered: "Perhaps it is because *I* love *them.*" In word, deed, and thought, the *Rosh Yeshiva* has demonstrated countless times this deep, abiding affection and concern for his fellow man and for *Klal Yisrael* in particular.

☙

REBBETZIN FEINSTEIN was very concerned. There was a wedding she had to attend, requiring that she be out of the house for several hours, and she disliked leaving the *Rosh Yeshiva* home alone. Reb Moshe refused to allow her to summon a relative or a student to stay with him and that meant no one would be around to screen his calls.

The Feinsteins' telephone was almost never silent. Calls routinely came in at every hour of the day and night from people seeking *piskei halacha,* advice on religious or personal matters, and assistance of every description; Reb Moshe responded to each one. He could never deny a caller his attention, despite his overcrowded schedule. The Rebbetzin, therefore, had taken to acting as his secretary, in an effort to insulate her husband to some degree from a demanding public.

Reb Moshe, she felt, was too kindhearted for his own good. He could not refuse anyone. Certainly, of the many calls he received, a majority were serious inquiries that required the *Rosh Yeshiva's* intercession, but there was a significant number of nuisance callers who apparently carried the Feinsteins' telephone number in their pocket and had no compunctions about dialing it whenever the mood struck them.

The *Rosh Yeshiva's* sensitive nature and his tremendous love for his people impelled him to devote time and energy even to the obviously deranged. How many hours he'd spent with these unfortunates over the years! she thought. And how many hours of precious sleep he'd forfeited to compensate for time lost from his studies and researches.

"I'm not going," she said at last.

"But you must!" the *Rosh Yeshiva* protested. "I'll be fine. Don't worry."

"How can you say you'll be fine when you know you can't turn anyone away? What if that unfortunate fellow phones — the one who called you a *gonnif* last week in front of the whole yeshiva, the one you invited to your office to chat for three quarters of an hour?"

"Oh, you know about that. Well, he was truly a troubled person and needed help. Could I turn him away?"

"No, you could not. And that's just the point. Your concern for the well-being of others often causes you to disregard your *own* well-being."

"And that's as it should be. What's a few moments of my time when a fellow-Jew is crying out for help? A small sacrifice, that's all."

"Like that *almanah?*

"You mean that poor, distressed woman who stopped

me in the middle of the street to tell me her troubles? But it is a mitzva to support widows and orphans. So I offered her a ride — is that so much?"

"You offered her *your* ride," the Rebbetzin reminded her husband gently, "while you walked home in the rain."

"I needed some time to myself anyway. I had to review my lecture for the next day. Besides, I don't recall that it was raining, at least not very hard."

"And what about the perpetual houseguests who've been eating here regularly for more than a *decade?*"

"It's the least I could do! *Hachnasas orchim* is a very basic mitzva, as you know."

"Of course I know it is," the Rebbetzin said with a smile, "and I'm delighted to have guests share Shabbos with us. I'm not complaining you understand, but wouldn't you say that having a guest for five hundred and twenty-six consecutive *Shabbosim* is perhaps carrying a good thing just a bit too far? Never mind. I've decided not to go to the wedding."

"But you *must!*"

"I've made up my mind. If I leave you here alone, you'll be on the phone the whole time I'm away and then you'll be awake half the night catching up on your writing. And you'll probably get up extra early in the morning in addition to get back to your *paperlach.*"

"But they're expecting you."

She knew he was right — as usual. "I'll only go if you promise not to answer the phone."

"Alright," the *Rosh Yeshiva* agreed with a twinkle in his eye

The Rebbetzin was still hesitant, but it was a family affair and, as Reb Moshe had pointed out, she had already notified her relatives that she would attend. Reluctantly, she consented to go, but only after Reb Moshe reiterated his assurance that he would not answer any calls.

S HE WAS NOT GONE five minutes when the telephone began to ring. Without even glancing up from his *sefer,* the *Rosh Yeshiva* stretched his hand out to lift the receiver. But there he stopped, suddenly remembering his promise to the Rebbetzin. He tried to ignore the ringing and return to his work, but it persisted for some time. He rose from his desk and went out of the room in order to put some distance between himself and temptation. The telephone bell, however, could be heard from every room of the Feinsteins' Lower East Side apartment.

"Perhaps it's an emergency, " he thought. "Some hapless Jew is suffering and needs solace. How can I deny him? Perhaps some neighborhood crisis has occurred, *chas v'shalom.* Surely the Rebbetzin will understand and forgive me." Only a few weeks earlier, the rabbi of a local shul had called in great distress. His shul had held a "Purim Carnival" for the youngsters and along with the various game booths, a "mock wedding" booth had been set up. To the rabbi's dismay, among the scores of children who had taken part in the "jest" were a dozen or more twelve- and thirteen-year-olds. Each boy had given a simulated gold ring to a girl and recited the *"Harei at."*

Their intention, of course, had been purely amusement and when the rabbi had become aware of what was transpiring in that booth, he had called an immediate halt to the festivities. Unless the *Rosh Yeshiva* knew of a *heter,* the "mock" *Kiddushin* were legitimate and binding; that is, the girls were, for all intents and purposes, married to the boys.

They would require a *get* to dissolve the marriage and would therefore be *grushos* — at the tender age of twelve! — and forbidden to *Cohanim.**

The report had been devastating. A foolish, childish prank had turned into a possible tragedy for perhaps a dozen neighborhood families. The ringing phone might *chalilah* be bringing word of a similar dilemma or of a catastrophe, one that could be prevented or mitigated by his intervention.

Reb Moshe hurried back to his desk and reached for the receiver. But just then, the phone stopped ringing. In a moment, he was again immersed in his work and his earlier concerns regarding the anonymous caller were forgotten.

BEFORE LONG, the telephone rang once more and once more his hand automatically moved to the receiver... and stopped." The Rebbetzin is right, of course," he told himself. "What would the caller do if I, too, had gone to the *chassanah?* He would solve his problem with the aid of some other rabbi, or come to my door in person, or call me later. I must pretend to myself that I'm not at home."

He knew that his Rebbetzin — like his children and other relations — had his best interests at heart. They tried to surround him with a protective shield to keep the possible "nudniks" at bay. During *Sukkos* one year, he recalled, at a relative's house in the suburbs, there had been a terrible commotion outside the *sukkah* and he'd asked his hosts repeatedly what the trouble was. His relatives had dismissed the ruckus as unimportant but when the *Rosh Yeshiva* had gone to the window to see for himself, a most astonishing sight appeared before his eyes. A group of *yidden* had literally been hanging from the branches of the

* The Torah forbids a *Cohain* to marry a divorcee. *Vayikra* 21:7

surrounding trees! Of course, he had greeted them — it was only right after the extremes they had gone to just to get a glimpse of him. The caller, too, might want nothing more than to hear a friendly voice, a kind word. How much time could that take from his work? Still, he had given the Rebbetzin his assurance.

T HE *ROSH YESHIVA* began to pace as he considered the problem and all the while the telephone rang persistently. "Perhaps it's an *agunah*," he thought, and his eyes filled with tears. There was no halachic solution for an actual *agunah* and each tragic case tore at his tender heart. "Or it may be one of those poor weak-minded individuals who are so put-upon by society, like that fellow who interrupted the *shiur* shouting 'Moishe! Moishe!' The boys wanted to throw him out, but I had him shown to my office. It only took an hour or so for him to calm down and I'm sure he felt better afterwards. I *must* answer. I know the Rebbetzin will understand."

But once more, the phone had stopped ringing by the time Reb Moshe reached for it and the *Rosh Yeshiva* returned to his labors. There was, as usual, a great deal of correspondence that required his attention and he was organizing the most recent *shailos* he'd received along with his *teshuvos* to be published as a new volume of *Igros Moshe*. In addition, he had to prepare his *daf shiur* and weekly *shiur klali*. It was fortunate that he had long ago accustomed himself to a barest minimum of sleep.

Then the phone rang for a third time.

He was unable to restrain himself. It might be the same desperate caller trying repeatedly to reach him. He grabbed the instrument. "Hallo?" he said.

A familiar voice came over the wire. "I thought we agreed that you were not to answer the phone!"

The Pious Patient

THE MOMENT Alice Murphy came on duty, she noticed that something had changed. She'd only been away for a week, yet the atmosphere in the hospital where she served as a "candy-striper" seemed different, less cold and antiseptic somehow and, well, friendly. She had waved to the switchboard operator when she'd entered the building and instead of the usual automatic return-wave, she'd received a brilliant smile in response.

Alice was about to ask, "To what do I owe this pleasure?" but the switchboard was flashing madly, and the operator only rolled her eyes skyward as she spoke into the headset. "Yes, thank God, his condition is stable... and God bless you too, sir. University Medical Center, good morning..." Alice hurried off to the bank of elevators.

One of Alice's responsibilities was the sorting and distribution of the patients' mail, a job that gave her enormous satisfaction because it enabled her to bring some joy to the infirm. But when she saw the huge pile of envelopes awaiting her attention, she was utterly confused. Had no one seen to the sorting in her absence? she wondered. A quick glance at the postmarks, however, revealed that the mail was all current. "What's going on here?" she asked a fellow volunteer.

"Why, nothing, Mrs. Murphy," the teenager replied. "The post delivery has been like that for days, but with God's help we've been able to manage even though we were shorthanded." That was twice in less than ten minutes she had heard the Deity's name invoked. Something peculiar was definitely afoot. Of that she was certain.

An intern wearing a *yarmulke* passed by her door and called, "Good morning, Mrs. Murphy. How was your vacation?"

"That does it!" she exclaimed. Although she was one of the few middle-aged "candy-stripers" at the hospital, her pink and white uniform had always cloaked her in invisibility. Rarely had any medical staff members so much as noticed her, let alone greeted her warmly. "Is something wrong with this place? Has everyone lost their marbles?"

"Not at all," the intern answered mildly. "Bless the Lord, everything is just fine."

Alice had a sneaking suspicion that "*He*" had checked in while she'd been away. Shrugging her shoulders, she bent to the task at hand, and soon it became apparent that the hospital was hosting a celebrity. Nearly a hundred cards, letters and telegrams were addressed to a single patient: Rabbi Moshe Feinstein. Arms piled high with mail, she strode off to see the "superstar" for herself.

WHEN SHE PUSHED open the door to his room, everything became clear. Propped up in bed like a monarch on his throne, the Rabbi was absorbed in a huge tome and surrounded by an almost palpable aura of spirituality. A snowy white beard spread down from his chin and a huge silk cap adorned his head, and when he glanced up from the text his face radiated such holiness as Alice Murphy had never seen before.

"And how are we feeling today, Rabbi?" she asked, trying to sound casual.

"*Baruch Hashem,*" Reb Moshe replied. His companion, a well-groomed young man, acted as translator. "Blessed be the Lord, I am well thank you. And yourself?"

Alice was awestruck. The patient clearly was *not* well: his room was crowded with medical apparatus and all of it was attached to him. Despite this, and unlike others who found themselves in similar circumstances, the Rabbi had voiced not a word of complaint but instead had inquired after *her* health. *And* his interest seemed genuine.

"I... I'm fine," she stammered.

"Please put down your burden," the Rabbi invited, noticing the load of mail she carried. "I'm so sorry to cause you such inconvenience."

"No, no, sir," she protested. "It's my pleasure!" She added her armload to the overflowing stack on the patient's nightstand and quietly withdrew. Even before she had reached the door, the Rabbi's face was buried again in the sacred volume. Alice Murphy knew she had been in the presence of greatness.

T HE *ROSH YESHIVA* had been brought to New York University Medical Center several weeks earlier in a very weak state, and the hospital had instantly been thrown into turmoil. With so many Jews on the staff who recognized the distinguished patient, the grapevine was soon humming with the news. From every department, noted physicians, whom the *Rosh Yeshiva* had consulted in the past on matters of *halacha*, flocked to his room to pay their respects, each deferentially donning a *yarmulke* before entering. Nurses vied for the privilege of attending him, and patients from every wing of the hospital gathered outside his room, hoping for a blessing for a *refu'ah sheleimah* or at least for a glimpse of the great man.

Each member of the staff who examined, served, tested, washed or injected the *Rosh Yeshiva* was rewarded with his gratitude, his blessing and his apology for the inconvenience. Each left his room wearing a dazed, glowing expression. The dietician who brought his breakfast was asked if she herself had eaten something nourishing that morning. The male nurse who dozed fitfully at Reb Moshe's bedside was offered a suggestion for a more practical arrangement of the chairs that would enable him to sleep more comfortably. And a certain lab technician learned the meaning of "*bitachon.*"

When the technician from Hematology came to draw a specimen of Reb Moshe's blood, her hands were trembling with trepidation. Skill and experience notwithstanding, drawing blood samples from geriatric patients is always a complicated procedure because of the presence of numerous weakened or collapsed veins. Locating a functional one on the first try is a veritable impossibility.

Although she prided herself on the almost painless technique she had perfected, the lab technician was sure that drawing this specimen would require several punctures. In addition to her own reluctance to cause further discomfort to an ailing patient, she was certain that to do so with this *particular* patient would elicit a severe reprimand from the attending physician, a tongue-lashing from the hematology resident and, quite possibly, a lecture from the hospital administrator.

As she approached his bed with tourniquet and hypodermic in hand, the *Rosh Yeshiva* looked up from his studies and confidently presented his arm. "It's alright," his eyes reassured her. Yet she hesitated. He gave her an encouraging smile as if to say "God will guide your hand. Have faith." She plunged the needle into his frail arm and watched in amazement as the syringe rapidly filled with bright red blood.

BY THE SEVENTH of Adar, which was Reb Moshe's ninetieth birthday — and not incidentally, that of Moshe *Rabeinu*, for whom he was named — the *Rosh Yeshiva's* condition had improved. Several of his relatives thoughtfully provided elaborately decorated cakes and tortes to mark the occasion. This day was not to pass unnoticed in New York University Medical Center — a vast hospital complex, occupying three square city blocks of midtown Manhattan, with hundreds of medical, technical, administrative and maintenance employees on its staff and a commensurate number of patients in its various wards.

The *Rosh Yeshiva,* whose restricted diet proscribes the consumption of foods with a high sugar content, could not allow the beautiful birthday confections to go to waste. In his halting English, he asked a patient from a nearby ward: "You vant some cake?"

Word went out that the Rabbi was dispensing birthday cake, and New York University Medical Center, staff and patients, lined up to wish Reb Moshe a "Happy Birthday" and receive their piece of the pie. It became a matter of pride and honor to be among the recipients of the portions which the pious patient graciously distributed, as these, rumor had it, had been blessed by the great man himself.

THE BUZZER sounded repeatedly at the nurses' station, and the lighted board blinked with urgency. It was room 1201: Mr. Hearst. The duty nurse did not interrupt her phone conversation, but eyebrow-signalled an aide to respond to the buzzer, and the girl hurried off down the corridor.

"When I want a *student* nurse," the irate patient fumed, "I'll *ask* for one. How long must a person ring in order to get some help around here?" William Randolph Hearst was unaccustomed to indifferent treatment.

"I'm sorry, sir, but everyone else is busy right now. There's an important patient on the floor."

"Well look around you, honey," Hearst instructed, implying that if there was anyone important at N.Y.U. Medical Center, it was William Randolph Hearst. "You think Medicaid paid for this suite?"

"No, no, of course not," the flustered girl replied. "I didn't mean..."

"Yeah, yeah. Forget it. Who is this big shot, anyway?"

"It's Rabbi Feinstein!" she whispered reverently.

"Who?" he demanded. Hearst was almost fully recovered from his illness and had reached the cantankerous stage. He was aware that his behavior was abominable, but orneriness, he felt, was the privilege of the affluent and influential.

"Rabbi Moses Feinstein," the student nurse explained, "the great rabbinic authority."

"Well, get him *in* here, girl. I'll give him a double-spread feature in one of my magazines. Tell him I'll make him famous."

The nurse dissolved in a fit of helpless giggling. Needless to say, the *Rosh Yeshiva* declined the offer.

TWO RELIGIOUS residents sat in the hospital cafeteria comparing notes on their illustrious patient. "When I did my internship at St. Vincent's Hospital, Reb Moshe was there," the first related, "and when they told him he'd need surgery to implant a pacemaker, he really got upset. I don't think I've ever seen him so distressed."

"It's not surprising," his colleague said. "Surgery can be a rather terrifying experience — especially for older people."

"Oh, he wasn't worried about the operation. He said that when the Redemption comes, he might be unable to fulfill his duty should the Messiah call upon him to serve in the *Sanhedrin*. The implant could render him a *baal mum* — legally 'blemished' — thereby disqualifying him for service in the *Sanhedrin*."

WHEN REB MOSHE learned that Senator Jacob Javits, who suffers from Lou Gehrig's Disease, had been admitted to the Medical Center, he immediately closed the volume in his lap. Over the vehement protests of his nurse, he climbed down from the hospital bed and into a wheelchair.

"What's the matter?" the male nurse cried in dismay. "Where are you going?"

"A Jew such as he, who has done so much for *Klal Yisrael,* is in the hospital — I must be *mevaker choleh*." And with that, the *Rosh Yeshiva* began to wheel himself out of the room.

༄

It is said that a man's true character is revealed in three areas: his finances, his flask, and his fury. When it comes to money matters, when he is "in his cups," and when he loses his temper, a man's rein on his natural impulses snaps and the opaque shield behind which he conceals his inner self becomes transparent.

There is, however, one more state wherein man is stripped of his defenses: his infirmity. Can a fevered brain control the words that escape slack lips? Can debilitated flesh be made to respond to the commands of the soul? The answer, obviously, is yes — when the soul has so saintly a master as Reb Moshe.

BOOK II

Introduction

THIS SECTION of '*SOULED!*' is designed for the edification and enjoyment of youngsters. Unlike the stories in Book I, these are not based on true events or real-life experiences, but on inspiring legends and Jewish lore. It is hoped that the occasionally difficult vocabulary will serve *not* as a deterrent for young readers, but as an inducement for them to read and discuss the stories with their parents.

On the advice of educators, the themes were chosen specifically for their relevance and appropriateness for children and the stories written in a style intended to capture their attention and stimulate their imagination. As in all the other stories in this volume, the settings and periods were carefully researched and depicted as accurately as possible.

BOOK II

Contents

three legends

למען ידעו דור אחרון בנים יולדו
יקמו ויספרו לבניהם.
תהילים עח:ו'

❀ So the generation to come may know them,
the children which should be born;
who should arise declare to their children

Psalms 78:6

Adrift

I T WAS SUNDAY MORNING, and the sky was black with angry thunderheads. The wind howled and rain poured down in icy sheets that stung like a thousand needles of steel. Waves as high as mountains crested, then crashed down upon the rolling deck. The sea, a seething witches' brew, foamed and churned with the great ship trapped in its hellish turbulence.

The vessel heaved and pitched violently, hurling crates and crockery about like chaff in a winnow. Zevulun ben Yissachar wrapped himself in oilskins and struggled up the slippery gangway to the upper deck. He watched in helpless terror as the storm tore relentlessly at the mainsail until it hung from the central mast in tatters.

The ocean slammed against the oaken hull. Lashed to the helm, the shipmaster fought a brave but futile battle to hold the schooner on course. It seemed that it could not be any worse than this — and then it was.

Fiery forks of lightning rent the heavens and struck the foremast a mighty blow. Despite its beer-barrel girth, the mast was felled like a sapling beneath the blade of a woodsman's axe. It smashed a hole in the deck the size of a cannonball and the cruel sea gushed in through the breach.

The captain cried "Abandon ship!" and all who dared, did, grabbing planks of wood and empty kegs as they leapt over the side. But Zevulun patted his pockets for the *tefillin* which he always kept on his person and then grabbed a coil of rope and swiftly tied himself to the rail. He was a poor swimmer and his fear of the ocean depths was keen. He prayed for a merciful death.

Z EVULUN BEN YISSACHAR was a merchant seaman by trade. Six months of every year he plied the waters from the Iberian coast to the Phoenician Gulf, buying and selling silks and spices, a profitable business which enabled him to spend the remainder of the year engaged in the study of the holy Torah. Would he ever touch those precious sacred books again? he wondered. Would he ever again see his beloved wife and children?

The bodies of his shipmates, swallowed whole and gone without a trace, failed to appease the ocean's fury. For two more days and nights the implacable tempest battered his ship, driving it at last onto the rocks. As the schooner broke up on the craggy coast of an uncharted island, Zevulun, still bound to the rail, was brutally thrown from the deck on impact. He floundered in the shallows, clutching flotsam from the wreck, until, sapped of strength, he washed up on the beach with the tide.

The storm subsided early Wednesday morning. Zevulun lay unconscious in the sand while the bright sun dried the shreds of clothing that clung to his limbs and torso. A freshening breeze ruffled his salt-caked hair. Zevulun stirred.

He dragged his pain-wracked body to the shelter of a tree

where he rested, gathering energy, and offered a prayer of thanksgiving to his Creator. His eyelids and lips were blistered, his tongue swollen from thirst, and crusts of dried blood covered his bare arms and feet. He doubted he could last long without sustenance. Grasping the bole of the tree for support, he hauled himself erect and began to forage for food.

On still shaky legs, with every bruised muscle screaming from the exertion, he headed inland. Dense foliage impeded his progress at every turn, indicating the presence of sweet water and the hope of fruit. But despite its abundance, the vegetation did not appear to be edible. The broad thorny leaves were like no leaves he had ever seen before and no fruit or nuts dangled from the lofty branches. Lush verdant bushes in every shade of green flourished among the trees, bare of berries; still he searched for the fresh water spring that fed them.

THE LEAF-LITTERED EARTH gave way abruptly to a neat, well-tended path. Zevulun followed the winding, narrow lane through the forest to a large clearing, in the heart of which stood dozens of small, wooden houses. He gazed upon the village in wonderment. Until that moment, he had been certain that the area was uninhabited. It was so odd an assumption to have made that he paused to analyze the thoughts which had led him to that conclusion.

The silence, he realized at once, yes, the absolute, utter silence of the place. Not a bird chirped in the trees, no sound of small, scurrying creatures reached his ears; neither the buzz of conversation nor the hum of industry, neither the tinkle of laughter nor the cry of a child penetrated the barrier of silence which enveloped him.

Yet the wooden structures appeared to be anything but

abandoned. Like the path, they were well-cared for, with small patches of garden in front and crisp curtains at the windows. "Hello!" he called, but no human voice responded. His eyes searched the village. There was no sign of life.

Zevulun was struck by his total isolation, the agony of his loneliness, the hopelessness of his situation. How he longed to see a face, to hear a voice besides his own! His need for human fellowship was as desperate as his hunger and thirst. Tears of sorrow coursed down his ravaged cheeks and he prayed to the Almighty for comfort and salvation.

He weakly made his way to the door of the first house and was just raising his hand to knock when he encountered a sight that filled him with awe. He rubbed his eyes with his fists, certain it had been an hallucination. But when he looked again, it was still there. He touched it with trembling fingers to convince himself that it was not a figment of his imagination.

"**I**T IS TRULY A MIRACLE," he said aloud, and indeed it was. For there on the doorpost of this modest hut in the midst of a clearing, in the depths of a forest on a deserted land, was a *mezuzah*.

With unbridled joy, he rapped his fist against the door, the pain and exhaustion gone from his body, the memory of his ordeal forgotten. He could barely contain his excitement. He banged at the door with all his might, but no one answered. He hurried to the next house and there, too, he found a *mezuzah*, but again no one answered his knock.

On every doorpost in the entire village a *mezuzah* was affixed, and Zevulun went from one house to the next, knocking and calling out and knocking again, until he practically collapsed from fatigue and frustration.

In despair, he grasped the nearest doorhandle, intending to break in if necessary, but to his astonishment the door yielded easily and swung open on silent hinges. He entered the house.

C LEARLY, the owners were absent, although signs of recent habitation were everywhere. Barely a speck of dust powdered the sparse furniture; a ruffled apron hung from a peg, its long ties still curved with the memory of a bow; an iron pot on the stove bore the still-discernible aroma of a pungent stew. And on the table stood a large bowl filled to overflowing with dried fruits and nuts.

Wordlessly, Zevulun thanked the absent homeowner and begged the man's forgiveness for his intrusion and presumptuousness. To partake of another's food without permission was a deplorable act, and had it not been a matter of survival, the idea would never have occurred to Zevulun. He praised God for His compassion and dined on the fruit as though it were the most sumptuous repast.

Sated at last, he lay down to await the owner's return, determined to recompense his unknown host in whatever way possible. In moments, Zevulun was asleep and when he awoke, a new day was dawning. It was Thursday, and thoughts of how he would celebrate — indeed observe, the coming Shabbos began to torment him. The absent homeowner had not returned.

The house, as well as the rest of the tiny village, remained silent. He went out to explore his surroundings, although his hopes of finding anyone had long since dimmed. With the remainder of the dried fruits and several handfuls of nuts tied in a scrap of cloth, Zevulun set out on the path leading through the forest.

By evening, however, his worst fears had been

confirmed. After a long trek, he discovered that he was indeed on an island, and even from the top of the highest tree he was unable to sight any nearby land mass. The only cultivated area was that of the abandoned village; all the rest of the small island was a virtually impenetrable forest. Dejected and disheartened, Zevulun followed the path "home."

A S HE NEARED the village, a strange sound caught his attention. He quickly turned towards the noise and discovered that the path branched off to the right. He had not noticed the fork earlier; now he followed it past an unusual rock formation and down a shallow incline, the strange sound growing increasingly louder as he went.

At the end of the path lay a large pool of clear water, rivulets trickling down to it from countless crevices in the surrounding rocks. Zevulun knelt at the edge of the pool, scooped water into his hand and tasted it. It was icy cold and sweeter than any wine he'd ever known. He sluiced his sunburned face in its coolness and slaked his terrible thirst.

On the far side of the pool stood a lone wooden structure similar in design to those in the village, but substantially larger. Thinking that perhaps the villagers were gathered in this building, Zevulun approached the imposing front door with a glimmer of hope. Here, too, a *mezuzah* was affixed to the doorpost.

Inside, Zevulun discovered a simple, but beautiful, *shul.* The last rays of the setting sun poured in through the windows as if the forest had parted to make way for the sunbeams. The *aron kodesh* was bathed in a Heavenly glow and Zevulun recited his evening prayers with great devotion.

An oil lamp, half-filled and still burning, illuminated the

interior even after sundown. Zevulun opened a worn, leather-bound volume and immersed himself in learning. He studied far into the night, dozing now and then on the hard bench.

At dawn he washed in the pool, then recited the morning service. He knew he must soon begin preparations for the Sabbath, but he could not think of how to go about it. Only a few small nuts remained in his cloth pouch and these he devoured slowly. His explorations of the island had uncovered no edible growth, and he was painfully aware that this might be his very last meal. If the villagers failed to return soon, he feared he would be compelled to raid yet another home, and even then, there was no assurance of finding anything.

He returned to his study of the sacred tome, hoping to delay the inevitable as long as he could. Hours passed. Suddenly, Zevulun looked up from the text, sensing a subtle change in the atmosphere. He ran to the window, but the tangled forest blocked his view of all but the limpid pool. The sound of trickling water had an extra intensity now, altered in some indefinable way.

His heart nearly burst with the joyful realization that the sound he heard was the sound of humanity. He raced down the path to the village. The sight that greeted him there was dazzling.

T HE TINY ABANDONED VILLAGE was completely transformed. Everywhere people were hurrying about their business: women scrubbed laundry in huge sudsy vats; men carried baskets and parcels with a purposeful stride; children swept doorsteps and scampered and sang merrily; and the air was full with the heady aromas of cooking and baking.

"Come," said a man as he passed Zevulun, handing him a cumbersome package. Zevulun, dumbstruck, followed obediently. A moment later, they entered the very house where Zevulun had discovered the bowl of fruit and nuts, but before he could speak, the lady of the house greeted him warmly.

"How wonderful! A guest for Shabbos!" She showed him to an alcove and laid out a clean suit of clothes upon a freshly-made bed. "Quickly," she said, "there isn't much time."

Zevulun began to stammer his thanks but the man swiftly drew the alcove curtain. He shucked his rags and donned the splendid attire his hosts had so graciously provided and reflected that had the villagers not returned, he would have had no way of celebrating the Sabbath properly.

The children of the household arrived. Through the curtain he heard the sounds of furniture being moved about, of tableware rattling, pots and pans banging, the bustle and hubbub of Shabbos preparations overlaid with the happy humming of Sabbath songs.

Although he had not lingered over his dressing, by the time he emerged from the alcove, the immaculate home was ready for Shabbos. The woman, a snowy apron over her long, dark dress and a lacy kerchief wrapped around her head, blessed the Sabbath oil lights and her husband and sons called "Good Shabbos" as they hurried out the door. The man gestured impatiently for Zevulun to join them, which he did.

THE VILLAGE SQUARE was as crowded as a marketplace with men and boys heading for the shul in the forest. Zevulun was struck by the warmth that radiated from all the smiling faces of the villagers, the hearty

"Good Shabbos" with which they hailed one another, and the orderly, ceremonial way they filed down the path past the pool.

"Ah, a guest!" each one said when he saw Zevulun. "Next Shabbos you'll stay with me." Zevulun smiled with pleasure at their hospitality and generosity towards a total stranger, wondering at the same time if indeed he was destined to remain on the island for so many weeks.

There was no doubt that the island and its inhabitants were most extraordinary. The possibility that it was all an illusion crossed Zevulun's mind, but he quickly rejected the thought. It was too real, too tangible to be a fantasy. His curiosity was overwhelming but he dared not disturb the serenity of the Sabbath by asking questions. What would he do if his inquisitiveness were to offend his benefactor or break the miraculous spell? He decided he must delay his interrogations until after Shabbos.

But why, he wondered, had no one thought to ask him whence he had come? Was it merely politeness, or a singular absence of curiosity? Was the sudden appearance of a stranger in their midst a commonplace occurrence? The beauty of the *tefillah* banished all care from his mind.

NEVER BEFORE had Zevulun heard the Friday night service sung so gloriously. The strains of *Lecha Dodi* filled the shul with joyous music, melodious and spiritual, the notes ascending straight to the Heavens. "Surely this is the way the angels sing," Zevulun thought to himself, for he could imagine nothing earthly to be so magnificent and inspirational. He could not fathom the Almighty's reasons for bringing him to this mysterious island, but, for Zevulun, to have been permitted to experience this uplifting *tefillah*, made the entire ordeal worth enduring.

Dinner Friday night at his host's table was no less sublime. The children, their cherubic faces gleaming in the glow of the Sabbath lights, politely questioned their father concerning the intricacies of the Torah and the ways of *mussar*. The *zemiros* they sang were as captivating as birdsong and the meal — a celestial feast — was indeed food for the *neshama yeseira*.

Shabbos morning was equally exhilarating. Throughout the *tefillah* the voices of the islanders blended together harmoniously in a virtual symphony of the soul. They heeded the Torah-reading avidly, appearing to absorb not only the words but the timeless lessons as well. The Sabbath meal was a celebration that nourished the spirit, with food fit for kings and ethereal, intoxicating songs.

Not a single profane or mundane matter intruded on the Shabbos tranquility. The afternoon was devoted to Torah study, followed by *mincha* services and a *seudah shlishis* that were the essence of sanctity and holiness. And as the Sabbath drew to a close, Zevulun was gripped with melancholy and a terrible sense of loss. The terror of the storm that had wrecked his ship, destroying his livelihood and casting him away on this remote island, the tragedy of his separation from his home and loved ones, all paled to insignificance alongside this incomparable Shabbos experience. He wished it would never end.

Zevulun prepared himself to offer up a *motzei Shabbos tefillah* that would convey his deep gratitude for the Almighty's benevolence. He prayed with greater devotion and fervor than ever before, concentrating his entire being on each word. So engrossed was he in his devotions that he did not notice when the other worshippers completed theirs. While he was yet immersed in the *Shemoneh Esrei*, the others recited the *Havdallah* service, lifting the candle high to light the way for the departing Sabbath Queen. Still

Zevulun lingered over his prayer, and when he was done, he found the shul deserted.

T HE PATH through the forest was eerily silent; starlight twinkled among the gnarled tree limbs and rustling leaves, illuminating his way. He hurried to the home of his generous host, anxious to express his appreciation for all the kindness and hospitality and to ask the questions which had seemed so unimportant throughout Shabbos but which now pressed with great urgency.

With an uneasy feeling, Zevulun rapped on the door. The village, which had been so recently a veritable hive of activity, was still. No one answered his knock. He ran to the next house, and the next, and the next, but all were as empty as they had been when he had first arrived. In desperation he opened door after door, calling out, begging the villagers not to hide from him, but his cries were met with silence.

He flew down the path to the beach, praying for a glimpse of the boats upon which the islanders had surely sailed, but there was only the glassy sea and the rising moon on the horizon. He fell to his knees and cried in anguish, "Please, I beseech you, do not abandon me! I cannot bear to be alone again!" But the only sound was the monotonous lapping of waves upon the sandy shore.

Despondent, he groped his way back to the shul to seek solace in the sacred texts. He opened a massive volume and quickly became engrossed in the complexities of the subject matter before him. Soon the pall of sorrow lifted. He studied through the night, napping briefly just before sunrise. When he awoke, he felt refreshed and not at all hungry. It was as though the Sabbath past continued to sustain and nurture him.

But his nerves found no respite. What was this enigma he was experiencing? he wondered. He searched the island again and again day after day, desperate to determine the whereabouts of its inhabitants. But he found not a single clue. It was hopeless. Only when his mind was completely occupied with exploring the ancient tomes was he at peace.

Occasionally, when he paused in his studies to drink at the pool and breathe the clean, fresh forest fragrances, he again considered the possibility that all that had transpired had been no more than an illusion, a dream which yet held him firmly in its grip. But such thoughts led nowhere and he hastily drove them from his mind and returned to his investigation of the Holy Scripture.

ONE THOUGHT, however, refused to be driven away. It pried relentlessly at the edges of his consciousness, demanding attention. It was the awareness of the approaching Sabbath and his hopeless inadequacy to celebrate it.

With neither wine nor challah on hand, how could he sanctify the holy day? How would his pathetic semblance of Shabbos compare with the villagers' undefiled, reverential Sabbath in the eyes of the Lord? The vision of a barren Shabbos table, a meal of plain water and stale nuts, devoid of moving *zemiros* and inspiring *divrei Torah*, tormented him.

On Friday afternoon, however, the welcome sounds of feverish activity drifted through the windows of the shul. With heart pounding, Zevulun sped to the village, overjoyed to find that the people had returned and that they were once again preparing to greet the Sabbath.

"Happy to see you!" a householder called cheerfully across his porch railing. "Don't forget, you promised to be our guest this week!" Zevulun was delighted to have been remembered.

Everything was as before: the prayers were as inspiring, the meals as delectable, the *divrei Torah* as edifying and the *zemiros* as dulcet as those of the previous week. Zevulun felt he had been blessed with a glimpse of Paradise — not once, but twice! Comfortably seated at his host's table surrounded by angelic children and enveloped in an aura of enchantment, Zevulun cast aside his curiosity. The very mention of the villagers' unexplained disappearance seemed a profanity. Such queries were best relegated to after Shabbos.

T HE SABBATH PASSED all too swiftly. As the time for *maariv* drew nearer, Zevulun rehearsed the questions he intended to pose, taking extreme care to phrase them as inoffensively as he could. But once again, his need to acknowledge his gratitude to the Almighty took precedence, and while the villagers chanted the *Havdallah* benedictions, Zevulun remained intent in prayer.

He praised his Creator for delivering him from the clutches of the cruel sea, for providing sustenance, for enabling him to experience celestial Sabbaths, and for allowing him to partake of the fruits of the World to Come. And when he emerged at last from his devotions, the villagers were gone.

Although he knew it was futile, he searched for them no less intensively than he had the previous week. He lit a torch from the flame of the shul's still-burning oil lamp and ran through the forest, this time in the direction away from the village. Perhaps a secret cave sheltered the people all week long, he wondered, or maybe they had repaired to another village, hidden among the trees?

"Stop," his inner voice rebuked him, "you know you search in vain! What use is the pursuit of specters and wraiths?" He did stop then, for he was certain his inner voice spoke the truth. The pious villagers could only be Heaven-born and Heaven-sent, Divine messengers dispatched to earth to demonstrate the spirituality of Shabbos.

The lesson was not lost on Zevulun. As he walked slowly back to the shul, his mind whirled with thoughts and plans. He knew now that he had been completely wrong about his inadequacy to celebrate the Sabbath in a way that would find favor in the eyes of the Lord. For more than the enjoyment of good fellowship, more than the splendor of sumptuous feasts, more than all the material pleasures, Shabbos was a celebration of the spirit.

Even if he were to have nothing but the water from the pool for *Kiddush*, it would be the water that God in His mercy provided, the cool, sweet draft which had refreshed his tortured body after the harrowing shipwreck and which continued to sustain him throughout the week. Even if his meals were to consist of no more than a handful of stale nuts, still he could sing joyous songs of praise to his Creator, still he could speak the words of Torah, though none would hear but the Almighty Himself.

Zevulun's delight at this discovery was marred only by the knowledge that he was destined to live out his days on this far-flung isle, bereft of his cherished family and severed from society. But it was not for him to question the ways of the Lord. He turned instead to the task before him.

All week long Zevulun prepared himself for the coming Shabbos. Each passage he studied in the ancient volumes took on new meaning, for now he considered the words not merely in the context of the explicit subject to which they related, but in the context of the whole of God's Creation.

When he drank at the pool, the glittering stars reflected therein heightened his awareness of the universe, the vastness and limitlessness of the Lords's domain and his own minuteness and insignificance within it.

WHEN *EREV SHABBOS* ARRIVED, it was not Zevulun who sought out the villagers, but the villagers who, entranced by the melodies emanating from the shul in the forest, sought out their erstwhile guest. They joined him in the stirring Friday night service, made even more exquisite by Zevulun's empassioned devotions. Throughout the Sabbath, he regaled them with brilliant *divrei Torah* and paeans of praise to the Almighty which he had composed.

After *mincha*, the villagers set up tables in the shul arrayed with every imaginable delicacy and together with Zevulun they feasted upon an otherworldly *seudah shlishis*. Then the eldest among them arose and addressed Zevulun in a sonorous voice:

"Honored visitor," he began, "we are aware that it was your respect for the sanctity of the Sabbath that prevented you from questioning us about our unusual existence. Now that you have demonstrated your ability to celebrate Shabbos as the Almighty intended, I am authorized to explain all that you have witnessed on our island.

"Many, many years ago, our ancestors were banished from the Holy Land by the wicked Nebuchadnezzar, and they escaped to this remote isle. Here they established a community steeped in Torah and devoted to service of the Holy One, blessed be He. They were only humble peasants with little money or material possessions, but here wealth had no significance. Their lives were dedicated to the study of the Divine Law.

"They cultivated the land and raised small crops in order to satisfy their simple needs, and dreamed fervently of one day returning to *Eretz Yisrael*. As the decades passed and word of the rebuilding of the Temple reached them, their longing to rest their eyes once more upon its golden splendor became all but endurable. It became the core of their existence.

"The enormous expense such a journey entailed, however, was far beyond their limited means. After much deliberation, it was decided that they would each contribute whatever they could to finance the journey of a handful of representatives, chosen by lot.

"And thus the tradition was born, a tradition carried on by generation after generation of our people, for hundreds of years, even until our own time. Each year money was pooled, lots were drawn and a delegation dispatched to the Holy Land. In some years, when the harvests were good, perhaps four or five islanders were able to embark on the voyage; in other years, only one or two could go.

"As was the custom, the Chosen Ones departed amid much fanfare and celebration and set sail in good time to reach the Holy Land before *Sukkos*. We would gather on the beach to bid them farewell and make them vow to relate to us every detail of *Yerushalayim*'s glory.

"They would bring sacrifices on behalf of our people on the Temple altars and sojourn for several weeks in the Holy City, in order to absorb its blessed beauty and wondrous sights. And we would anxiously await their return, posting scouts in the treetops to announce their ship's approach.

"Upon their return, the Chosen Ones were greeted with jubilation such as you have never seen. For three days and three nights they would tell of their experiences in the glorious Land of our dreams, about how the *Leviim* had sung and the *Cohanim* had performed the *avodah*. They would describe the drawing of waters at the *Simchas Bais HaShoeva*, the hosts of worshippers at the Temple, and the joy that suffused every day of the feast.

"ONE YEAR, three Chosen Ones embarked on the annual pilgrimage, but within weeks the sails of their returning ship were sighted on the horizon. This was an unheard of occurrence as the delegation was not meant to return until much later. We hurriedly assembled on the beach to welcome our brethren in our customary festive fashion, waving and singing our usual songs of welcome.

"Before long, the ship itself came into view, but the Chosen Ones were nowhere to be seen. We dared not think what dire fate had befallen our brothers. The ship anchored far out at sea and a rowboat was lowered. Three men dressed in sackcloth boarded the boat and were rowed towards the shore. Surely these could not be our Chosen Ones, we thought, for the delegation was always clothed in finery, as befitted the occasion. But as the boat drew nearer, we recognized them.

"We continued to wave as hard as we could, even though our comrades did not respond. With stoic expressions they sat motionless in their rowboat and finally climbed down. With none of the usual rush and excitement, they waded to the beach and we could see the desolate pallor of their faces, the ashes upon their heads and the immeasurable sorrow in their eyes. They would not speak; they could not. We begged and beseeched them to explain why they were so sad. At last, they tearfully reported the devastating destruction of our beloved Temple; how they had seen it aflame and the Jews driven into exile. The Chosen Ones described in horrid detail the Holy City laid waste.

"A great wailing rose up from our people, a moaning and keening that fairly rent the heavens. So enormous was our anguish that one by one we fell to the ground, every man, woman and child among us, without the breath of life.

"WHEN OUR SOULS arrived at the gates of Heaven, our appearance seemed to create a problem. Our lives had terminated, yet our deaths were premature, brought about by our everlasting love for *Eretz Yisrael* and deep devotion to the *Bais HaMikdash*.

"The Heavenly Court decided that, in the merit of our reverence for the Holy Land and for the Divine Torah, we would be permitted to live out our years one Shabbos at a time — Shabbos being akin to the World to Come — until the number of Sabbaths equalled the number of days we were each allotted. Thus, every *erev Shabbos*, our souls return to earth to celebrate the sacred Day of Rest in the manner of the Heavenly Beings.

"Now, you, Zevulun ben Yissachar, have been privileged to witness a Celestial Sabbath. Go back to your home and emulate all that you have seen."

"Wait!" Zevulun cried. "How...," but the elderly villager interrupted him. "It is almost time for us to depart," he said, "and we must *daven maariv* and recite the *Havdallah* service before we go." Immediately, the service commenced and Zevulun was prevented from asking the most vital question of all.

As the *Havdallah* candle sizzled out in a puddle of sweet wine, the elder pressed a scrap of parchment into Zevulun's hand. "When you are ready to leave our island," he whispered, "go down to the beach and think of your loved ones. Read that which is written here and then cast this parchment into the sea." And with those words, the elder and all of the islanders disappeared like the smoke of the candle.

ZEVULUN DID NOT hurry down to the beach — not that night. He sat on the bench in the shul in the forest and sang to the departing Sabbath Queen. He recited *divrei Torah* to console his spirit for the loss it suffered when Shabbos ended.

After the *melave malka*, he walked through the forest inhaling the spicy fragrance of the foliage and drank again the sweet waters of the pool. All through the night and all the next day he studied the sacred texts and relived in his mind the weeks he had spent on the island, an island sanctified by the lives of those who truly yearned for *Eretz Yisrael* — by those who knew how to observe the Day of Rest.

Finally, his heart filled with the joys of Sabbath Island, he strolled slowly down to the shore, retracing the path where his heavenly adventure had begun.

He gazed out upon the calm sea, so vast and yet, a mere droplet in God's mighty hand, to lie tranquil or rise up in mountainous waves at His command. Zevulun thought of his home and loved ones, of telling them and everyone he knew about the way the angels celebrate Shabbos. Then he read the Ineffable Name inscribed on the parchment. A tear rolled down his cheek and fell upon the inscription, and the parchment began to dissolve. Quickly he cast it into the seafoam, and Zevulun ben Yissachar left Sabbath Island — where Shabbos, *Eretz Yisrael* and the World to Come were one — forever.

Baruch and the Pasha's Sword

IFTY CHASSIDIM sat at the Rebbe's *tisch* celebrating the birth of his first grandson. It was a *shalom zachor* as only chassidim can devise: the table fairly groaned beneath the weight of cakes and confections, fruit and nuts, and the wine and whiskey flowed unchecked. There was no dearth of gaiety and merriment, either. Centuries-old *niggunim* were sung with inimitable chassidic exuberance, and the crystal chandelier rang in tuneful accompaniment as the lusty voices bombarded the room with sound.

The festivities were sure to last far into the night, for this was no ordinary *simcha*: the grandchild, the first male born to one of the Rebbe's seven daughters, was the heir-apparent, the crown prince who would assure the family's dynastic succession and bear the name of the Rebbe's father, Dovid, may his sainted memory be blessed. Accordingly, the chassidim offered the Rebbe their own humble blessing, that the infant who would bear the name of David, King of Israel, would herald the coming of the Messiah.

At these words, the Rebbe signalled for silence, a familiar temple-tapping gesture which his disciples recognized as an indication that their mentor had recalled a parable appropriate to the occasion. A hush fell over the room. With a leisurely, hypnotic cadence, the Rebbe began to spin his tale:

IN THE DAYS of Ottoman supremacy, the Sultan of Turkey frequently dispatched emissaries to the remote lands that comprised his vast empire, there to oversee the orderly collection of taxes, quash civil disobedience, settle juridical disputes, or simply to demonstrate by a show of force the far-reaching power of the mighty ruler. Regardless of the reason for his visit, whenever the Sultan's Pasha came to town, it did not bode well for the Jews. The moment the Pasha's entourage was sighted, with its score of caparisoned riders and horses and the regal sedan chair borne by a dozen turbaned slaves, the Jewish inhabitants of Jerusalem wisely sought refuge behind shuttered windows and barred doors. This occasion was no exception.

The leaders of the Moslem community, in order to curry favor with the Sultan, prepared a lavish welcome for the Pasha and escorted him on a grand tour of the city. The Pasha, stifling a yawn, accorded only cursory attention to the holy places and historical sites. It was clear that he viewed the tour as no more than a tiresome prerequisite to the evening's sumptuous feast and exciting entertainment; nonetheless, he fulfilled this odious obligation with a maximum of pomp.

The Pasha was short in stature and bandylegged, and his girth bore witness to a life of gastronomic excess, but his attire endowed him with majesty. A voluminous turban was perched on his head and in its center a ruby gleamed like a sanguinary third eye. His flowing robes were exquisitely tailored of silken cloth shot with gold and silver threads and contrived to display to best advantage the Pasha's most prized possession: a jewel-encrusted sword presented to him by the Sultan himself.

A superb piece of workmanship, the keen-edged sword had a golden haft set with myriad precious and semi-precious stones that glittered richly in the brilliant sunlight. Despite the ponderous weight of the blade, the Pasha brandished his burden with savage pride. None doubted his readiness to employ that sword in meting out Ottoman justice.

AS THE TOUR neared its end uneventfully, the Jews allowed themselves a collective sigh of relief. Their sense of tranquility, however, was premature. On the outskirts of the city, the guides pointed out to the Pasha a crumbling, dried-up well believed to be the burial place of King David, and the Pasha, whose tour had thus far been long on tedium and short on recreation, seized the opportunity for diversion. He leaned over the edge of the well and called derisively: "David, oh David, can you hear me?" to the delight of his audience.

The Moslem leaders laughed dutifully, although bitter experience and their own superstitions had long since taught them to beware of jests at the Jews' expense. The Pasha, clearly enjoying himself, repeated the performance.

He bent over the edge a second time, and suddenly, all laughter died. Unnoticed, the buckle of the Pasha's scabbard had somehow become undone, the scabbard which held his cherished gift from the Sultan, and as the crowd watched in horror, the jewel-encrusted sword plummeted clangorously down the shaft.

AN OMINOUS SILENCE ensued. The crowd was thunderstruck by this unforeseen turn of events, certain it augured ill for every one of them. No benign plenipotentiary, the Pasha had more than once exhibited a vile and implacable temper, but no one present could have predicted the emissary's reaction.

He slapped his palms smartly against the lip of the well and cried, "No, no, *no!*" over and over. He snatched the turban off his head and stomped on it in fury and frustration until it lay unraveled in the earth like the desquamated skin of a rare white serpent. He threw his hands heavenward and screamed like an overindulged child denied his favorite treat: "My sword, my sword, *I want my sword!*"

Had their fear been less intense, those assembled would likely have dissolved in paroxysms of laughter. As it was, they awaited the subsidence of the Pasha's rage with great trepidation. When at last he regained a measure of composure, he commanded that the longest, sturdiest rope in the entire city be brought to him. This was accomplished in short order and the rope was firmly secured to the waist of a hapless Turkish soldier.

With several of his comrades gripping the thickly-plaited rope, the soldier was lowered slowly down the shaft. As soon as he had the sword in hand, he was to tug twice on the rope. This seemed a simple enough instruction to follow, so when the prearranged signal failed to be received after what was deemed a reasonable interval, the Pasha lost all restraint. He screamed the order to pull up the rope.

The soldiers quickly complied, heedless of the oddly flaccid weight at the end of the line and without regard for the possible consequences of slamming their associate repeatedly against the stone walls of the shaft. In moments the body of the sword-retriever was unceremoniously hauled over the edge of the well — with neither the sword in his hand nor the breath of life on his lips.

"Fool!" the Pasha raged. "Imbecile!" he shrieked, delivering a swift kick to the soldier's insensate remains. "Off with his head!" He drew the scimitar of the nearest servant to carry out his own command.

"But, sire," ventured one of the Moslem leaders, "the man is already dead, and," he continued, "appears to have been so for some time!"

"You cretin!" shouted the Pasha, turning on the first of the rope-haulers. "You killed him by dragging him up too fast and caused him to drop my sword! It is *your* fault!"

"No, sire, no! He was already..."

"Silence, idiot! You will go down there in his stead." The rope was untied from the dead soldier and secured to the live one, the severity of his trembling impeding the swift implementation of the task. Then, as his comrade before him, the soldier was lowered into King David's well, with a brief but fervent prayer to "Allah."

ONCE AGAIN the arrayed soldiers anxiously awaited the prearranged signal, but nary a quiver was felt on the line. The Pasha's rein on his patience snapped. "Up!" he shouted. "Up, up, *UP!*"

The soldiers obeyed, yanking the rope hand-over-hand until the body — or, more correctly, the corpse of their confrere emerged from the well. A gasp of awe arose from the crowd.

One of the Moslems stepped forward. "Forgive me, sire, but I am a doctor." He knelt at the soldier's side and examined his lifeless form. "Not only is this man dead," he pronounced, "but his body is cold. I believe that his death occurred even before he reached the bottom of the shaft. Furthermore," he went on, "there is not a mark on him. It was not a blow which killed him, but something else. Perhaps he died of fright, or..." The doctor made the two-fingered sign to ward off the "evil eye" and gripped his *hamsa* amulet tightly in his hand.

THE PASHA'S WRATH boiled over. He turned to the next soldier in line. The ranks shrank from his gaze in the barren hope of being swallowed up by the earth before the finger of fate pointed in their direction. They wailed and writhed and clawed their cheeks in terror. The emissary looked upon them with disgust. "Cowards! You muddleheaded nincompoops would be incapable of retrieving your own sandals if they were attached to your feet!" He spun around. "You — doctor!" he bellowed. The Arab physician began to quake. "Tie him up and send him down."

The soldiers were only too grateful to have been passed over for the dubious honor and quickly bent to the task. "Wait!" cried the Arab in desperation. "This site is holy to the Jews. If it is their ancestor who haunts the well, then only a Jew can safely enter it." Not for naught was this Moslem's extensive education. "Only a Jew can retrieve your sword," he added, pressing home his point.

The Pasha hesitated and considered the suggestion. The argument seemed valid. "Agreed," he said. "Bring me a Jew!" The troops scattered to do their commander's bidding, but the Jews, as it may be remembered, had wisely removed themselves from the Pasha's presence. Much time elapsed while the Pasha paced and fumed and his dragomen nervously gnawed their fingernails to ruins. At last the soldiers returned with their captive.

T HE APPREHENSION OF BARUCH, the *Shammas* had proved less difficult than the soldiers would have surmised. Unlike all his co-religionists, Baruch had not abandoned his post upon the arrival of the Pasha in Jerusalem. In fact, Baruch was entirely oblivious to the goings-on. While the Jews had hurriedly barricaded themselves in their subterranean retreats, Baruch had persevered in his assigned duties.

His chores were numerous: he had to arrange the chairs in the synagogue, replace the prayer books, and other *sefarim*, organize the *minyanim* and schedule the *shiurim*. All these responsibilities and more received Baruch's dedicated attention and only when his chores were satisfactorily completed could Baruch devote himself to his favorite pastime: the study of Torah.

Unknown to the members of the Jewish community, Baruch whiled away his many free hours engaged in plumbing the depths of Holy Scripture, and thus had he been occupied when the Pasha's troops had burst into the shul. Their exhaustive search had, until that moment, proved fruitless but they had not dared return emptyhanded to their irate master. They had seized Baruch with unnecessary force and dragged their bewildered prisoner to the site of the well.

The Turkish envoy was well pleased with his minions' success. Without further ado, Baruch was hoisted to the lip of the well and bound with the heavy rope. The dragomen interpreted the Pasha's instructions: retrieve the sword, tug twice, prepare to be hauled up. Understood?

"No," Baruch replied simply. The Pasha became rabid with fury. The interpreters reiterated the instructions.

"I cannot do it," said Baruch. "I cannot and I *will* not." The Pasha's face suffused with scarlet. A vein in his forehead bulged and throbbed.

"You *can,*" he shrieked hysterically. "You *can* and you *will.* Do you not know who I am? I am the Sultan's personal ambassador. My order is the *Sultan's* order. I command you to obey this instant or your miserable, worthless life will come to an immediate and horrible end!"

Baruch was unmoved by the Pasha's rantings. "I am but a humble beadle. I take orders only from the rabbi of the synagogue. If he says I must go down into the well, then so I shall."

The Pasha was beside himself. Never had he heard such insolence! But without the scoundrel's cooperation, all would be lost. He dispatched criers to announce the imminent execution of Baruch the Beadle, and thereby — quite cleverly — lured the rabbi from his own hiding place.

T HE RABBI could not permit the simpleminded *shammas* to be victimized by a ruthless Turk. He sped to the well. The Moslem guides quickly explained the situation and directed the rabbi to instruct Baruch to obey the Pasha's orders.

"No, no, no," the rabbi declared. "This is a holy site and Baruch was correct to refuse. His presence would defile King David's sacred burial place and his punishment would be far more severe than any mortal man could devise." The rabbi pondered the problem for several moments while the Pasha's fury went from red to white.

At last the rabbi emerged from his meditations. "I am not certain that Baruch is the man for the job. He is, well, a simpleton, and the task may demand more wisdom than he possesses. The choice of a messenger should rightly be left to the Almighty and this will be accomplished by the drawing of lots.

"In addition," the rabbi continued, "the individual thus selected must cleanse and purify himself for three days so that he will not desecrate the sanctity of the tomb. On the afternoon of the fourth day, we shall meet again at this location and the mission will be carried out."

For all his fulminating, the Pasha was essentially a spineless blusterer and the thought of antagonizing the Jews' cleric who might be instrumental in saving his sword filled him with dread. At the same time, he dared not expose himself to their ridicule. Therefore, although he had already decided to accede to the rabbi's demands, he assumed an air of contemplation before rendering his decision.

"Granted," the Turk proclaimed, "but let there be no mistake: if you fail to appear in three days' time, woe unto you and your entire community!"

The rabbi and Baruch made a hasty retreat. Before an hour had passed, all the Jews assembled in the courtyard of the shul and were apprised of the calamitous predicament. "We have no recourse," the rabbi announced, "but to appeal to God for deliverance. Let us all fast and spend these days in prayer and supplication.

"On the evening of the third day, lots will be cast among all men over twenty years of age, including myself, and he who is chosen will cleanse and purify himself and present himself before the Pasha."

For three days and three nights the Jews of Jerusalem sought the Almighty's guidance through abnegation and fervent supplication. None abstained from the communal effort, for the ramifications were too awesome to consider. On the third day, the lots were drawn and the rabbi stared in wonder at the name inscribed on the scrap of parchment in his palm: it was none other than Baruch, the *Shammas*.

THERE WAS no collective sigh of relief this time, no expressions of gratitude at having been spared, for everyone present was aware that the fate of the community was linked with Baruch's own. No longer was he merely the town simpleton; the Almighty had selected him for this most dangerous mission and by that very fact was he worthy of their honor and trust.

"You see," the Rebbe told his spellbound chassidim, "this fellow Baruch was a secret tzaddik. *For this reason, the Almighty selected him not once, but twice. Only when the lots were cast did the people begin to grasp the saintliness of the beadle." The Rebbe sipped from his chalice and his eyes glistened as he continued his story.*

After *mincha* on the fourth day, Baruch walked humbly to the *aron kodesh,* embraced the *paroches,* and then departed for the well. There, it seemed, the entire population of Jerusalem had gathered to witness the event. Many faces bore the bloodthirsty expression of those who would delight in the beadle's failure, for the Pasha was certain to exact revenge from the Jews. The more degenerate among them had honed their blades in anticipation of joining in the massacre.

The rabbi approached the Pasha but made no gesture of obeisance. In a firm voice he declared: "This man was appointed to fulfill your mission and he will do so, with the Almighty's help, on condition that he be allowed ample time for the task. Not before sunset may the rope be raised or you will never see your sword again."

"Sunset! How *dare* you..." the Turk spluttered, "of all the temerity...*sunset!*" Hatred added vehemence to his anger. These cursed wretches were making a mockery of him before thousands of witnesses, he thought, but what alternative was there? How else could he regain his precious

sword? "So be it," he roared, "but if he fails, the streets of Jerusalem will run with rivers of Jewish blood!"

Baruch was lowered into the well and the noise of the crowd rose to an uproar. Wagering was heavy both in favor of and against his success and several resourceful entrepreneurs made fortunes selling mementos of the occasion. A tent was pitched to shelter the Pasha from the merciless Mediterranean sun and trays of grapes and flasks of wine were brought to quench his thirst. Musicians and jugglers, magicians and conjurers entertained the envoy throughout the long afternoon and all the while the Jews prayed for salvation.

When the sun sank below the horizon, the raucous crowd fell silent. Torches were lit and the Pasha positioned himself at the edge of the well to await the signal. The rope-haulers had been relieved hourly by replacement troops, but none had reported so much as a twitch or a quiver on the line.

The Pasha clapped his hands together twice and the soldiers began hauling in the rope. The crowd vibrated with excitement. Suddenly, the line came free of the stone lip and there, glittering in the torchlight, was the Pasha's jewel-encrusted sword, tied to the end of the rope with a careless knot.

Baruch was nowhere to be seen.

THE CROWD CHEERED ecstatically, although many had lost tidy sums in the wagering and others were denied the satisfaction of their blood-lust. But the Jews were horror-stricken. What had befallen poor Baruch, the *Shammas*, they asked one another in vain. They called his name into the well, but their cries were answered only with echoes. They relowered the rope, hoping the beadle would grab hold, but their efforts proved futile.

The Pasha, overjoyed at the return of his cherished treasure, promptly forgot about the Jews and their role in its retrieval. Exhausted by the day's events, he and his retinue retired to their quarters and the crowd soon dispersed. Still Baruch had not reappeared.

Five Jews stationed themselves at the well to man the rope, in the event that the *shammas* should signal, and the rest repaired to the synagogue to pray for Baruch.

The Rebbe tossed a handful of arbes *into his mouth and chewed them thoughtfully. "Rebbe," a young chassid cried anxiously, "what became of Baruch? A* tzaddik *such as he had to give his life to salvage the plaything of a* soneh Yisrael?!"

"My son," the Rebbe said with infinite patience, "Baruch didn't save the Pasha's sword, he saved the Jewish community." The chassid's gaze fell to his lap in embarrassment. "And who said the shammas *died?"*

When the Jews reached the synagogue, they were utterly astonished to find their Baruch hard at work, setting up the chairs. It was a miracle!

"What...? How...? Where...?" they gasped, crowding around the *shammas,* but Baruch only raised his hand and clapped it down upon the *shulchan,* crying *"Maariv, maariv!"* Surely there was cause for rejoicing, but the evening service took precedence. The congregants recited prayers of thanksgiving for Baruch's and their own redemption and deferred the satisfaction of their curiosity until after *maariv.*

Upon completion of the service, however, Baruch pointedly occupied himself with arranging the tables for the rabbi's *shiur* and the people understood that the *shammas* had no intention of revealing his secret. On many occasions after that, individuals or groups would approach him with burning questions, but each time Baruch suddenly became too busy to reply. After a time, they stopped asking.

U NTIL HIS DYING DAY, Baruch guarded the secret, but when he lay upon his death bed, the urge to unburden himself became irresistible. He summoned the *Chevra Kadisha* and in their presence recounted the amazing incident of years and years before. Although few of the assembled were old enough to have witnessed the event, there was not a single Jew in all of Jerusalem — or perhaps in all of Israel — who was unaware of what had happened at the site of King David's well.

But not a single Jew in all of Jerusalem — or anywhere on this earth — knew what had transpired *inside* King David's well...save Baruch.

"When I reached the bottom of the shaft," he began, his voice weary with age, "I noticed a tunnel leading away from where I stood. At the far end of the long, winding path, I spied a dim light, so I unfastened the rope and headed in that direction.

"The light, I discovered, was coming from a lamp imbedded in a niche in the wall, and the tunnel widened at its end to form a sort of anteroom. There seemed to be another chamber beyond that, a much larger one, I sensed, although I was unable to see into it as the light was quite weak.

"Now, in this anteroom was a small table and upon the table stood a basin, a pitcher of water and a clean, fresh towel. Other than these things, the room was virtually empty.

"I lifted the lamp from its niche and stepped to the

connecting doorway, holding the light so that it illuminated the room beyond. The sight my eyes beheld was too amazing to be believed. I crossed the threshold to get a better look and there before me was an enormous bed with a great fur coverlet."

The *shammas* hitched his wasted body higher on the pillows, but then a violent coughing fit seized him, and the *Chevra Kadisha* feared his life would end before his revelations were concluded. However, the *shammas* went on.

"I TOOK ANOTHER STEP forward and raised the lamp. There was a figure in the bed, a most elegantly clad, sleeping figure, in robes of the finest weave. And his head was adorned with a small gold crown.

"As I stood gaping at this eerie apparition, he suddenly thrust out his hands over the edge of the bed. There was no mistaking the loose-fisted gesture: it was the posture of one awaiting ablution. I was speechless, but could not refrain from complying with the regal figure's unspoken request. I threw the towel over my shoulder, snatched the basin and pitcher, and hurried to his bedside.

"I had positioned the basin beneath his fists and was just about to pour the water over his hands when all at once I received a stunning blow to my arm. The pitcher went flying and smashed to pieces against the wall.

"I turned in horror to find an elderly man towering over me, a man with a long, flowing beard and fire in his eyes. 'What are you doing?!' he demanded. I was never so terrified in all my life. I stammered my reply, that I was merely washing the fellow's hands, for he had indicated that he wished I do so.

"The old man became even more irate. 'It is forbidden!' he bellowed at me and his voice echoed loudly in the hollow chamber. 'How did you get here? This place is not for people like you!' he declared, and as his anger grew, so did my fear.

I N AN INSTANT, though, his fury subsided, to be replaced by a kindly, almost fatherly smile. 'No matter,' he said, 'the mere fact that you *are* here, and alive, is a sign that you are no ordinary being.' I assure you, at that moment, I felt the most ordinary urge to faint. 'Nevertheless,' he continued, 'you must leave at once!' Nothing would have pleased me more.

"Then I remembered my mission and somehow found the courage to explain that I could not return without the Pasha's sword lest the Jews of Jerusalem suffer a dire fate. He nodded and said the matter would be seen to. And all this time, the sleeping figure slept on, undisturbed

"The old man then led me through a labyrinth of tunnels and passageways until we reached a crevice in the rock. I could see starlight there. He told me I must leave through that crevice and never return, that I must not look back but walk two hundred paces in a straight line away from the exit, and only then might I return home."

The telling of the story exacted a high price of the dying *shammas*. His eyelids fluttered and his breathing became labored. The end was very near, but he could not depart from this world before completing his tale. The *Chevra Kadisha* members edged closer to Baruch; his voice was nearly inaudible.

"I slipped through the narrow crevice," he whispered, "and found myself a great distance from the city. I had not taken ten paces when suddenly the earth beneath my feet began to shake. The force hurled me to the ground. I could hear and feel a deep rumbling below the surface.

"I knew then that the paths to that mysterious chamber had been sealed off and that no other eyes would see what mine had seen." And with those words, the *shammas* breathed his final breath.

"Oy," the Rebbe sighed wistfully. "If only... if only..."

"Yes, Rebbe?" the chassidim encouraged.

"If only Baruch, the tzaddik *had disregarded the old man's instructions – but of course he could not. The man might have been... Eliyahu Hanavi. But if Baruch had completed the act of washing the King's hands, who can say? It might have hastened the arrival of the Messiah." The Rebbe began to sway with the rhythm of the niggun in his head. With his eyes closed, he pounded the table and once more the room resounded with the strains of an ancient song.*

"Achakeh lo," *they sang,* "achakeh lo," *and their rejoicing was mingled with tears.*

Look Not
Upon the Flask

ince the two great Rebbes were honored guests at the *chassanah,* they could allow themselves certain liberties, and as the entertainer had thrice dropped the bottles he was juggling and was more than likely to burn the town down with the lighted paper cone he was trying to balance on his nose, they withdrew to a quiet, safer corner of the square. The waiter was signalled and a fresh quart was brought to their table.

"I have a daughter, you know," said the Amdinover as he filled his colleague's glass.

"So I've heard," the Brezhinover replied, lifting his drink in salute. "A *ba'alas chessed.* And a wonderful *balabusta.*"

The Amdinover drained his glass and refilled it. "That she is," he said, "and more. You have a son, yes?"

The *Klezmer* were off-key and overloud, but with the conversation taking so serious a turn, neither of the Rebbes appeared disturbed. A group of heavy-footed dancers lurched past their table bearing the white-faced *chassan* aloft in a singularly graceless pose. "Look not upon the flask," the Brezhinover remarked, "but upon its contents."

His learned companion considered this somewhat irrelevant Mishnaic comment for a moment. Surely, he thought, the Rebbe had not referred to the truly vile concoction they were imbibing; neither the flask *nor* its contents were noteworthy, except perhaps, for their common vulgarity. He inferred, therefore, that the remark related to the pallid *chassan,* a boy who was known to have difficulty holding his *Gemara* the right way around and who looked now, on the night of his wedding, more like a sacrificial lamb than a happy bridegroom. Perhaps, the Rebbe concluded, there was more to this young fellow than met the eye.

But this was of no interest, not when the subject at hand concerned a union between the two greatest chassidic houses in all of Europe. He steered the conversation back on course. "I've heard your son is a great *talmid chacham,*" he said, "an *ilui.*" He knew he was overstating the case, but the stakes were very high. The Brezhinover raised an eyebrow. With that one small word, his colleague had, perhaps knowingly, substantially raised the price of the dowry. Negotiations now began in earnest.

The level of liquor in the bottle had descended to a point just above the false bottom by the time the terms of the *shidduch* were agreed upon and the Rebbes were both immensely pleased with the bargain they had struck. They drank a final "*le'chaim*" to seal the agreement, clapped one another heartily on the shoulder, and, offering their warmest blessings to the *mechutanim,* hastily departed for home.

IN EVERY SHTETL, in every corner of Europe, the upcoming wedding between the son of the Brezhinover and the daughter of the Amdinover became front page news, so to speak. The thought of uniting the two most esteemed courts flamed imaginations and kindled hopes for the *Geulah*. It would be the affair of a lifetime, the gossips proclaimed, nay — the affair of the century! Every member of chassidic nobility was sure to attend, and it was rumored that the *Tzaddik* of Sassov *bich'vodo u've'atzmo* would officiate.

"I heard from my cousin Mottel, the son-in-law of the baker of Amdinov," reported one of the more reliable tale bearers, "that two thousand loaves of challah have been ordered, and a cake more than two meters high!"

"My great-aunt's dressmaker's assistant," pronounced another, "has been sewing pearls onto the lace of the *kallah's* gown for two months without respite. She says there must be as many pearls on the gown as there are in the Sea of Japan!"

The grapevine relayed word that not a cow nor calf would remain in all of the Austro-Hungarian empire after the *shechting* was done for the bridal feast. The most trustworthy butchers and cooks were being brought in from five major cities. Orchards were being picked clean of fruit for miles around. Trainloads of wine and whiskey were already en route from the most reputable vineyards and refineries.

"It is said," whispered an itinerant peddler from Grodsk, "that the wedding gifts thus far received are greater in value than the combined treasure houses of Franz-Josef and Tsar Nikolai! And the presents have only *begun* to arrive!"

For once, it seemed, the rumor-mongers had not exaggerated.

A S THE DAY of the great *chassanah* neared, excitement rose to a fevered pitch. In the shtetls, it was enough for a humble villager to have *touched* one of the honored invitees for him to be endowed with glory. "Reb Shmelke gave me a kopek to shine his boots for the wedding!" an old cobbler announced proudly. "Ooh," his audience moaned ecstatically. "Aahh," they cried, "ah sguleh!"

But none enjoyed more adulation than Huddel the sheitel-macher who had personally laid eyes on the kallah. "Mere words cannot describe such beauty," she gushed. "An artist could not do her justice."

"It is a match made in heaven," said Yuske the melamed. "The Rebbe's son was a child prodigy and has grown to become such an outstanding Torah scholar that even misnagdim run to ask him shailos!"

"The offspring of this union will be doubly blessed," predicted Yentl the midwife, whose oracular pronouncements were rarely off the mark. "They will have their mother's face and their father's brains!"

Only one cynical misanthrope dared to point out that the bride and groom had never met. "What a farce!" he chuckled derisively. "They might despise one another on sight!"

He only just escaped with his life.

BECAUSE OF THE GREAT DISTANCE that separated the towns of Amdinov and Brezhinov, this not-insignificant matter had indeed been neglected. Of course the chassan-kallah were unlikely to defy their fathers' express wishes; still it was customary — indeed halachically mandated — for the prospective bride and groom to be introduced at some time before the solemn moment, even if only as a formality. Provision was therefore made for the two young people to meet eight days prior to the wedding.

But, as it is said, "Man toils; God foils," and the train carrying the youthful *chassan* was derailed many kilometers from Ovinsk, where a coach that was to take him to Amdinov awaited. Fortunately, there were no injuries, although the delay cost the groom and his party three days traveling time. And when the train at last pulled into the station at Ovinsk, the coach was nowhere to be found.

A wagon and driver were hired — the only available transport in Ovinsk — and the *chassan* and his family hastily boarded, knowing full well that the rag-tag conveyance would make a somewhat undignified entrance at Amdinov. Still, it couldn't be helped. Were they to await the return of the coach, they might be forced to spend Shabbos among total strangers; moreover, they could not allow any further delay. Time-honored custom forbade encounters between bride and groom during the week prior to the *chassanah*, and, as it was, they were far behind schedule.

Outside a remote village some two days' ride from Amdinov, the wagon lost a wheel and the only wheelwright in that town was a drunkard sleeping off the previous evening's bender. "Like clay beneath the potter's hand, thus man conforms to God's command," it is written, and clearly God had not intended for the groom's journey to be uneventful. By the time the wagon was roadworthy once again, yet another two days had come and gone, and the *chassan* arrived only minutes before his own *chassanah*.

The thousands of invited guests, notables and townspeople, were in a most agitated state when the driver reined in the horses in the center of the village square. Although riders had been sent on ahead to convey the message of the *chassan's* unfortunate delay to the *kallah's* anxious family, tension had been mounting with every passing hour. The bridegroom's arrival was therefore greeted with uninhibited cheering and jubilation.

The bride, dressed in a gown the exquisiteness of which outshone even the gossip's description, hurried to the window of the upstairs parlor. As she watched, her *chassan's* baggage was lowered from the wagon, his family members were helped from their seats, and finally, the young man himself alit. All at once, a look of horror came over the bride's lovely features and her hand flew to her lips in dismay. She spun on her delicate heels, lifted her frothy lace skirts and ran from the room.

WORD OF THE *KALLAH'S* refusal to go through with the ceremony spread as swiftly as the wagging tongues could carry it. Delegations of sisters, cousins and aunts were dispatched to appeal to her through her locked bedroom door, but their pleas fell on deaf ears. The bride's anguished sobbing was all the response they received. Even aging Tante Shprintza, who had travelled for the occasion all the way from Reisha, could not coax her grandniece out of the boudoir.

Down in the square, pandemonium reigned. The *mechutanim* tried desperately to bear the disgrace in a manner befitting Rebbes of their stature, but it was all too apparent that a scandal could not be avoided unless drastic measures were taken to rectify the situation. The *kallah's* refusal to go through with the *shidduch* was unfathomable, not to mention inexcusable! Nowhere in the Empire could she hope to find a young man of finer virtue or nobler character. At last, the Amdinover himself went to petition his recalcitrant daughter.

"You deceived me!" the young woman cried when her father knocked.

"Deceived you?!" the Rebbe exclaimed, genuinely surprised. "How can you say that? Is the Brezhinover's son and heir not a great *talmid chacham*? Is he not a *ba'al midos*? Is he not destined for greatness?"

"Yes, *Tatteh*, he is all those things," the bride conceded through a veil of tears, "and he is also *lame*! Nothing you could say would make me marry a *cripple*!"

Only the bridegroom, that unequalled *ben Torah*, that present *ilui* and future *gadol*, received her rebuff with equanimity. Over the raucous din of the crowd, he called for silence. "I must be allowed to speak with the *kallah* myself," he said, and several female guests swooned.

It was unheard of! That the *chassan* and *kallah* should meet during the wedding week was nearly as scandalous as the last-minute cancellation of the nuptials itself! Reputations had been destroyed over less brazen acts. Despite this, and after a lengthy consultation, the Rebbes granted their permission.

W HEN THE *KALLAH* unlocked the door of her room, she was thunderstruck to find her rejected suitor standing alone on the threshold. She covered her tear-stained face in shame — as much at the humiliation of having been betrothed to a cripple, as at her own disgraceful behavior.

"I have come to tell you something important," the *chassan* said gently, but the *kallah's* mortification knew no bounds. She began to weep again, deep tortured cries, and the *chassan* waited patiently for her sobbing to subside.

At last, red-eyed but composed, the beautiful *kallah* lowered her hands and forced herself to look upon the boy whom she had so mercilessly spurned.

"Matches are not made on earth," the young man began, "but in the corridors of Heaven. The Talmud relates that forty days before the creation of a child, a voice from Above proclaims: 'This daughter of so-and-so shall wed so-and-so.'" The bride nodded mutely, knowing he spoke the truth.

"Forty days before the birth of my match, a vision came to me," the *chassan* continued. "In it, I learned that my *kallah* would be not only a woman of valor but the daughter of an illustrious family. She would be a *ba'alas chessed* and would raise our children to be God-fearing. And..." He paused to allow the impact of his next words to penetrate, "... she would be lame."

"But-but..." the bride stammered in confusion. The bridegroom went on. "When I learned that my *kallah* would suffer such a fate, I cried bitter tears — not for myself, but for this unfortunate girl whose entire life would be marred by a deformity.

"I fasted and prayed with all my heart that *I* be the one to receive this decree, that the deformity should be *mine* and not hers. And *baruch Hashem*, my fervent prayers were answered."

The wedding of the House of Amdinov and the House of Brezhinov took place, *b'sha'a tova u'mutzlachas*, right on schedule.

three on allegiance

...וְנֶפֶשׁ יְהוֹנָתָן נִקְשְׁרָה בְּנֶפֶשׁ דָּוִד
וַיֶּאֱהָבֵהוּ יְהוֹנָתָן כְּנַפְשׁוֹ.
שמואל א : יח:א

❧ ...the soul of Yehonasan was bound
to the soul of David, and Yehonasan
loved him as his own soul.

Samuel I 18:1

One-and-a-Half Friends

AV NISSIM was worried about his son. Or rather about the company his son was keeping. Saadya seemed to gravitate to the most disreputable of his contemporaries. His friends were rowdy, disobedient, and a terrible influence. Patiently, Rav Nissim tried to explain that friendship is more than just companionship, that it is one heart in two bodies. And that the cement of a long-term relationship is equality. If a "friend" is interested only in the personal gain he can derive from the relationship, he went on, then the friendship becomes a charade.

"My son, heed my words. Such 'friends' will only bring you down, for you will become like your associates."

But Saadya refused to listen to his father. His friends, he insisted, were genuine and caring. They did not take advantage of his generous nature and they would never hesitate to assist him if he needed their help.

"**I** WONDER," said Rav Nissim. "You boast about your many friends, and I have but one-and-a-half friends. But among all of your friends, I doubt that any would pass the test of true friendship!"

"Then, Father, put them to the test and you will see that they will demonstrate their fidelity."

"Very well. Only when one is truly in need can friendship be accurately tested. We shall see."

Rav Nissim pondered a moment and then went to the pantry. He returned with a large gourd and a pot of thick red elderberry sauce. Saadya watched him in bewilderment as he poured the sauce over the gourd and placed it in a canvas sack. "Now then," said Rav Nissim, giving the sack to Saadya. "Here is what you must do..."

Late that night, Saadya walked stealthily to the house of one of his closest friends carrying the sack through which the viscous fluid was beginning to seep.

He knocked furtively on the door of his best friend. "It's me — Saadya," he whispered. "Don't be alarmed." The door opened a crack.

"Saadya! What are you doing here at this hour? Do you know what time it is?"

"I am here because I need your help, dear friend. I have just murdered the son of the Mayor of Constantinople and I am seeking refuge. The police are surely already searching for the assailant, and here — look! — I have his head."

The friend took one glance at the gruesome-looking sack and Saadya sensed the door, still only slightly open, begin to close. "Saadya, you know that I am your friend," he said hesitantly, "but harboring a murderer, well, that is simply too dangerous. The authorities might accuse me of being an accomplice and jail me for life. I'm very sorry," he blurted out and quickly shut the door. Saadya heard the bolt being rammed home.

DISILLUSIONED, SAADYA TURNED to his next friend, who lived two streets away. He knocked on the door. "It's me — Saadya. Please let me in, quickly. I'm in terrible trouble."

"What have you got there? It is saturated with blood!"

"This," Saadya whispered, "is the head of the Mayor's son. Hurry, let me in. They're looking for me."

"I... I... I'm glad that you killed that scoundrel, but what if the police trace you to here? What about my wife and children? How can I jeopardize their future? I hope you understand, Saadya." The door slammed shut

One after the other, Saadya put his "friends" to the test. Each expressed regret at his perilous predicament, but not one was willing to open his door and offer his wholehearted assistance. Saadya was crushed.

His only comfort as he returned despondently home was the thought that if his own friends had let him down, surely his father's friends, even if they be only "one-and-a-half", would have behaved no differently. But his father disagreed.

Now it was Saadya's turn to throw down the challenge: "Who are these one-and-a-half friends of yours? Let's see if they would act any differently."

"My one friend doesn't live here," replied his father. "In Constantinople I only have my half friend, but you may try him if you wish."

THAT VERY NIGHT, just a few hours before sunrise, Saadya set out for the house of his father's half friend. He knocked loudly on the door and woke up the elderly fellow.

"Who is it?" came a sleepy grunt from the window.

"It is Saadya, the son of Rav Nissim, the Rabbi of Constantinople."

The man came to the door in the gloomy pre-dawn. "What do you want?" he asked.

"I have just killed the son of the Mayor," said Saadya, displaying the bag which now appeared thoroughly bloody. "I need a place to hide for the night."

"I shouldn't do this," said the man, shooting surreptitious glances out into the darkness, and at the same time, drawing Saadya into his home. "But you are Rav Nissim's son. Do you realize that what you did could cause a pogrom against the Jews of this country? Here, come, you can sleep in this bed. But first let's get rid of the evidence."

Saadya returned home humbled. "You were right, my Father, but why do you call such an intimate acquaintance only a 'half friend?'"

"This man let you into his house, but he said that he shouldn't have. A full friend would never say that."

"Then I must meet your 'whole friend.' Who is he?"

"As I said, my 'whole' friend doesn't live here. I have not seen him for many years. His name is Aziz Elfandri, and he works in a bank in Alexandria."

"It doesn't matter where he lives. I must meet him. Please, I don't care how long a trip is involved."

"I am glad, my son, that you now have an idea what a true

friend is. If you will make up your mind never to mix with such associates as yours in the future, then I will be happy to send you to my friend. But I must insist on one condition: I am sure that you will be well taken care of in Alexandria, but I ask that you give me your word that you will return within a year."

Saadya agreed, and one week later, after bidding his family farewell, he set out on the long and arduous trip to Alexandria. He travelled light, and all he had to help him find his destination was a name and an address.

S AADYA DISCOVERED that his father's information was not completely correct. His father's friend did, indeed, work in a bank in Alexandria, but he was actually far more than an ordinary bank official.

In the middle of the morning he arrived at Aziz Elfandri's bank address. It was an imposing, sprawling, white stuccoed building, in the very center of town. Saadya entered and asked if his father's friend was in. The receptionist answered that Mr. Elfandri was in the middle of an important meeting. He certainly could not be disturbed. Elfandri, as it turned out, was a banker's banker — one of the wealthiest and most successful in all of Egypt. Financiers and merchants came to him from all over the area to do business with him and seek his advice.

"Whom shall I say is calling? Which bank do you represent?" asked the receptionist courteously.

"My name is Saadya, the son of Rabbi Nissim of Constantinople."

"Well then, I will let him know you are here, but I imagine that you will have to wait until late next week for an appointment."

A minute later, Saadya saw the door of the conference room fly open and heard a man announce "meeting adjourned." An elegantly attired man rushed toward him with an outstretched hand. "I am Aziz Elfandri. I'm delighted to meet you."

"Why, you didn't have to disturb your meeting just for me!" said Saadya.

"What are you talking about! You are my friend's son — I would do *anything* for him. Let me take you to my house and give you something to eat."

Elfandri strode out of his office, one hand protectively around Saadya, the other gesturing to all of the secretaries who tried to catch his attention to pass on messages. He brought Saadya to his luxurious mansion, and soon, the two were sitting down to a sumptuous meal. Then Elfandri showed Saadya to an elegant room. "These will be your quarters for as long as you care to stay. But now," said the gracious host, "you must rest. I will be right here waiting for you when you awake."

THAT AFTERNOON Elfandri took Saadya on a tour of Alexandria. He spared no expense and lavished his young guest with gifts and souvenirs. At dinner that evening, Saadya was informed in no uncertain terms that the entire Elfandri household was at his disposal. "Do not hesitate to make any request that will make your stay more comfortable," his host insisted.

Then Aziz Elfandri announced that he was taking an entire week off work to spend time with Saadya, to keep him company and to ensure that everything would be to his satisfaction. After a week of wondrous entertainment and thrilling excursions, Elfandri took Saadya aside to speak to him. Very apologetically, he explained that although he would gladly abandon his work indefinitely if he could in order to attend to the needs of his friend's son, the demands of business required that he return to his office. He requested Saadya's permission to do so, but said he would willingly extend his leave of absence if his guest so wished.

Saadya replied that he was quite overwhelmed by the hospitality that had been extended to him. The last thing he wanted was for his host's business to suffer. As for the reason for his trip — to appreciate the meaning of true friendship — he had already seen more than he felt capable of comprehending. Nonetheless, he was in no hurry to leave the company of his father's friend.

"I shall go back to work now," Elfandri told him the next morning, "but I want to leave you the keys to my house — you are after all the son of my friend and therefore all that is mine is yours. Feel free to explore any room you please."

During the day, Saadya wandered through the house matching the keys to the seemingly endless number of rooms. Fascinated by the treasures he uncovered, he spent many hours in one room filled with globes and maps of distant lands, and in another decorated with antique paintings.

When Elfandri returned from work that evening, he asked Saadya about the things he had seen that day. Saadya described his discoveries and Elfandri set about explaining where and how he had acquired the many priceless treasures.

The next day, Saadya resumed his tour of the rooms. He discovered a room full of intricately carved toys and elaborate games; another hung with fine silks and tapestries. Yet another contained ornate religious items. And once again, after Elfandri came home, Saadya described the discoveries he had made that day.

By the end of the week, Saadya had inspected every room in the house — except one. There was one key for which he could not find a door. Saadya was sure that he had explored the house thoroughly, and so his curiosity was aroused. He scoured the house for the door he must have missed. Once, twice, he went through the house, and still he found no room which the key would unlock.

He was about to give up his search when suddenly he detected it — cleverly camouflaged in the woodwork but unmistakable once discovered: a tiny keyhole. If he had not scrutinized every inch of the house so carefully, he would surely never have spotted it. He tried the final key in the lock and the door opened instantly.

HE DID NOT KNOW what to expect, but he was totally unprepared for the sight that greeted him. For there before his eyes lay a beautiful little garden enclosed by a high stone wall. Now Saadya's curiosity was really piqued.

He examined the garden carefully, wondering why it should be so well-protected. Then he noticed a small hole close to the top of the stone wall. Saadya clambered up the wall and peered through. What he saw took his breath away. Beyond the small garden was yet another garden, this one much larger with a vast green lawn enclosed by a high fence. And in the center of this verdant splendor stood a small house.

Just then, the door to the house opened and several school-age girls came running out to play in the garden. For many hours Saadya stood watching in wonder. He could hardly believe his eyes.

That evening, Aziz Elfandri asked him once again how he had spent his day and what he had discovered. Saadya remained silent. Elfandri immediately understood the silence. "I see that you have found the room which leads to the garden." Saadya nodded his head. "Did you see anything move?" Elfandri asked somewhat nervously.

Saadya nodded again. "As it happens," he said, "through the hole in the far wall I was able to see into the next garden."

Elfandri looked at Saadya directly: "What else did you see?" he asked.

"I saw girls coming out of the house in the center of the lawn."

F OR SOME TIME, Elfandri sat in silent thought, then he looked up suddenly as though he had made a difficult decision. "Since you are my friend's son," he said, "I cannot hold anything back from you. The origin of that house, or rather school, goes back many years. It goes back to a time when we were extremely poor, so poor that we had hardly anything to eat, and our children cried out regularly from hunger.

"One *erev Shabbos*, we didn't have a morsel to eat. Usually, we were somehow able to put something on the table for Shabbos, either by borrowing or by receiving some hand-outs. But that week the table was empty. I cannot describe to you how sad and despondent we were. We sat and cried. We did not know where to turn.

"Then my wife went to the chest of drawers and took out the diamond earrings she had received as an inheritance from her grandmother. 'Take these,' she said, 'and see what you can get for them. We have no choice.' I protested. 'These are heirlooms,' I said, 'not something we can sell.' But she insisted. 'We have no alternative,' she said. 'Hurry, it is *erev Shabbos* and there is much for you to buy.'

"The diamond earrings actually had more than sentimental value. Before I became involved in banking, I was a diamond appraiser by profession, and I knew precisely how much those earrings were worth. I was also well aware that I would not be getting anything near their real value in my Friday afternoon rush.

"I was walking dejectedly towards the center of town when I was suddenly accosted by a burly sailor with a little girl at his side. 'Jew!' he yelled. I turned toward him and he gestured at the little girl. 'She is a Jew, and I am giving you the last chance to redeem her from me. I asked the other Jews I came across in this town and no one was willing to pay for her. If you don't come up with the money right now I am going to throw her into the sea.'

"**A**T FIRST I TREMBLED at the thought, for I didn't have any money. And then I realized that I was carrying my wife's diamond earrings in my hand. I knew that my wife would be beside herself if, instead of bringing home the desperately needed food, I brought home another mouth to feed. But what else could I do?

"So I gave the pirate the two diamond earrings. He examined them and then handed the girl over to me. I hadn't taken more than three steps with my new ward when a stranger rushed over to me: 'Do you know where I can find an appraiser of diamonds at this hour? I am in a great hurry.'

"'I am an appraiser,' I told him, 'but I charge for my services.'

"'It doesn't matter,' replied the stranger, 'I must know exactly how much these diamonds are worth — right now.'

"I looked at the diamonds and told him their exact value. I was also able to tell him precisely where he would be able to get the highest price for them and where he should avoid selling them.

"The fellow paid me handsomely for my appraisal and advice, and just as I was recounting once again the blessed money he had given me, another man who had overheard our conversation came over to me and also asked for an appraisal. The stream of clients didn't stop. I appraised the value of each of their diamonds and told them exactly where they should go in order to sell them. Some of them would profit nicely from the local market; I suggested to others that they sell their diamonds abroad.

"I returned home just a few minutes before candle-lighting, but my arms were laden with groceries — and I had a lot of money left over. As soon as Shabbos ended, people began knocking on my door, asking me to evaluate their diamonds. By the time the week was over, I had amassed a small fortune. It was clear that this little girl had brought us an auspicious change of *mazel*.

"We took good care of her, and God took good care of us. I became so wealthy appraising diamonds that I became a financial consultant, and after a number of years, I had become a banker's banker — with clients throughout the Middle East.

"But we had one problem. The little girl we had adopted had grown to be inordinately beautiful. And in the course of time her beauty presented us with a very serious dilemma.

"She was so attractive we felt that we could not expose her to the local populace — we feared for her safety. But on the other hand, we had no idea how to protect her. That is, until we thought of creating a complete, miniature society for her. We had the financial means to achieve it, and after all, we owed all we had to her.

"It was simply unfair to keep her secluded from other

children so we decided to build in the garden a school for her, attended by classmates her own age. The whole project, of course, is a closely-guarded secret, and were it not for the fact that you are my friend's son, I would never have revealed it to you."

FROM THEN ON Saadya was able to pass freely through all the doors in the house and no room or garden was closed to him. After some weeks, he approached Elfandri and told him what was on his mind. "I wish to marry the girl," he said simply.

Elfandri and his wife were delighted. They had grown to love Saadya, and this would also solve the problem of marrying their ward without revealing their secret.

Saadya sent word of the news to his parents. He knew that they would not be able to make the long and gruelling journey, but he was sure that they would be happy to hear that he was marrying the adopted daughter of his father's best friend.

Not long after the wedding, Saadya remembered his pledge to his father that he would return to Constantinople within a year. The Elfandris' were disappointed to hear that he was leaving, but they would do nothing to dissuade him from fulfilling his promise to his father.

The parting was very sad, for the Elfandris could not imagine life without the young couple. But the departure of the young couple was not the only adjustment that the Elfandris had to make in their lives.

NO SOONER HAD SAADYA and his new wife left them, than the wheel of fortune began to turn once again. Elfandri's banking enterprise began to lose customers and his assets plummeted in value. One day, he realized he could no longer pay his workers' salaries.

Daily the situation grew worse. Within a short time he was forced to sell both his office and his mansion. Elfandri, once again, had a hard time putting food on the table. Incredibly, it seemed, their *mazel* had left them along with their adopted daughter.

Mrs. Elfandri insisted that her husband write to his friend in Constantinople. "You must ask him to bring the girl back," she urged. "Or at least to send us something in return for all we gave him." But her husband would not hear of it. "Saadya and his father are my friends," he said, "and I would never take advantage of their friendship."

But his wife insisted, and her demands were bolstered by their dire financial straits. Under mounting pressure he finally decided to compromise: he did not actually write the letter she had wanted, but he attempted to convey his predicament in vague hints and cryptic terms.

Life had not been the same since she had left, he wrote, and both he and his wife had lost a lot of weight. They seemed to be wearing the same clothes all the time now, he added, and they had moved to more intimate and less expensive surroundings.

The Elfandris never received a response to their letter. Although Mrs. Elfandri pressed her husband to write again, and this time make a very explicit appeal, her husband refused. He was confident that he would receive some kind of response soon from his friend. But he was mistaken.

Mrs. Elfandri had heard more than enough from her husband about how inappropriate it was to ask a favor from a friend, and she demanded that he travel to Constantinople immediately to seek the relief they needed — and deserved. Elfandri vehemently opposed making the trip. But gradually, his wife's pleas and his hardships eroded his opposition.

Wearing a ragged suit — the only one he still owned — and carrying no other possessions, Elfandri set out on the long trip. As soon as he arrived in Constantinople, hungry and desperate, he went directly to meet his close friend. Elfandri stood hesitantly on the doorstep. Only his sorrowful plight and urgent need helped him overcome his greatest shame: having to beg assistance from his friend.

HE KNOCKED ON the door of the Rabbi's house, told the attendant who he was and asked to be allowed in. A few minutes later, the attendant returned. His master, he said, was not at home. Elfandri was astonished. After the rigors of his journey, it took all his willpower to control himself. He turned from the door and stumbled away. It just cannot be, he thought.

As evening fell, Elfandri knocked once again on the door to the Rabbi's house. The Rabbi was still away, said the attendant. He walked away from the house and sat down on a park bench. He simply had nowhere else to go or to spend the night. Alone and bedraggled, with hopelessness and despair written in the lines of his ashen face, Elfandri could hardly bear to contemplate the bleak future. What troubled him above all else were the thoughts of resentment he could not help but feel towards Rav Nissim whose son he had so welcomed into his home.

Rav Nissim too was having thoughts about his friend, but these were thoughts of aching sympathy and concern for his plight. As he peered out from behind the curtains of the first-floor window of his house at the despondent figure of Elfandri slumped on a bench in the nearby park, he had to restrain himself from running out to embrace him. But he had made his arrangements and knew what he had to do to save his friend the embarrassment of begging charity.

Try as he might, Elfandri could find no glimmer of promise to brighten his prospects. Finally he decided that rather than harbor the tormenting thoughts of his friend's betrayal, he would go to the great synagogue to seek solace in prayer. Spurred on by the hope that penitence might bring relief, he strode swiftly towards the imposing edifice.

A S HE CLIMBED DOWN the synagogue steps, his attention was drawn to a furious argument between two men standing nearby. The argument was over the value of a diamond, and the men did not seem to mind if anyone overheard.

Elfandri walked down from the steps and told them that he could ascertain the exact value of the diamond and tell them where they could get the best price for it.

The men took him up on his offer and were highly impressed by his obvious expertise. They paid him a generous fee and promised to recommend him to others. Before long, a stream of men were lining up to have their diamonds appraised. In a matter of hours, Elfandri's empty pockets were filled with money.

A feeling of elation filled his soul. He walked into a clothing store and purchased a new suit, glad to be rid of the rags which he had been reduced to wearing. And with his self-respect restored, he decided once more, although he no longer needed assistance from his friend, to visit the Rabbi of Constantinople.

Elfandri knocked on the door and Rav Nissim himself joyfully ushered his *whole* friend in. Saadya and his wife greeted Elfandri with surprise and joy. He could not restrain his excitement at seeing his friend again and told him of his stroke of luck, unaware of the role Rav Nissim had played in arranging the scenario that had gotten the wheel of fortune spinning once again. Rav Nissim smiled, happy that Aziz Elfandri would never be embarrassed by knowing of his debt to his whole and caring friend.

Out of the Woods

THEY HAD KNOWN each other all their lives. From childhood days spent in the *cheder* of their small Ukranian shtetl, Hersh and Nosson were the best of friends. Even when forced by necessity to abandon their studies and help their fathers eke out a living harvesting rented fields, they were inseparable.

Side by side they often toiled in the late summer sun, perspiration pouring from their brows and dripping down their short *payos*. But what was heard from the fields where Hersh and Nosson worked was not the grunts and groans of physical labor, but the sing-song learning of the *Mishnayos* they knew by heart. Self-appointed *chevrusos* at a precociously early age, the two pledged that neither the sowing of seeds, nor the harvesting of potatoes, nor even the coming of the Cossacks would deter them from their mission of immersing themselves in Torah.

It was precisely this shared quixotic nature that precipitated their enrollment in the Novardok yeshiva. What else could have caused them to undertake such a *nissayon* so willingly? Even the youngest *bochur* in the most remote yeshiva had heard awesome tales of the great demands of Novardok, not to mention the deplorable conditions, and the ascetic regimen. The *Rosh Yeshiva* was known for encouraging his disciples to subsist on but a single meal each day. One wondered if this insistence was respected more because of the absence of any alternative than for its idealistic roots.

But if tenacity was needed in order to live up to Reb Yoizel's* standards in suppressing material desires, his spiritual demands required even more than that. Woe to the student whose spiritual appetite allowed itself to be sated. In matters of Torah law, the *Rosh Yeshiva*'s level of observance was unequivocally stringent and his school was a virtual testing ground of faith, where through rigorous self-development one achieved a level of exclusive reliance on none but the Almighty.

The one and only thing that Novardok students had in rich measure was an insatiable love of Torah and a desire to lead an exemplary life. It was a desire both Hersh and Nosson shared. In *mussar* classes, they excelled.

Their two years at the yeshiva saw a tremendous growth in both the *bochurim* themselves and in the depth of their friendship. The bond was further strengthened by the strictures of Novardok, and the deprivations were made far less traumatic by the shared experience.

THE NOVARDOK REGIMEN mandated long hours of study, endless sessions of self-criticism and not least important, *hisbodedus*: long periods of total isolation and introspection. The goal was to become a *ba'al bitachon*, a title conferred only on those who truly became "masters of trust in God." *Hisbodedus* provided the

* Rosh Yeshiva and founder of the Novardok yeshiva network.

opportunity to examine how close one truly was to achieving the Novardok ideal. Except for these periods of isolation, Hersh and Nosson remained inseparable, as always.

At this time, in early twentieth-century Russia, total privacy from the yeshiva meant retreating into the forest amid the unfolding Bolshevik Revolution. It was a period when Jews were always on the run, both from the revolutionary Red Army (the Bolsheviks), and the counter-revolutionary White Army. The Red Army was comprised of peasants who by nature hated the Jews, and the White Army was comprised of Cossacks whose hatred of Jews was a matter of ideology. The difference was academic, for both groups perpetrated acts of pillage, plunder and rape, and carried out pogroms on the Jews.

Novardok, for all its few hundred *bochurim*, was an impenetrable fortress against the most ruthless onslaughts. The reason was simple: they were not afraid. Instead of anguished cries, ghastly expressions of fright and passionate pleas for mercy, the Novardokers demonstrated — in the image of their founder, Reb Yoizel — that their only fear was that of Heaven itself. On more than one occasion, their uncanny bravery so unnerved the attacking Communists that the persecutors turned tail and scuttled away. Eventually, Reb Yoizel would realize that the yeshiva had to flee to independent Poland, but until that time he continued to disseminate Torah and *mussar*, undaunted by the dangers presented by the warring forces.

The lessons of the Revolution were not lost on Hersh and Nosson. Although they were naturally apprehensive about their future and the lot of all Jews in those treacherous times, they devoted their energy to their studies and adopted Novardok's most stalwart policy: always place your trust in God. In reality, they were not even in a position to worry, since they were both destitute. Escape without money — and a considerable sum was needed — was inconceivable.

Still, dreams of release from the constant horrors of their situation pervaded the thoughts of every Jew living in those times, yeshiva students included. Although opportunities were very rare, when they *did* present themselves, there was usually no time to think about anyone but oneself. For the Novardoker student, "escape" became the acid test of friendship: If you waited to inform others of the chance, most likely the opportunity would no longer be available. Even during *hisbodedus,* when one's introspection was to be exclusively devoted to bettering oneself and caring more for others, thoughts of a lone escape occasionally surfaced.

HERSH AND NOSSON strove hard to live up to the standards advocated by the Novardok doctrine. One brisk afternoon in 1917, as Hersh left for his period of *hisbodedus* in the forest, it was thoughts of *mussar* which filled his mind.

If there was one lesson which Reb Yoizel inculcated in his students, it was *sheviras hamidos,* that is, the shattering of one's imperfect character traits. For the *Rosh Yeshiva* of Novardok, *sheviras hamidos* entailed the uprooting and total annihilation of all worldly passions, the negation of lusts and desires for money and power.

To facilitate the shattering of these unseemly traits, Reb Yoizel devised several "*mussar* exercises". To render a student oblivious to the criticism of others and undeterred from his responsibilities by the comments of others, the students were instructed to act on occasion in a deliberately peculiar manner. It was not uncommon, for example, to witness a Novardoker asking for a slice of cheese at the hardware store or a railroad ticket at the post office. Non sequiturs spouted from their mouths, and they would often interrupt a serious discussion to offer a totally irrelevant comment. These, along with a host of other exercises, were designed by the Rebbe to help build fortitude among his students and to enable them to withstand the disdain of others.

Personally, Hersh felt that his greatest weakness lay in his desire for money, an entity he was totally unfamiliar with, as he had never possessed a kopek in his life. By standards accepted outside the world of Novardok, his desire was wholly legitimate. He only wanted the means to buy himself a pair of decent shoes, a little food to supplement his meager meals and a blanket to alleviate the cold which kept him awake through most of the night. Of course, a little extra money to keep with him in case the chance of escape ever arose would be his greatest dream — but that was no more than a distant fantasy.

DEEP INTO THE FOREST by this time, Hersh thought about Nosson. If Nosson came by any money, would he share it with Hersh? Immediately Hersh was ashamed that he had even asked himself the question. The answer, he knew, was "yes." He dismissed all thoughts of money he could not hope to see and worked on achieving the state of *hisbodedus* which Reb Yoizel so often espoused. In his intense meditation he was oblivious to the rustling sound coming from the distant underbrush.

How far he had wandered out into the woods Hersh could not say; there was no way of knowing. For periods of *hisbodedus*, it was not unusual for the Novardokers to venture kilometers into the forest to ensure total privacy. During this particular session, Hersh made the mistake of thinking he was all alone. But he was wrong.

A few meters away, a rattlesnake slithered swiftly through the brush towards a defenseless cripple who was about to become its victim. The cripple was none other than the Grand Duke of Hesse-Darmstadt and a high officer in the White army. So wealthy and prestigious was the Duke that he was able to bestow the honorific "Baron" upon whomever he chose. But for all of his might, he was rendered powerless as he lay on the forest bed, both legs fractured and splayed from his knees like limbs on a rag doll. Glaring menacingly into the eyes of his victim, the rattlesnake hissed excitedly, charged with venom and poised to strike.

Minutes earlier, the Duke had been literally riding on top of the world, for he had been in the saddle of his giant black stallion when the snake had lunged at the animal. Paralyzed by pain and stunned with fear, the horse had stopped dead in its tracks, hurtling its rider in a forward thrust with the velocity of a cannonball. The stallion managed to sprint away; the rider fared far worse, abandoned to a near-certain and gruesome death. As the snake swayed to and fro in the air, displaying a pair of drooling fangs, the Duke, with what he thought was his last breath, let out a bloodcurdling scream.

Whether it was the sheer volume of the Duke's anguished cry or the subtle rattling of the venomous snake stimulating some deep-seated instinct for self-preservation, Hersh's consciousness was finally penetrated. As only a Novardoker could, he reacted to the situation without fear. With a detached calm, Hersh swiftly took hold of the largest rock in sight and hurled it at the snake. In a stroke of *mazel* reserved for those who trust in the Above, Hersh scored a direct hit. There would not have been time for a second attempt.

Wounded by the blow and no longer in a position to

attack, the serpent beat a hasty retreat. The Duke quivered. The pain in his legs, temporarily blocked by the overriding peril which could not have loomed closer, returned. Teetering on the edge of delirium, the Duke was stunned back to reality at his first sight of Hersh.

"How did you...? How could you...?" he stammered at the young yeshiva *bochur*. He stared at his savior with a look of awe mixed with genuine gratitude and imploring agony. Hersh, unaccustomed to acknowledging the existence of Russian soldiers, let alone communicating with them, remained mute.

T HE DUKE began to panic as the full impact of his predicament dawned anew. With two broken legs he'd been helplessly stranded, and if abandoned once again, he would surely fall victim to other elements of the forest. Even without the Duke's hasty explanations, Hersh immediately grasped his plight. Finding his tongue, he switched from the familiar Yiddish of a Jew's cordoned existence to the local Slavic dialect.

"Please do not thank me. I only did what had to be done." As he spoke, Hersh slid his arms under the man's chest. As gently as he could, he raised the Duke onto his shoulders and headed for the main road. Resting every few meters, he followed the directions of the Duke, who knew the paths of the forest well.

They had not walked more than a kilometer when night began to fall. But more alarming than the total darkness, was the muffled sound of galloping hooves in the distance. Although almost any cavalry traveling through the woods should have been subordinate to the Grand Duke of Hesse-Darmstadt, there was always the danger that the horsemen would be troops loyal to the Red Army. The Duke, driven beyond the point of rationality by his pain, wanted to position himself directly in their path to call for help. Hersh reasoned, however, that if the troops were the revolutionaries, it would surely mean trouble for them both.

"Come, let us rest in the soft moss while we wait," Hersh coaxed hoarsely as he deposited the Duke in the shadows alongside the path. From this vantage point, he hoped to discern whether the approaching troops were friend or foe.

The seconds ticked by in anxious silence. As the sound of the pounding hooves grew closer, it became apparent that a dozen or more riders were galloping toward them at breakneck speed. Still, Hersh and the Duke did not know where their fate lay. Both troops knew the route by sheer instinct, having been raised since childhood in this very forest. The darkness and their speed left no clue as to their loyalties.

Trepidation mounted as the Duke, himself, became aware of their perilous position. "What if they..." the Duke began, but Hersh was already propping him up again and vigorously shaking his head to indicate silence.

Supported by the Novardok *bochur*, the Duke strained to see the group of soldiers racing toward them, many more than both had imagined. To Hersh, who as a Jew was accustomed to abuse from all sides, they appeared like apparitions from *Gehinnom* itself.

Suddenly the Duke cried out with glee, "They're ours! They're ours!" Together with Hersh, he shouted at them to stop. But the din of the twenty or more horses galloping by in oblivion, left no possibility for the riders to hear the feeble, exhausted cries emanating from the roadside.

"There is no point in our sitting here sulking," Hersh urged quietly. "We must continue."

THE HUNGER and pain which racked the Duke's crippled body were now joined by heartache and despair. But not so for Hersh. He knew the physical world was only transitory and understood full well that God had a good reason for them to be stranded in the forest. The Duke, amazed and bewildered by Hersh's composure, began to view his small companion as an unearthly savior, whose behavior was like nothing he had ever encountered before in his life.

The Duke was in agony, and in dire need of medical attention. But as long as this boy was willing to carry him to town, he could not refuse; he was helpless and totally dependent upon Hersh's assistance. And honest enough to admit to himself that were the tables turned and were he in a similar situation, he would have neither the patience nor the compassion this boy had to help a stranger — certainly not if the stranger were a Jew.

The most astonishing detail of all to the Duke was that this boy had no idea whom he was helping. Earlier, while waiting out the horses, he had tried to convey to Hersh that he was a high officer in the White Army. But the boy was either uninterested, or uncomprehending. The idea that this Jew was helping him without thought of remuneration, baffled him entirely. Indeed, all the Duke's promises that he would one day repay him were met with indifference. Although he had no way of knowing, perhaps no two ideologies could be more antithetical than those of the Duke and the Novardoker.

Shortly before dawn, they reached the edge of the forest. Exhausted to the point where it was nearly impossible to carry on, Hersh managed to trudge slowly down the dirt road. His spirits buoyed as his feet were relieved of the gnarled paths of the forest. Surely that was one aspect of the Almighty's world he had previously overlooked. He made a mental note to add thanks for this pleasure in his daily prayers.

At this moment, a milk wagon en route to a nearby farm appeared out of the early morning fog.

"Stop! Help!" they shouted. The driver's attention was immediately riveted in the stillness of the hour to the two barely discernible figures in the distant haze.

"I am the Grand Duke of Hesse-Darmstadt," the wounded man announced. "You are to take me at once to the village doctor."

The driver and Hersh loaded the Duke onto the cart. "My friend!" the suffering officer called to Hersh who had turned to depart. "Where are you going?"

"I must return to yeshiva immediately. I am sure they are worried about me."

"Before you go, take this," the Duke said, pressing a bundle of notes into the boy's hand, "and remember my name. The day may come when you need to use it. You might wish to leave this village, travel far away... I shall not forget you, for you have saved my life." He then twisted around towards the driver and told him to proceed.

I N THE DIM LIGHT of the morning, Hersh could not make out the denomination of the bills, but he was certain he held in his hand more money then he had ever seen in his life. The exhaustion of his ordeal was suddenly dissipated; he ran towards the yeshiva thinking only about the wealth he now possessed.

Energy charged through his tired, hungry body. "I can buy myself shoes," he thought to himself. "I can buy myself food, a blanket and maybe have enough left over to put some aside." His thoughts kept pace with his racing legs. "It will be a whole new life for me now."

A sudden thought stopped him short. Nosson.

"How? How could I be so self-centered as to forget Nosson?" he chastised himself. "Certainly I must share my wealth with the friend with whom I have shared everything my entire life."

The moment he contemplated sharing the treasure with his friend, he became suffused with a warm feeling of pride at his generosity. "I've done it, I've done it!" he shouted triumphantly. "I do not wish it all for myself. I am willing to share it with my friend!" And, pleased with his own altruism, he hurried on, towards the yeshiva.

Hersh could now see the *Beis Midrash* in the distance. His pace quickened. Before the doors of that humble building, he stopped to catch his breath and count the wad of notes he was gripping tightly. His eyes opened wide and his jaw dropped in disbelief.

He was holding one hundred rubles, a sum so enormous it made him shudder. Hersh was so overcome by the amount that for a moment he forgot about his pledge to his friend and his mind began to wander to thoughts of how he would spend so much. But soon he remembered Nosson.

Initially, Hersh had envisioned presenting Nosson with one or two rubles. Little had he realized then, that the Duke had presented him with a small fortune. It was now unthinkable to give his friend such an insignificant amount. But then again, how could he hand him a large sum without embarrassing him or making him feel indebted? The best way of giving, Hersh reasoned, was anonymously, and once again he savored the thought of the mitzva he was about to perform.

"Hurry!" his inner voice instructed him. "While everyone is still sleeping, do the deed." But how much should I give, he still wondered. Hersh was aware that anything over five rubles was a considerable sum. He considered the matter for a while.

REMOVING TEN RUBLES from his cache, he stealthily tiptoed into Nosson's room. He placed the money under Nosson's pillow, where his friend was sure to find it when he awoke. Then, as quietly as he had entered the room, he left, and made his way to the *Beis Midrash*.

The time had come to thank God for the kindness which had been bestowed upon him. As tired as he was, Hersh was eager to perform this solemn duty. In forty minutes, he would be joined by the rest of the yeshiva for the morning services; now was his chance to offer his private prayers of gratitude.

After the *bochurim* had *davened* together, Hersh was besieged by questions. He allayed their fears that he had met up with local Cossacks who might easily have decided to make sport of him, and explained his lengthy disappearance and told how he had assisted the stricken Duke.

Hersh then headed to his bed for some desperately needed rest. Alone in his room, he reviewed the events of the previous day, finally recalling his generous deed of giving a tenth of his fortune to his friend, who had surely found the surprise under his pillow.

Wearing only his threadbare nightshirt, Hersh lay down on the bare mattress, a mattress which he knew would soon be graced with a blanket. He reached for his pillow and found beneath it five rubles. It had been placed there by an anonymous friend.

Friends 'til the End

**Y WHAT CRITERIA** is true friendship measured? Is a real friend someone who would give you the shirt off his back; who would share with you his most cherished possession; who is there to lend a hand when you need his help the most? Our Heritage illuminates the special relationship that existed between David and Jonathan, a friendship so rare that it has become the standard against which society judges all such human alliances and allegiances. It was a friendship in which the parties willingly risked life and limb for one another.

The heroes of our tale are called Mendel and Laibel, but their names are not important. Neither is the setting or the century, for the story is timeless and could have taken place anywhere. What *is* significant is the depth of feeling and genuine affection of one friend for the other and the sacrifice each is prepared to make in the name of friendship.

MENDEL AND LAIBEL had been life-long friends. From earliest childhood, throughout their school years and up until the day each had wed, they had been inseparable. Even after marriage, they had continued to live and work in the same city, and their friendship had extended to envelop their wives and children as well. But, despite their affirmations to the contrary, it finally came time for a parting of the ways. An irresistible job offer in a distant city was to tear Laibel away from his companion of twenty-six years.

Their farewell was fraught with emotion. Any parting between close friends is difficult, but the pain for Laibel and Mendel was especially acute. Few had achieved their depth of friendship. Moreover, they both knew that from this time on reunions would be brief and sporadic: they would, after all, be living thousands of kilometers apart.

Laibel and Mendel undertook the same pledges all friends make on parting. The difference was that for them, these were not mere words or empty promises. It was understood that they would correspond regularly and send regards with any courier heading in the right direction.

But inevitably, time and distance took their toll on the relationship. The letters ceased flowing regularly and even the memories of their years of companionship began to fade. The letters were replaced by greeting cards before holidays. And even those later dwindled to hastily-penned good wishes before every Rosh Hashanah.

ONE YEAR, however, as he was writing his New Year greeting to Laibel, Mendel suddenly — inexplicably — decided that it was not enough. He simply had to visit his dear friend, despite the expense and hardship of the journey. After making his travel arrangements, he set off, looking forward to a grand reunion.

After over two weeks of travelling, Mendel finally arrived in the far-off city. As he walked down the main street he noticed an unusually large crowd gathered in the town square. Although his curiosity was aroused Mendel could not stop now: he had travelled all this way in order to visit his friend and nothing could distract or deter him from his mission.

With some difficulty, Mendel found his way to Laibel's street, a great distance from the heart of town. He could no longer contain his excitement. This was the moment about which he had dreamed for so many years. Without even realizing it, he was running, his heart thumping. "Laibel! Laibel!" he heard himself cry out as he raced to greet his closest and dearest friend.

Mendel followed the numbers down the road and spotted the house in the distance. He rushed up to the door and knocked anxiously. After a few moments, which seemed like hours, Laibel's wife answered the door. She was a terrible sight. Her eyes were puffy from crying and her voice was barely audible.

"Where's Laibel?" Mendel asked anxiously, suddenly uneasy.

"You don't know? Everyone knows by now. They took him from the house not five minutes ago."

"Where? Who took him?"

"The police. He's been arrested and accused of grand larceny. They've taken him to the town square to hang him."

"Hang him?!" Mendel exclaimed. "But surely Laibel is innocent!"

"Of course!" Laibel's wife replied. "He was framed."

Mendel turned on his heels and raced back to the center of town. So that was what the excitement had been about!

Now all that concerned him was that he should see his friend once more.

IN THE MEANTIME, under the approving gaze of the Mayor of the city, the hangman was making the usual offer to the condemned man. "Do you have one last request?"

The response took everyone by surprise. "I want to return home to bid farewell to my family. I was hauled out in such haste that I didn't even have a chance to say goodbye to my wife and kiss my children."

The executioner roared with laughter: "Ha ha, do you think we're new at this job? I can give you a cigarette or arrange a bowl of cherries, but do you imagine we would be naive enough to allow you to return home? A man as clever as yourself, who eluded capture for so long, would surely find a way to escape."

"But I give you my word of honor that I will return!" Laibel pleaded. Again the hangman laughed. "How much is the word of a condemned thief worth? The one way — the only way — that I could grant your request would be if somebody would agree to be your guarantor. But who in the world would be foolish enough to stake his life on the unlikely gamble that you would return for your death? "

A faint "I" was heard from the edge of the crowd.

"Let's get on with it," the Mayor ordered impatiently.

"I," the small voice repeated.

SLOWLY, HEADS BEGAN to turn toward the source of the voice. "What's all the commotion about?" asked the Mayor, anxious for the spectacle to begin.

"Everyone is to remain silent," the executioner yelled, "I

need to concentrate on my work."

"I, I," came the insistent voice again, drawing closer to the gallows.

"'I' what?" demanded the hangman, trying to locate the source of the turmoil amid the raucous crowd.

"You asked who would be willing to be a guarantor," Mendel said firmly, "and I answered that I would. I will guarantee with my life that Laibel will return here after he bids his family farewell."

"Do you mean," asked the Mayor in disbelief, "that if he does not come back — which is more likely than not — then we can kill you instead?"

"That is correct."

"Step up here," the executioner ordered, lowering the noose from his hand.

Laibel now saw who it was that had offered to be his guarantor and his mouth fell open. "What are you doing here?" he asked in amazement.

"What are you doing here?" Mendel countered.

"I was framed, but all of that is irrelevant now. You see what kind of justice they dispense around here."

"Cut the conversation," the hangman growled. "What is this, 'social hour?' Just tell me," he said, turning toward Laibel, "how long will it take you to say goodbye? And it had better not be long, because I never like to keep my audience waiting."

"About an hour."

"No 'abouts'," the executioner retorted. "You'd better be back in exactly one hour or your friend will get it," and he made a choking motion with his hand.

ONE HOUR LATER, Laibel had not returned. Everyone watched the road that led to his home to see if he was coming, but there was no sign of him.

"Come up here," the executioner ordered Mendel. It was obvious, though, that even the hangman felt uneasy about the unusual situation. How could he expect to get job satisfaction from executing a stand-in? He stood on his toes and tried to spot Laibel in the distance. Minutes ticked by. "We will give him ten more minutes," he said looking at the Mayor for his approval. The Mayor nodded.

Ten minutes later, the executioner was more anxious than ever. Beads of sweat covered his ruddy face. The Mayor signalled to him to wait five more minutes. Still, there was no sign of Laibel. All eyes were now turned in the direction of his house, but the road remained empty and silent.

"All right, Mister," the executioner said, turning to Mendel, "your friend fixed you up but good. Step over here." Mendel approached the hangman and the noose was slipped around his neck. "No final requests for you — we made that mistake once already today." As the executioner was making his adjustments and tightening the rope, a breathless shout was heard in the distance.

"Hey! Hey!" the voice cried, panting.

THE THRONG ASSEMBLED to witness an execution craned their necks with annoyance to see who was causing yet another disturbance. It was none other than Laibel running as fast as he could towards the gallows.

"Where have you been?" the executioner growled. Laibel was easily making his way to the platform as the crowd parted to let him through. "My horse had a flat," he responded lamely, and climbed up to the gallows.

"What matters is that I'm back, a little late, but back. I said my goodbyes, so now you may take my life if you must."

"Hey, just one second there," Mendel protested. "A deal is a deal. You said that you would be back in an hour and you didn't keep your word. You have forfeited your right to die."

"What do you mean, 'I forfeited my right'? It's *me* they framed and it's *me* they want to hang, not *you*."

"Listen here, Laibel. We have been friends all our lives. You can't go back on your word now."

"What do you mean, 'I can't go back on my word'? I only agreed to allow you to be my guarantor, not my pinch hitter!" He lifted the noose from Mendel's neck and draped it around his own.

The executioner wanted to intervene, but didn't know exactly what to do.

Mendel jerked the noose off Laibel's neck and replaced it on his own. Laibel fought to take it back. No one — including the hangman and the Mayor — had ever witnessed anything like it: two men fighting over the privilege of dying.

AT THE SIGHT of this amazing spectacle, the Mayor stepped over to the gallows and separated the two with his outstretched hands. "Stop this," he said. "Stop this, this instant. Never in my life have I seen such a friendship.

"And as disappointed as this fine audience may be, when I see two friends that are willing to die for one another, how can I not pardon them — and let them live for one another?"

three on leadership

מי כהחכם ומי יודע פשר דבר
חכמת אדם תאיר פניו ועז פניו ישנא.
קהלת ח:א

❀ *Who is like the wise man?*
and who knows the meaning of a thing?
A man's wisdom makes his face shine,
and the boldness of his face is changed.

Koheles 8:1

The Tzup

NEVER HAD SO MANY Jews been seen in Prague before. Even the Rosh Hashanah crowds — when the Jewish residents of the Czechoslovakian capital all streamed down for *Tashlich* to the banks of the river which neatly divided the town — were dwarfed by the current assemblage. Every man, woman and child of that large and prestigious community was there. All, that is, except one.

What the onlookers did not know was that this day represented the culmination of fifteen months of a painstaking and arduous search. After fifteen months of scouring Europe for a scholar whose reputation, erudition and character would befit a community such as Prague, the appropriate candidate had finally been selected.

Rumors of his scholarship long preceded his arrival. Glowing reports circulated about the man's genius and piety. There was therefore little wonder that they had all gathered to give due honor to the long-awaited Rav of Prague. All except one.

The summer heat bore down on the assembled gathering

as they sweltered in their holiday finery. The men fanned their hats back and forth in an attempt to create a little breeze, while the women headed for the meager shade afforded by scattered trees. But even the heat could not dampen the holiday spirit of the Jews, whose expectations were raised to a tantalizing pitch. And when the horse-led wagon came into view, pandemonium broke out.

The seven *Tuvai Ha'Ir* rushed forward to greet the Rav while the ecstatic crowds pressed closer and closer. The distinguished ambassadors of the town literally ran to the approaching carriage and unharnessed the four stallions which were drawing the impressive stage. And then against the vehement protests of the scholar — whose humility equalled his erudition — they drew the wagon into town by hand.

The Rav repeatedly tried to stop the seven notables, but to no avail. They were determined to bring the Rav over the threshold of their city by their own efforts. And soon they were joined by thousands of others, all dancing and singing, trying their hardest to give the wagon a little shove so that they, too, could feel that they had shared in the honor of escorting their new Rav into his new home.

The Jews of Prague pledged their allegiance to the Rav. The intensity of their welcome reflected their long and troubled search for a leader and their yearning for a man to fill that prestigious post.

AND YET, amid all the overflowing joy and the festivities, one man continued to hold back. He was Leib-Itzik ben Yosef, but to one and all he was known simply as "the Tzup". He had acquired this epithet from the long *tzup* or braid which he made from his uncut hair and which he fashioned into a bun, tucked beneath his *yarmulke*.

While all were unable to contain their elation and excitement, the Tzup went through town spreading the word that the new Rav was not what he had been made out to be. He was hardly a scholar and far from a pious individual, the Tzup warned. Rather than being given a tumultuous welcome, he went on, the newcomer — posing falsely as one versed in Torah knowledge — should be driven out of town.

Needless to say, the Jews of Prague did not take kindly to the Tzup's derision. They reported his mockery to the Rav, who refused to pay any attention. Why should he take this eccentric seriously?

THE RAV DISMISSED the matter from his mind, until one Friday, when, as was the custom every *erev Shabbos*, three *baalei battim* visited the Talmud Torah to test the *cheder* children. On this particular Friday, one member of the delegation was none other than the Tzup.

One of the children in the room, he noticed, was Avreimeleh, the new Rav's youngest son. The Tzup's lips began to tremble with rage and he ordered the child to read the *Gemara*.

Avreimeleh stood up and began, "*Tannu rabbanan... di Rabbanan habben gelernt...*" The Tzup turned white with anger, his eyes bulged with fury, and he slapped the boy mightily across the face.

"*Nein,*" he shouted. "*Nisht, 'di Rabbanan habben gelernt,' nor, 'TANNU – ven mir lernt, dan is RABBANAN!'* [Not, 'we have learned from the Rabbis,' but '*Tannu,* when you learn, only *then,* do you become a rabbi.'] Go home and tell your father, that *am haaretz,* that he himself must first learn before he can claim to be a Rav!"

The boy, smarting from the stinging blow, ran home with

tears cascading down his cheeks. He had been so shamed in front of all his classmates that he thought that he would never be able to face them again.

By the time Avreimeleh arrived home, his cheek had become swollen and he could barely talk. Between convulsive sobs, he told his father all that had occurred. The Rav's face turned grave as his son recounted that morning's encounter in the Talmud Torah.

The Rav could no longer afford to disregard the Tzup. He had been sure that in the course of time the Tzup would have found that his ridicule fell on deaf ears and would have given up what was obviously a losing battle. But now he knew that he could no longer be oblivious to the man's hatred. Dressing the bruise on his child's face and sensing the pain in the boy's little heart, the Rav realized that he had to put an end to the Tzup's insolence.

HE SUMMONED HIS *shammas:* "It appears I have no choice," the Rav announced. "I must silence the Tzup's criticism once and for all. I want you to go and tell him that I invite him to test me publicly on *Shas*. He may raise absolutely any question that bothers him in *Bavli* or *Yerushalmi*. But let it be known that if I succeed in answering his questions, then his lips must remain forever sealed regarding my position as Rav.

"On the other hand, if I fail to answer the questions then I will give up my post at once and leave Prague.

"Go," he told his *shammas,* "and relay my message to the Tzup. You will find him in the Meisels Shul. Tell him the public *farheir* will be held one week from today, Friday, at nine o'clock in the morning, in the Altneu Shul."

The *shammas* raced off to fulfill the Rav's request and found the Tzup just where the Rav said he would be. The *shammas* repeated the instructions the Rav had given him. The dozens of men present in the shul were astonished, but the Tzup rocked back and forth in derisive laughter. "That *am haaretz* expects me to test him on anything in *Shas* that bothers me, does he? What a joke! You go back and tell your so-called 'Rav' that I don't have to test him on all of *Shas* to prove his ignorance."

Now the Tzup's face was contorted in a malevolent snicker. His whole body showed his contempt for the Rav: "I want you to tell him," the Tzup said, "exactly which *Mesechta,* which *Perek,* and precisely which page." The Tzup cited a page of *Gemara* and chortled. "He has exactly a week to prepare... let's see if your '*Gaon*' can handle this."

The embarrassed *shammas* walked humbly back to the Rav and related the Tzup's response. "So be it," the Rav agreed. "In just one week we shall see. And you have my permission to publicize the *farheir* to all the residents of Prague."

ALL WEEK LONG, the Rav ignored the coming *farheir,* although it had become the talk of the town. Since he was such a tremendous *Gaon,* well-versed in all the intricacies of the Torah, one page of *Gemara* was certainly nothing to intimidate or worry him. He attended to his rabbinical duties as usual, not giving a single stray thought to the showdown that was destined for the coming Friday.

On Thursday night, however — *mishmar* night — just as the Rav was about to go to bed, he decided to take a glance at the *Gemara* on which he would be tested the following day. He removed the volume from his bookcase, placed it on his table and opened it to the proper page. The Rav's fingers raced quickly down the page through the *Mishna* and into the *Gemara*. There did not seem to be anything complex about this page of *Gemara*, and *Rashi* and *Tosafos* proved equally straightforward. But just in case, the Rav decided to go through it once more to make absolutely sure that there was not some hidden difficulty which had escaped him. Only when he was convinced that he had entirely mastered the material did he replace the *Gemara* on the shelf and make his way to bed.

But the Rav had not taken more than four steps out of his study when he heard a thump from the room he had just left. He went back and saw that the *Gemara* which he had replaced was lying on the floor open to the very page that he had studied. Somewhat puzzled, he picked it up lovingly, kissed it, and replaced it on the shelf — this time being sure to place it there with extra care.

As soon as the Rav had turned his back, there was another thump: the *Gemara* had once again fallen to the ground. And when he bent to pick it up he found it had again fallen open to the very same page. Mystified, yet hoping this was not an omen, he picked up the volume and was careful to place it even more securely on the shelf.

The Rav walked out of the room, but before he could get very far he again heard what was now a familiar thud. He turned around, and there on the floor lay the *Gemara* that he would be tested on the next morning. Again it was open at the same place.

This time it was impossible to simply dismiss the occurrences. He placed the *Gemara* on his *shtender* to take another look at it.

And so, once again, he set about relearning the *Gemara*, starting with the *Mishna*, working his way down the *Gemara*, referring to both the *Rashi* and *Tosafos*. Yet as deliberately and carefully as he went, he could not detect anything particularly complex or perplexing. He thought it over one more time to be sure — and it seemed as plain as before.

But, as the Rav bent down to kiss his *Gemara* before closing it, he was suddenly struck — as though by a bolt of lightning — by a startling realization. He clapped his hand to his head as his mind raced in a fury. He simply could not believe it... The *Mishna* on the page he had just learned was explicitly contradicted by another *Mishna* in a different *Mesechta!* It was a contradiction both striking and blatant, yet no one had ever called attention to it before.

The Rav's mind began to accelerate, and intellectual gears were rapidly becoming engaged. Surely this elusive contradiction was what the Tzup had intended to use in order to trip him up and humiliate him. All of the appropriate *Gemaras* were now flashing through his mind, and sweat poured from every pore as he concentrated all his energies on the task before him. But just as he began to sense a breakthrough in understanding a concept, he heard a light tap on his door.

I T WAS 1:30 in the morning, and he knew that if he got up to answer the door it would totally interrupt his train of thought. But he also knew that he was still the Rav of the town, and if someone knocked at that hour then it must truly be an emergency requiring rabbinic assistance.

When the Rav opened the door, he found an old lady clutching a handkerchief to her eyes. "My poor, sick husband," she wept. "He is gasping for breath on his death-bed."

The Rav ran for his hat and frock coat and followed her out into the pitch-black night. At her home, several members of the family were gathered around the bed, while the woman's son was dispatched to try to summon a *minyan*. There was no mistaking the gravity of the situation, and the Rav immediately set about reciting the appropriate verses to the dying man. After the old man passed away, he stayed to comfort the grieving family.

It was already four o'clock in the morning, and it was clear to the Rav that his presence was still necessary. Yet the great *farheir* was to take place in just five hours, and he had neither slept nor been able to apply himself to resolving the contradiction with which he would inevitably be confronted.

But there was nothing to be done. His rabbinic responsibilities took precedence over a personal squabble — even though his future as Rav now hinged on his being able to make a brilliant impression at the *farheir*. At five-thirty in the morning he felt that he had done all he could and promised the widow that he would eulogize her husband at the funeral, arrange *minyanim*, and visit her again before Shabbos.

THOROUGHLY EXHAUSTED, he returned home and tried to re-examine the *Gemara*. But by this time, both his emotion and his power of concentration were spent. He struggled vainly to keep his eyes open; his weary body ached from complete exhaustion. Sadly, he realized that there was no point in trying to resolve the contradiction. He simply could not muster the mental energy necessary for the task. Moreover, he was beginning to see that there was, in fact, no resolution to the contradiction. Every attempt at an answer raised even more serious problems and greater contradictions. The problem in the *Mishna* was paradoxical and could not be given the kind of answer conventionally offered by the *Rishonim* and *Acharonim*.

With a devastating feeling of defeat, the Rav went to bed

for a short rest. At seven o'clock he would have to be up for the main *minyan* in Prague, where *baalei battim* frequently attended just so that they could ask him their *shailos.*

But as he fell asleep, his mind began to wander to the far corners of the universe, to spheres beyond human understanding. And as he travelled through this mental stratosphere, he saw a bright light shimmering in the dense fog that clouded the distance. Almost imperceptibly, the light drifted towards him through the fog, and he was now beginning to discern an image within the rays. The awesome apparition rapidly drew nearer to the Rav, and then, staring in wonder at the center of this aurora, he saw the shining face of his sainted father.

The figure moved forward and extended a frail hand. His father's long grey beard billowed with the current of air rushing against it; his pale blue eyes stared directly ahead. The hand came down and caressed the head of the Rav. "My dear son, my child," whispered the old man in a sonorous voice. "You must know that the Tzup is a very holy and righteous man. Where I am, we are well aware of his great piety. Furthermore, he is a *talmid chacham* of unrivaled excellence. Every evening he stays up late into the night studying the words of the Torah with burning diligence, allowing himself little rest or sleep.

"This is why he has a *tzup,* for when he learns at night in his cellar, away from the public eye, he unravels his braid and pins it to the wall. Thus, if he dozes off or his head droops forward, it is yanked back by his *tzup,* rousing him so that he may resume his learning with even greater fervor.

"He speaks of you with contempt simply because he realizes that as outstanding as you are, you still have not achieved a scintilla of what you are capable of achieving. This is his only motivation.

"I see that you are perplexed about why he hurts you so. Well, my son, his methods may be improper, but his intentions are wholly altruistic, and you must respect him and accord him the highest deference, for he is indeed the greater scholar.

"As for the contradiction which you noticed in the *Mishna,* there is in fact no answer to the problem in *yeshiva shel matta.* No one below, barring the Tzup, has even noticed it before. But I will share with you how we reconcile this conflict of *Mishnayos* in *yeshiva shel maala...*"

The Rav's father began to explain a series of concepts that were fundamental to answering the question. The underpinnings of what was being asserted were so fantastic, so incisive, that he felt that his mind was exploding. It was as if sparks of fire were bombarding his brain in a relentless assault. Each step wove into the next in a tapestry of exquisite reasoning. It was like nothing he had ever heard before. The Rav clearly understood that what he was hearing was *divrei Elokim chaim,* the words of Torah of the living God.

BUT BEFORE his father could complete his answer, the Rav was jolted awake by the *shammas'* knocking at the front door: it was already seven o'clock. Awakened from his sleep by the noise, he realized that he would never have an opportunity to hear the conclusion of the answer — not in *this* world. The same feeling of defeat which had weighed down his spirit when he had gone to bed now returned in strong measure.

He washed his hands and hurried to shul to pray to God to save him from a humiliating debacle later that morning. By the time the *davening* was over, the Altneu Shul had already begun to fill with men who had come to witness the anxiously awaited contest. Well before the appointed time of the *farheir,* the shul was packed. There was not a spare seat, and hundreds gathered in the street outside.

At exactly nine o'clock, the Rav walked into the shul with a *Gemara* under his arm. Those who were seated jumped to their feet in deference. But the Tzup, leaning against the doorpost at the far end of the shul, jeered out loud. The Rav stopped when he got to the *bima,* opened his *Gemara* and began to read.

In his clear, readily understandable style, the Rav went through the *Mishna* and *Gemara,* explaining it as he went along with the interpretations of *Rashi* and *Tosafos.* All the while, the Tzup stood with arms folded, a cynical smirk on his face and a mean look in his eyes.

"*Rabbosai,*" the Rav concluded, "as you can see there really seems to be nothing exceptional about this *Gemara.*" The Tzup's face lit up and he grinned broadly, showing every tooth in his mouth. His eyes seemed to be taunting the Rav, while his eyebrows arched with unmasked scorn. The Tzup tapped his fingers against his arms impatiently, preparing to devour a great feast.

"**H**OWEVER," the Rav quickly added, "there is yet one question that may be raised." The Tzup's expression changed. His nostrils flared, and his shoulders hunched instinctively in defense. His ruddy complexion was even more accentuated now, and he nodded his head as if to say, "So you *did* find the question after all." The Tzup's sense of anticipation was apparent as he took a step closer, his entire being now tensed with expectation.

"The question," the Rav continued, "is that our *Mishna* appears to contradict a different *Mishna* which says..." The *lomdim* in the shul put their hands to their heads in disbelief because they had never noticed this contradiction, an inconsistency which now seemed so obvious. "Actually," the Rav continued, "in our realm there is no answer to this polemic, but perhaps we could learn thus..." But now the Rav was playing for time — he had not heard the complete answer and did not know how to resolve the problem. Perhaps, he thought, he would yet acquire some insight and be able to finish off that which his father had started to explain.

He proceeded to repeat the explanation he had heard in his dream that morning. All the scholars in the shul were spellbound by what they heard, sitting on the edge of their seats and following every word. They were mesmerized by the Rav's words; they had never heard anything like this before. Their minds reeled from the extraordinary performance.

But as hard as the Rav tried, he was unable to complete the answer. He was stuck and fell silent in the midst of his recitation, his eyes closed in intense concentration.

T HE TZUP didn't waste a second. His cheeks went red with fury, his lips turned a tinge of purple. His eyes shot flames and he raised his clenched fists. In a horrible voice, raucous and barely human, the Tzup screamed, "*Am haaretz!* Get out of town!"

Without saying a word the Rav stepped down from the *bima* and amid the gasps of the congregation, started walking towards the door. With each step the stunned men of the shul parted, reluctantly allowing the Rav to pass through. His head hung low and his frame drooped heavily as he reached the door to leave the illustrious shul for the last time. But suddenly he was arrested by a sharp cry.

"Stop!" shouted the Tzup. "We made a deal that if there

was any question in *Shas* that bothered me which you could not answer, you would leave town. But it was not a question in *Shas*..." a small, abashed smile appeared on the Tzup's face. "It was your *Rabbanus* that bothered me... and we never made any deals about that."

As the onlookers stood in silent amazement, the Tzup walked across the full length of the shul towards the Rav and embraced him warmly, paying his belated but humble respects to the rightful Rabbi of Prague.

An Affair of Honor

T WAS SEVERAL HOURS into the humid night in the Yemen town of Sa'na but there was still a flurry of activity at the court of Mori Salim ben Amnon. Mori Salim, Chief Rabbi of Sa'na, had left long before, at dusk, and his followers on the *Beit Din* were now anxiously debating what should be done with the urgent telegram which had just arrived from Aleppo, Syria.

"Shall we go and wake him up?" asked one of the men.

"You know how old and feeble he is," replied Mori Salim's grandson, who also served in the *Beit Din*. "He needs his rest."

"But many lives are at stake. We must act immediately. Come let us hurry!"

Clutching the telegram they had just received from the Rav of Aleppo, the men rushed through the deserted, narrow streets of Sa'na to the house of Mori Salim. It took the wise, rheumy-eyed octogenarian a few moments to recognize his late-night visitors after being dragged from a deep sleep. "What is the trouble?" he asked in alarm. His grandson began to read the contents of the telegram aloud:

"'To His Honor, the venerable and revered Rav, Mori Salim ben...'"

"Leave out the formalities," interrupted Mori Salim, "and read the message. It must be urgent."

His grandson continued: "'Great danger has struck our community in Aleppo. A respected local glassmaker — al-Bedawiya — has been accused of murdering his rival, ibn Khatib.

"'The only witnesses to the alleged crime are two Jewish boys, the Farhi brothers. Fearing retribution from the powerful al-Bedawiya family, they have fled all the way to Sa'na to seek refuge until the trial begins. If al-Bedawiya is found guilty, there will certainly be a pogrom here in Aleppo. His family has already made that clear to us.

"'My dear colleague, the trial is to commence soon. I beseech you to find the two brothers and cross-examine them. If you cannot find some flaw in their testimony and write to the authorities discrediting them as witnesses, then who knows what will become of us?

"'Signed: The revered sage Rav Yih'ya Sama'yas of Aleppo.'"

For several minutes Mori Salim sat motionless, considering the contents of the telegram. "Perhaps it is not quite as urgent as we thought, after all," he mused.

T HE VISITORS looked at him in astonishment and one could not hold back his reaction: "But surely we must find these witnesses and question them immediately," he burst out.

"Very well," responded the Rav calmly. "Please report back to me with your findings."

The men rushed out of Mori Salim's house, each in a different direction in search of the Farhi brothers. By late that evening the brothers had been found and the questioning commenced: "My dear friends," the grandson began earnestly, "do you realize the peril that now faces the Aleppo Jewish community? You must tell us exactly what you witnessed and what made you flee to Sa'na."

The brothers repeated their story, insisting that they had clearly witnessed the murder of ibn Khatib by al-Bedawiya. They would not alter one word of their testimony.

Dissapointed but not dissuaded from their plan, the men hurried back to report to Mori Salim. They had already mentally composed the telegram they would send to the authorities in Aleppo, stating that they had found that the testimony of the Farhi brothers was inconsistent and unreliable. True, they had not actually been able to disprove the account of the brothers, but their obligation to save their brethren in Aleppo from the horrors that would follow the conviction of al-Bedawiya was more important. Mori Salim, they were sure, could only concur with their reasoning.

They found the old Rav engaged in the study of the Kabbalah. Apart from the few hours he grudgingly allowed himself for sleeping and eating, Mori Salim could always be found delving into the words of the Torah — even late into the night.

"Honored teacher," they began. "The brothers who have fled here from Aleppo adhere to their story and refuse to alter it, or even admit that they might be mistaken."

"What, then, would you suppose that we do?" asked the Rav.

"We must dispatch a telegram at once stating that we questioned the Farhi brothers and that they are now very doubtful about their original testimony given in Aleppo. Clearly, we have no other choice."

MORI SALIM RAISED his frail hands to signal his protest. "My dear colleagues," he whispered in a soft, barely audible tone, "the reason I asked you to investigate this matter is that from the outset I suspected the telegram might not be genuine. And now that you have told me what the Farhi brothers had to say, I am all the more convinced that the telegram we received is fraudulent."

The men were aghast. They leapt to their feet to object, but found no words, not knowing exactly how they could contradict the words of their revered master.

"Honored Teacher," one of them said, summoning up all his courage, "but what if the telegram is indeed real? How can we take the responsibility for the pillage and plunder which will undoubtedly befall our hapless brethren in Aleppo? The Rav knows that there is scant refuge for a Jew in Syria, and the Arabs of Aleppo are notoriously savage." His colleagues nodded their heads in manifest agreement.

"True," Mori Salim replied slowly, "I know all that you are saying. Our greatest concern must indeed be for the lives of our brethren in Aleppo. It is for this very reason I recommend that we do not send a reply to this telegram but that we let events run their course."

The members of the *Beit Din* were vexed. It even occurred to them that their master might be showing signs of senility. But what could they do? Defying a directive from Mori Salim was inconceivable. On the other hand, ignoring the plight of their brethren might be worse.

Mori Salim detected their discomfort at his response to the telegram. "My friends," suggested the venerable Rav, "if you feel unable to fulfill my instructions and still feel that word should be sent to Aleppo to discredit the testimony of the Farhi brothers, then I recommend that you consult with the famed Mori Rahamim ben Nehemia, Rav of Manakheh."

The men could not argue. All knew of Mori Rahamim's reputation as a great scholar, well versed in both the intracies of *halachah* and the depths of Kabbalah. The Jews of the small village, Manakheh, were indeed fortunate to have such a sage in their town. And the very fact that Mori Salim recommended that they travel to Manakheh to seek the advice of a man many years his junior was an enormous tribute to Mori Rahamim's erudition.

Spurred on by the urgency of their mission, the men left immediately. They travelled through the rest of the night and most of the next day taking only the shortest breaks to rest their camels and partake of some refreshment.

"AH, WELCOME, my friends." Mori Rahamim rose from his studies and greeted them warmly. "How can I be of assistance to you?" After bestowing the greetings of Mori Salim, they wasted no time in explaining the nature and the urgency of their visit.

Mori Rahamim took the telegram and, after scanning it briefly, looked up in surprise. "But why have you come to me?" he asked. "The cable is addressed to the Rav of Sa'na."

"True," one of the men answered. "But our master is old and feels he is unable to deal with such matters anymore. He therefore recommended that we seek your counsel."

Mori Rahamim nodded pensively and returned his attention to the telegram, which he now addressed with greater concentration. The men from Sa'na could hardly wait for him to finish. "Should we seek out the Farhi brothers," they asked, "and bring them to Mori Rahamim for questioning?"

"No, I would not rush to do that," Mori Rahamim replied carefully, looking intently at his visitors from Sa'na. "You see, I believe that this telegram is not genuine. I believe it was actually sent by the al-Bedawiya family in an attempt to save the accused. Instead, I do not think we should send a reply, and wait to let events take their course."

The men were dumbstruck. Two great *rabbanim* had responded in exactly the same manner. Awed by a logic beyond their comprehension, the shocked men remained rooted in their place. Mori Rahamim was puzzled. "Have I said something that troubles you?" he asked.

"No, no," answered the men. "It is just that you respond to the query in precisely the same way as our Mori Salim does." They thanked him profusely, promised to carry out his instructions, and returned to Sa'na.

BACK IN SA'NA, the men returned to see their Rav. "Mori Salim," they began, "we offer our humble apologies. Mori Rahamim agrees with you in all that you told us. We shall send no telegram to the authorities in Aleppo and wait to see the outcome." The men did, however, send a worried letter to the Rav in Aleppo, expressing their concern for the welfare of his community in light of the forthcoming murder trial. Several weeks later, reports arrived from Aleppo saying that al-Bedawiya had been convicted of the murder of ibn Khatib and that there had been no outbreak of violence in the city.

"How did the Rav *and* Mori Rahamim both know that the telegram was a forgery?" The members of the *Beit Din* asked Mori Salim. They were astounded at this glimpse of how immersion in Torah study had so sharpened the minds and perception of these two great *rabbanim*.

Mori Salim smiled. "Humility speaks far louder than praise," he said. "The telegram was signed: 'The revered sage Rav Yih'ya Sama'yas of Aleppo.' Rav Yih'ya is indeed revered and a sage, but his humility is such that he would never use these words to describe himself. It is this absence of humility that showed the telegram to be a forgery and warned me not to reply. Who knows what harm might have befallen the Jews of Aleppo had we been accomplices in false testimony?"

The very same day, a letter arrived from the Rav of Aleppo in response to the letter he had received from the *Beit Din,* confirming that no violence had erupted. "But had you interfered with the testimony of the Farhi brothers," it continued, "then the ibn Khatib family would indeed have wreaked a pogrom against our community. The letter was signed simply: "Yih'ya Sama'yas of Aleppo."

Money Talks

EB ZUNDEL sighed heavily. Early every morning he made his trek to the shul to deliver his daily *shiur* for the *baalei battim,* and his slouched figure, silhouetted against the white-walled houses lining the narrow streets, was by now a familiar sight.

His drooping shoulders did not reflect unwillingness or apathy. Quite the contrary, they were weighed down by the heavy burden of his congregational responsibilities. The troubles of his community had left a visible imprint on his physical appearance. Each wrinkle of his well-lined face reflected the *tzores* of a member of his *Kehilla.* If ever a Rav cared for his fellow Jew, it was Reb Zundel.

Reb Zundel's concern for the plight of his townspeople was legendary. And for this reason his most trivial recommendations commanded the respect and almost blind obedience of his congregants. Nor was this relationship, the fruit of twenty years of dedicated service, unknown outside his community...

THIS MORNING, as he turned down the path to the shul, he suddenly noticed someone beckoning to him from the far side of the street. Reb Zundel was astonished to see two husky fellows clutching a man who was bound and gagged. He recognized the captive, a newcomer to the area who had come to Reb Zundel's shul once or twice.

"Hey you," one of the men called out to him. "We got us a Jew, and you got until four o'clock to buy him back. Four o'clock and not a minute later. We'll be just outside town, near the old well in the woods. The price is two hundred rubles." And then, more ominously, he added: "Two hundred rubles — or else!" The two, almost as though they had rehearsed the scene, passed their fingers menacingly across their throats, just to make sure that their threat was clearly understood.

Reb Zundel's heart pounded. What a predicament! What a sum! He knew that there was no way to bargain with the abductors, to try to reduce the ransom or to extend the deadline. They looked eminently capable and willing to carry out their threat: Noncompliance with their demands would result in the captive's certain death.

Reb Zundel rushed into the shul and sent a messenger to summon his *gabbai* before addressing the men who had gathered for the *shiur*. "I regret that our *shiur* will have to be postponed," he announced. "It is a matter of *pikuach nefesh*. I hope we will be able to meet later today."

Within a few minutes the *gabbai* hurried breathlessly into the shul to answer Reb Zundel's urgent call. "Reb Yankel," cried the Rabbi, taking hold of the *gabbai*'s wrist, "they have grabbed a *Yid* and he must be ransomed by four o'clock this afternoon! Hurry, get a piece of paper. We must make a list.

"The only way that we can raise this enormous sum in such a short time is by appealing to the wealthiest members of our community for help."

Reb Yankel did as his Rabbi instructed. "I am sure that in

this case they will be willing to give generously," he said.

"I hope you are right, my dear *gabbai*. But no one is ever in a rush to part with his hard-earned savings. Everyone tends to worry about his own physical well-being and other people's souls. If only we would worry more about our *own* souls and the physical well-being of *others*. Raising money is one area in which I have never been very successful." Reb Zundel shook his head ruefully. "But now is not the time to *discuss* the problem. We must try to *solve* it. Come, let us draw up a list and pray that we can raise the money quickly."

W HEN THEY HAD FINISHED making up the list, the two men raced to the home of the first *guir* on their list in the hope that he would contribute the hefty sum of ten rubles without too much resistance. Remarkably, the Rabbi hadn't even finished his hurried appeal when the *guir* whipped twenty-five rubles out of his pocket. "Go try my brother-in-law who lives up the block. He, too, would want to share in this mitzva."

The Rabbi and *gabbai* thanked the *guir* profusely and were only too happy to take him up on his suggestion. They found the *guir*'s brother-in-law at home, and he, too, was very receptive to the plight of the unfortunate Jew who was being held for ransom. And once again, before the Rabbi had had a chance to suggest an amount he might donate, the brother-in-law removed fifteen rubles from his living room bureau and handed it cheerfully to the *gabbai*.

Reb Zundel and the *gabbai* were elated. They blinked in amazement at each other as if to say, "we might just make it," before racing off to the next house on their list. Wherever they went, they were greeted by displays of magnanimous philanthropy, more than the Rabbi had ever imagined he would encounter. Many of the donors even offered to add to the amount they had contributed in the event that Reb Zundel was unable to raise the necessary amount by four o'clock.

"This is a powerful lesson for me," Reb Zundel chastised himself. "We should never prejudge our fellow Jew." The gabbai nodded solemnly in agreement.

By one-thirty that afternoon, they had collected the full two hundred rubles, and they still had not approached even half of the people on their list. Reb Zundel returned to the shul happy but thoughtful. "I will be able to deliver my shiur after all," he thought to himself as he entered the shul and found the men inside still waiting for him. "But something seems not quite right to me."

WHEN HE FINISHED the shiur, it was almost three o'clock and the gabbai was waiting impatiently for him. "My esteemed Rabbi," he said, "I believe that it would be in everyone's interest that we not delay paying the ransom until the last minute. That poor Jew is probably desperately worried about his fate, and we rely on the whims of the kidnappers to keep their word to wait until the deadline? The very thought of what they could be doing to him right now terrifies me."

"My distinguished gabbai," replied the Rabbi, "I have also been thinking about his plight. Now, I want you to follow my instructions carefully: Take the money, together with the list on which you wrote down each congregant's contribution, and return every last kopek to the donors."

Reb Yankel could not believe what he had heard. "But... Rabbi," he protested, "surely you are joking. It is only one hour until the deadline!"

"I am perfectly serious. Do as I say and come back to me as soon as you are finished."

The Rabbi's ruling was final. Reb Yankel could not understand what was happening, and his mind reeled with confusion. Still, he reluctantly obeyed, although he did allow himself the liberty of asking each donor to whom he returned the money if he might come back to them once again for the very same sum in the event that the Rabbi changed his mind. They all agreed.

The *gabbai* returned to the shul after completing his strange mission and reported to Reb Zundel his willingness and that of all the donors to repeat the fundraising effort, should the Rabbi so desire. But Reb Zundel was adamant. "The money is not to be collected again. Nor is the ransom to be paid," he stated emphatically.

"And now," he continued, "I want you to go to the yeshiva and select ten of the brawniest students. Tell them to go to the well in the woods just outside of town. I will meet them there and tell them what they must do."

The *gabbai* wanted to object, but he held back: how could he contradict Reb Zundel? It was all a horrible dream, he told himself. Such directives were completely out of character for the Rabbi! Did not all of Reb Zundel's fame emanate from the succor he provided in situations just like this? And now, after he had already amassed the entire sum, he chose to turn his back on that poor victim...

The Rabbi's command was obeyed, and the students were dispatched from the yeshiva. Bursting with curiosity they arrived at the well where Reb Zundel waited for them. He carefully explained his plan, but the students were still doubtful. They had never been given an assignment quite like this before, and they approached it with mixed feelings.

AT EXACTLY four o'clock, the kidnappers arrived at the well with their captive. The students were nowhere to be seen. Then all of a sudden, at a prearranged signal, they appeared from their hiding places and slowly, menacingly, began to close in. The kidnappers were terrified. Little did they know that the students were equally afraid.

Reb Zundel had instructed them to overwhelm the thugs, using violence if necessary. It was unclear how thorough a job the Rabbi expected of them if it came to a fight, but they decided to be extra stringent just in case.

Above all, they were fearful that the kidnappers would use force on their captive, although Reb Zundel had assured them that there was no reason for concern. The students surrounded the thugs and were about to strike the first blow, when the kidnappers raised their arms in a gesture of surrender and cried out, "We confess, we confess!"

Curious to know what the kidnappers were babbling about, the yeshiva students grabbed them and demanded they explain.

"Please!" they implored on bended knees. "We aren't really kidnappers. This Jew hired us to tie him up and appear as kidnappers so that he would be able to collect his own ransom money."

The "victim" lowered his eyes to the ground. Word of what happened spread quickly, and all who heard marvelled at Reb Zundel's clairvoyance. How could he have known?

"The very fact," the Rabbi replied, "that the money was collected so rapidly, with neither protest nor resistance, indicated that something was amiss.

"The greater the mitzva, the greater the yetzer hara acting to discourage mankind from fulfillment of the mitzva. A mitzva as important and sacred as pidyon shevuyim — the redemption of prisoners — could never be so easily bought."

Glossary

The following glossary provides a partial explanation of some of the foreign words and phrases used in this book. The spelling, tense, and explanations reflect the way the specific word is used in 'SOULED!' Often, there are alternate spellings and meanings for the words. Foreign words and phrases which are immediately followed by a translation in the text are not included in this section.

ACHAKEH LO — I await him [the Messiah]

ACHARONIM — talmudic scholars of the last five hundred years

AGUNAH — lit. a "chained woman;" refers to a woman whose marriage has been terminated *de facto* but not *de jure,* and is therefore unable to remarry because she is still technically married to her absent husband

AM HAARETZ — ignoramus

ARBES — chick peas; delicacy traditionally served at a SHALOM ZACHOR

ARON KODESH — lit. holy ark; ark containing the Torah scrolls

AU REVOIR — (Fr.) good-bye

AVODAH — ritual worship performed in the Holy Temple

BAALAS CHESSED — (f.) individual with a generous, giving nature

BAALEI BATTIM — lay individuals

BAAL MIDOS — virtuous individual

BAAL MUM — individual who is halachically blemished

BALABUSTA — (Yid., colloq.) efficient, capable housekeeper

BARUCH HASHEM — lit. the Lord is blessed; thank God

BARUCH MECHAYEH HAMEISIM — lit. blessed be the Reviver of the dead; blessing recited upon being reunited with someone neither seen nor heard from in more than a year

BASHERT — (Yid.) destined

BAVLI — Babylonian Talmud

B'EZER HASHEM — (colloq. form of b'ezras Hashem) with God's help

BEHAIMES — (colloq. form of behaimos) animals

BEIS HAMIKDASH — the Holy Temple

BEIS MIDRASH — house of study used for both Torah study and prayer

BEIT DIN — (Sefaradit Hebrew form of beis din) court of Jewish law

BEN TORAH — lit. son of Torah; person imbued with Torah values and committed to its study

BICHVODO U'V'ATZMO — lit. in his honor and his very being; in person

BIEN SUR — (Fr.) of course

BIMA — platform located in the center of the synagogue, from where the Torah is read

BITACHON — trust [in God]

BLI AYIN HARA — lit. without the "evil eye"; expression invoking Divine protection for children, good health, good fortune, etc.

BOCHUR(IM) — unmarried yeshiva student

B'SHA'A TOVA U'MUTZLACHAS — lit. in a good and successful hour; expresses hope that the time of a particular event will be propitious.

BUBBE — (Yid.) grandmother

CA DOIT ETRE LUI — (Fr.) It is he!

CHASDEI HASHEM KI LO SAMNU — through God's grace were we not annihilated

CHASSAN — groom

CHASSANAH — (Yid.) wedding

CHAS VE'CHALILAH — God forbid

CHAS V'SHALOM — God forbid

CHAZZAN — cantor; the leader of public worship

CHEDER — lit. room; yeshiva elementary school

CHEVRA KADISHA — lit. Holy Society; a group which

provides for the religious needs of the community, particularly in the area of the care and rites of the dead

CHEVRUSOS — study partners

CHIDDUSHIM — novellae; new insights in Torah interpretation;

COHANIM — male decendants from the priestly family of Aaron

DAF SHIUR — GEMARA lesson focussed on the page being studied

DAVEN — (Yid.) pray

DINEI TORAH — (pl.) cases brought for adjudication according to Jewish law

DIVREI ELOKIM CHAIM — the words of the living God

DIVREI TORAH — Torah thoughts

EMUNAH SHELEIMAH — complete faith

ERETZ YISRAEL (YISRUEL) — the land of Israel (Yid., colloq.)

EREV — eve

EREV SHABBOS — Sabbath eve

EXCUSEZ MOI — (Fr.) pardon me

FARHEIR — (Yid.) oral examination in GEMARA

FARSHLUGGENER — (Yid.,colloq.) beat-up

GABBAI — warden of the synagogue who collects and dispenses charity

GADOL — lit. great one; refers to a giant in Torah scholarship

GAON — lit. brilliant one; honorific for a distinguished sage

GARTEL — (Yid.) belt worn by some men, particularly chassidim, during prayer

GEHINNOM — hell

GEMACH — contraction of GEMILUS CHASSADIM; interest-free loan society

GEMARA — 1.commentary on the MISHNA (together they comprise the Talmud); 2. a volume of the Talmud

GEMILUS CHASSADIM — performance of good works

GET (GITTIN) — (pl.) divorce documents

GEULAH — final Redemption

GEZEIRA — decree

GLUZ TAY — (Yid.) glass of tea

GOIMEL-BENCHER — (Yid.,colloq.) an event over which reciting *Bircas Hagomel* is indicated; (*Bircas Hagomel* is the blessing recited after being spared from harm)

GOTT IN HIMMEL — (Yid.) God in Heaven

GOTT TZU DANKEN — (Yid.) thank God

GUTT YONTIFF — (Yid.) a good holiday

GVIR — man of substantial means

HACHNASAS ORCHIM — hospitality

HALACHA — Jewish law

HAMSA — amulet in the shape of a hand believed to ward off the "evil eye"

HAREI AT — opening words of wedding formula said by the groom to his bride

HAVDALLAH — lit. separation; service to conclude the Shabbos

HETER — halachic dispensation

HOSHANNA RABBA — the seventh day of Sukkos

ILUI — genius; towering Torah scholar

JE VOUS PRIE — (Fr.) I beg of you

KADDISH — prayer in praise of God recited by mourners for their deceased

KALLAH — bride

KASHRUS — Jewish dietary laws

KIDDUSHIN — marriage ceremony

KEHILLA — organized community; congregation

KIDDUSH — sanctification; prayer recited over wine to usher in the Sabbath and festivals

K'NA HARA — (Yid.) see BLI AYIN HARA

KLAL YISRAEL — community of Israel; all Jewry

KLEZMER — musicians

KOLLEL — post-graduate yeshiva, the student body of which is usually comprised of young married students who receive stipends

KRAITZ — (Yid.) lower part of the back

KUGELS — noodle puddings

LAISHEV BASUKKAH — blessing recited upon sitting in a Sukkah

LECHA DODI — a song in the Friday night service, composed by Solomon Alkabetz HaLevi; it depicts the Sabbath as the bride of the Jewish people

LE'CHAIM — to life (a toast)

LEVIIM — (pl.) Levites

LOMDIM — (colloq.) scholars

MAARIV — the evening prayer service

MADAME — (Fr.) Mrs.

MAMMALEH — (Yid.) lit. little mother; affectionate sobriquet

MASHGIACH RUCHANI — dean of students in a yeshiva who acts as a spiritual guide and advisor

MAYAIN OLAM HABA — like the World to Come

MAZEL — luck; fortune

MECHUTANIM — the two sets of parents of a married couple or couple about to wed

MELAMED — teacher

MELAVE MALKA — lit. escorting the Queen; the Saturday night meal at which the Sabbath is bid farewell

MERCI BEAUCOUP — (Fr.) Thank you very much

MESECHTA — talmudic volume

MESHULACH — lit. messenger; itinerent fundraiser for a charitable institution

MEZOINES — (colloq.) lit. grain; rolls which do not require washing of the hands before eating, as bread does

MEVAKER CHOLEH — visit the infirm

MIESSA MESHUNEHDIGGE — (Yid.) lit. like a macabre death; a vile color

MIKVE — a ritual bath used for the purpose of ritual purification

MINCHA — the afternoon prayer service

MIN HASHOMAYIM — lit. from Heaven; Divinely inspired

MINYAN — quorum of ten adult Jewish males; the basic unit of community for certain religious purposes, including prayer

MISHMAR — lit. watch; an all-night Torah study session

MISHNA(YOS) — the earliest codification of Jewish oral law by Rabbi Yehudah HaNassi

MISNAGDIM — (pl.) opposers of the Chassidic Movement

MITZVOS — (pl.) lit. commandments; applied to good deeds

MONSIEUR — (Fr.) Mr.

MORAH — (f.) teacher

MOSHE RABEINU — Moses, our teacher

MOTEK — (colloq.) sweetie

MOTZEI SHABBOS — end of the Sabbath

MUSSAR — 1. school of thought emphasizing ethical performance; 2. moral teachings; 3. ethical lecture

NEBBACH — (Yid.) unfortunately

NEIN — (Yid.) — no

NESHAMA YESEIRA — "extra soul" provided on Shabbos

NIGGUN — song, tune

NISHT — (Yid.) not

NISSAYON — trial of faith

OUI — (Fr.) yes

OY MEIN GOTT — (Yid.) Oh my God!

OY VEY (Yid.) — Oh, agony!

OY VEY'S MIR — (Yid.) Oh, woe unto me!

PAPERLACH — (Yid.,colloq.) snippets of paper

PAROCHES — curtain of the ark containing the Torah scrolls

PAYOS — sidelocks

PEREK — chapter

PIKUACH NEFESH — matter of life and death

PISKEI HALACHA — halachic rulings

RABBANIM — rabbis

RABBANUS — the rabbinate

RABBIN — (Fr.) rabbi

RASHI — leading commentator on the Bible and Talmud

RAV — Rabbi

REBBETZIN — wife of a rabbi

REFUAH SHELEIMAH — a complete recovery

RISHONIM — lit. first ones; European scholars of the eleventh through the fifteenth century

ROSH KEHILLA — head of the community

ROSH KOLLEL — head of the KOLLEL

ROSH YESHIVA — yeshiva dean

SANHEDRIN — the highest judicial and ecclesiastical court of the Jewish nation

SECHEL — mind; intelligence

SEFER (SEFARIM) — book of religious content

SEUDAH SHLISHLIS — the third Sabbath meal, usually begun just before sunset and lasting past nightfall

SGULEH — (Yid.,colloq.) auspicious sign

SHACHARIS — the morning prayer service

SHAILOS — (pl.) lit. questions; halachic queries

SHALOM ALEICHEM — lit. peace be upon you; greetings!

SHALOM ZACHOR — the celebration held on the Friday night following the birth of a baby boy

SHAMMAS — synagogue caretaker; rabbi's assistant

SHAS — lit. the six orders of the MISHNA; the Talmud

SHE'AYRIS HAPLAITA — remnants of the Nation

SHECHTING — (Yid.) slaughtering

SHEITEL-MACHER — (Yid.) wig maker

SHEMA YISRAEL HASHEM ELOKEINU HASHEM

ECHAD — prayer recited daily proclaiming the oneness of God and affirming faith in Him and His Torah

SHEMINI ATZERES — the eighth day of Sukkos

SHEMONEH ESREI — lit. eighteen; the central prayer in Jewish liturgy which is recited three times daily

SHIDDUCH — a (matrimonial) match

SHIKTZA — (Yid.) non-Jewish girl

SHIN-BET — Israel's secret service and intelligence agency

SHIUR(IM) — Torah lecture

SHIUR KLALI — lit. general lecture; advanced lecture usually delivered by the senior ROSH YESHIVA

SHIVA — lit. seven; the seven day period of mourning following death

SHLEPPING — (Yid.) dragging

SHOMREI MITZVOS — (pl.) lit. observers of the commandments; religious Jews

SHTIEBLACH — (Yid.) small, informal, intimate room for prayer and study

SHTENDER — (Yid.) lectern, used in place of desks in many yeshivos

SHUL — (Yid.) synagogue

SHULCHAN — table where the Torah is placed during its reading

SIDDUR — prayerbook

SI JE PEUX VOUS CORRIGER — (Fr.) if I may correct you

SIMCHA — lit. joy; celebration

SIMCHAS BEIS HASHOEVA — festival of the "drawing of

water" which took place in the Holy Temple during the Sukkos holiday

SIMCHAS TORAH — the holiday of the rejoicing of the Torah

SIYATA D'SHMAYA — Heavenly assistance

SMICHA — rabbinic ordination

SONEH YISRAEL — anti-Semite

SUKKAH — temporary dwelling which is a central requirement of the holiday of Sukkos

SUKKOS — week-long Autumn festival during which time one dwells in a SUKKAH

TALLIS — four-cornered prayer shawl with fringes at each corner worn by men during morning prayers

TALMID CHACHAM — Torah scholar

TALMIDIM — students

TASHLICH — prayer recited alongside a body of water on the afternoon of the first day of Rosh Hashana

TEFILLAH — prayer; prayer service

TEFILLIN — black leather boxes containing verses from the Bible bound to the arm and head of a man during morning prayers

TEHILLIM — Psalms; Book of Psalms

TISCH — (Yid.) Rebbe's table

TOSAFOS — early annotations and commentaries on the Talmud

TREIFE — (Yid.) lit. torn; non-kosher; unacceptable

TSUK — (Yid.) draft; strong breeze

TUVAI HA'IR — distinguished citizens

TZADDIK — righteous man

TZIPPALEH — (Yid., colloq.) little one

VAYS-ALLES — (Yid.) "Mr. Know-it-all"

VIDUY — confessional prayer

YAHRZEIT — (Yid.) anniversary of a death

YARMULKE — (Yid.) skullcap; head covering worn by religious Jews

YERUSHALMI — Jerusalem Talmud; earlier edition of the Babylonian Talmud

YESHIVA SHEL MAALA — lit. Heavenly assembly; place of TZADDIKIM in Heaven

YESHIVA SHEL MATTA — lit. earthly assembly; where mankind meets to study Torah

YIBANEH HAMIKDASH — may the Holy Temple be restored

YEMACH SHEMAM V'ZICHRAM — may their name and memories be eradicated

YOM TOV — holiday

ZEESKEIT — (Yid., colloq.) sweetness

ZEMIROS — songs traditionally sung at the Sabbath table

ZT"L — abbreviation for "may the memory of the TZADDIK be blessed"